GUIDE TO JEWISH FILMS ON VIDEO

Larry Anklewicz

KTAV Publishing House, Inc.
Hoboken, NJ 07030

Library of Congress Cataloging-in-Publicaton Data

Anklewicz, Larry.
Guide to Jewish films on video / by Larry Anklewicz.
p. cm.
Includes bibliographical references.
ISBN 0-88125-618-8 — ISBN 0-88125-605-6 (pbk.)
1. Jews in motion pictures. 2. Motion pictures--Catalogs. 3. Video recordings--Catalogs. I. Title.

PN1995.9J46 A55 2000
791.43'65203924--dc21 99-058433

Distributed by
KTAV Publishing House, Inc.
900 Jefferson Street
Hoboken, NJ 07030

Dedication

This book is dedicated to my loving and devoted family—my children, Michael (Moti), Shira, and Adam (Avi), and especially my wife Gerry—all of whom have provided me with the unstinting support that has made this book possible.

TABLE OF CONTENTS

GUIDE TO JEWISH FILMS

Prologue

What is a Jewish Film? And what makes a film Jewish?

Obviously it is not a question of Jewish actors, producers, or directors, otherwise most Hollywood films would be Jewish.

This is a question that doesn't always have a clear-cut answer. The best way to look at this is through the film's storyline or whether the film has recognizably Jewish characters.

If we look at storylines, then it is obvious that any film about the Holocaust, about Israel, or about anti-Semitism could be considered Jewish. For example, *Europa, Europa*, about a Jewish youngster passing himself off as a non-Jew during World War II, would be a Jewish film, as would *Schindler's List*, although the main character is not Jewish. Both of these films have universal relevance, but each is very Jewish in its own way.

The same is true of films about Israel. *Exodus* and *Cast a Giant Shadow* are Jewish films. Both deal with the creation of the State of Israel. *Jerusalem*, the recent Scandinavian film about a group of Swedish Christians moving to Jerusalem in the heat of religious fervor, is not a Jewish film.

Films with Jewish content or storylines would include *Gentleman's Agreement* and *School Ties*, both of which deal with anti-Semitism, but might also include such films as *Independence Day* and *The Birdcage*, because both feature central characters who are Jewish.

In *Independence Day*, David Levinson, played by Jeff Goldblum, is the character who finally cracks the secret to defeating the aliens and flies into the mother ship to ensure its destruction. Levinson's Jewishness is affirmed when his father gives him a Jewish prayer book and a yarmulke to take with him on the dangerous mission.

In *The Birdcage*, Robin Williams plays Armand Goldman. When Goldman realizes that his son's future in-laws are coming over for dinner, and that the prospective father-in-law is an archconservative, he tries to deny his Jewishness. But at the end a rabbi co-officiates at the wedding ceremony and the groom wears a yarmulke. Not a very satisfactory ending for many Jews, but probably quite in vogue in Hollywood.

In many ways, whether a film is Jewish or not is in the eyes of the viewer. To some, a film like *Dirty Dancing* is very Jewish, but others would never notice the Jewish connotations hidden beneath the surface. Everyone is free to decide.

For myself, the films listed in this book are Jewish. They vary from *The Chosen* to *Annie Hall* to *Dirty Dancing* to *The Proprietor.*

There is no simple formula for determining whether a film is Jewish. Each film must be judged on its own merits, and the final decision is highly subjective.

It should also be pointed out that most of the films in this Guide are American-produced. This is partly because Hollywood dominates the world film industry, and because Jews are so prominent in the American film industry.

But a large number of excellent Jewish films have come out of Europe, and these too are discussed and described in this Guide.

Some people claim that Hollywood is controlled by Jews

That's an exaggeration, but the fact is that Jews play an important role in the film industry, and always have. Jews helped to create the cinematic world that we think of as Hollywood; they have been active in film making from the outset, and still are today. Until very recently, though, very few Jewish characters and Jewish stories made it onto the big screen.

In the early days of Hollywood, Samuel Goldwyn, Louis B. Mayer, Irving Thalberg, Harry Cohn, Carl Laemmle, William Fox, and Jack Warner, among others, founded studios and helped make the movies a major industry.

In the past two or three decades many of the new generation of owners, executives, producers, directors, writers, and actors have changed Hollywood since the early days of this century when it first became the center of the American film industry. In those days, Hollywood was an isolated backwater, half a world away from the political and financial centers of North America. Today it is the focus of the world's entertainment industry.

There are many new faces in today's Hollywood, but some of the current power brokers are still Jewish: people such as Steven Spielberg (Dream Works), Michael Eisner (Disney), Gerald Levin (Warner), Edgar Bronfman, Jr. (Universal), and so on down the line.

There are several reasons why Jews have gravitated to Hollywood over the years.

The film industry, in the early days, was easy to get into. Movies were in their infancy and there were no ingrained barriers against Jews, as there were in many other professions and businesses. Anyone with talent and imagination and anyone who could raise a few dollars could enter the business and might even succeed.

As a result, Hollywood beckoned to people who were creative and entrepreneurial. And it didn't matter what their background was. If they had talent and/or chutzpah, they could try their luck.

That's not to say there was no anti-Semitism in the United States or even in Hollywood. There was, but there was no defined system of discrimination against Jews. Unlike Europe, no pogroms forced Jews to fear for their lives in America.

In the United States, the greatest challenge to the Jewish community has been assimilation, not persecution. As a result, Jews could try new things and reap the rewards of their efforts.

The Jewish population of the United States integrated into the business and social classes of their adopted country and became indistinguishable from their gentile countrymen unless they chose to remain different and apart.

This was the goal of the early pioneers in the film industry. Although many were Jewish, they wanted to move up in social class, increase their wealth, and become indistinguishable from their neighbors in the same social class.

These Jewish trailblazers pursued assimilation, or Americanization, with a passion. They often anglicized their names. They often broke ties with their families. They wanted to be successes in the eyes of their non-Jewish friends and associates. And they wanted to make sure that their children would be "Americans," and not "Jewish-Americans" or "American Jews." Many lost all touch with their religious and ethnic background. They frequently married non-Jewish spouses and raised their children with little or no ties to Judaism.

Many aspects of this desire to disappear or to maintain a low profile were reflected in the material Hollywood's Jews put on the screen.

In the early decades of the 20th century the Hollywood pioneers restricted the Jewish presence on screen to films with biblical themes. This was a safe area because the Jews in these films were far removed from present-day reality and it was unnecessary to point out that they were Jews. Or they used one-dimensional stereotypes that bore little resemblance to real-life Jews.

The Silent Age

In Hollywood's early years, approximately 1900 to 1929, filmmakers produced a number of adaptations of classic literary works like *The Merchant of Venice* and *Oliver Twist*, many of which included Jewish characters and Jewish story elements. The fact that the Jews in these works were often described in a derogatory manner did not appear to offend the Jewish film moguls.

Other Jewish characters often had very stereotypical physical characteristics and occupations, and were portrayed as villains, usurers, and cheats.

Jewish characters in silent films, when they did appear, were usually in low-prestige occupations, such as clothing dealer, sweatshop worker, peddler, pawnbroker, etc.

In this, the film world offered an accurate picture of the situation. At that time, the bulk of the Jewish population in the United States consisted mainly of first-generation Americans struggling to make ends meet and trying to collect enough capital to launch their children on the path of success.

As the Jewish population grew and integrated itself in American life, many entered show business, and an increasing number ventured to the West Coast, where they became involved in the film industry.

Show business was a relatively easy way to enter mainstream American society, and success did not depend upon one's ancestry but on one's talent and ability. As a result, the period from 1900 to 1929 saw a host of Jewish entertainers gain acceptance and fame, among them Al Jolson, George Gershwin, the Marx Brothers, Eddie Cantor, Sophie Tucker, Irving Berlin, Fannie Brice, Jack Benny, George Burns, and Milton Berle.

At the same time, a number of Jews moved into positions of prominence and power behind the scenes in Hollywood—men like Goldwyn, Mayer, and the Warnor brothers.

In the rush to establish and consolidate their cinema empires, the Jewish moguls paid little attention to their Jewish roots and were willing to cater to the prejudices and stereotypes of the non-Jewish world. Films in the first three decades of this century tended to depict Jews as overly clever, immoral, and dishonest (some Jewish characters burned down their own stores for the insurance money or regularly defrauded non-Jews). Other Jewish characters were fools and buffoons.

The Jazz Singer (1927), the first talking film, flew in the face of Jewish customs and sensibilities, and even seemed to relish the idea of going against Jewish religious law. It supported both intermarriage and the eating of non-kosher foods.

At the same time, films began to develop as the conscience of society and some of them mirrored the concerns of the time. Several early Hollywood films showed the crowded tenements and the problems of poverty that made life difficult for the urban masses, most of the country's Jews among them. But behind all this there was an ongoing effort to encourage assimilation and the wiping out of the differences that set Jews apart from the non-Jewish population.

This push toward assimilation and the desire not to be noticed for their Jewishness pushed the Jew off the screen after talking pictures became the mainstay of the film industry. Except for *The Jazz Singer* and its rather dubious message, the silver screen was for a long time without Jewish plots and characters.

The Movies Break the Sound Barrier

When literary works containing Jewish characters were adapted for the screen, they were sanitized of all Jewish references. When Jewish characters appeared in the films of the 1930s and 1940s, they were either one-dimensional or their Jewish aspects were ignored.

In films like *The Life of Emile Zola* (1937) and *Rhapsody in Blue* (1945), for instance, there was little or no reference to the fact that a central character was a Jew. Film producers did not want to draw attention to their own ethnic background and feared that films with identifiably Jewish features would not appeal to non-Jewish moviegoers.

Their position is evidenced by the comments of Columbia studio head Harry Cohn about an actor: "He looks too Jewish. . . . Around this studio the only Jews we put into pictures play Indians."[1]

Or as MGM head Louis B. Mayer told Danny Kaye: "I would put you under contract right now but you look too Jewish. Have some surgery to straighten out your nose and then we'll talk."[2]

As a result, many Jewish performers, in an attempt to "pass," changed their names. Julius Garfinkle became John Garfield, Emmanuel Goldberg became Edward G. Robinson, Marion Levy became Paulette Goddard, and so on. Some even changed their appearance.

As writer Michael Blankfort described the Jews in Hollywood: "They were accidental Jews, terribly frightened Jews, who rejected their background to become super-Americans. They were interested in power and profit. They would hardly ever touch a story with a Jewish character, and if they did, they would cast a gentile for the part."[3]

It wasn't only actors and producers who were afraid to admit or display their Jewish origins. When novels or magazine stories were adapted for films, Jewish characters had their names changed and their ethnicity removed.

Although times have changed, this still sometimes happens today. *Roommates* (1995) was about a young man who was raised by his grandfather. The two men lived together for many years, and the book upon which the movie was based makes it clear they were both Jewish. The film adaptation transforms the grandfather into a Polish Catholic.

The 1930s and 1940s were a time when Jew-baiting was a great deal more acceptable than it is today. The Hollywood moguls lived in a world where fascism was on the rise, and where the United States was an isolationist country in which attacks against Hitler or Mussolini could be construed as an attempt to get the United States into a foreign war.

The 1930s, 1940s, and early 1950s also saw a fear of Communism sweep through the United States and a wave of anti-Communist paranoia which tried to link Jews and Communism.

America's entry into World War II made it possible, at last, to emphasize ethnic issues. But the focus was on the old American cliches: the melting pot and the desire of ethnics to assimilate and be just like the stereotypical American. This led to an increased interest in Hollywood films on assimilation. So although war films featured multi-ethnic military units, most of the Jewish characters were not really that much different from their Polish, Italian, or Irish buddies, except for superficial matters.

But once again there were two streams in Hollywood. While some focused on assimilation, a few took up the challenge of anti-Semitism and persecution.

Lubitsch's comedy *To Be or Not to Be* (1942) and Chaplin's The Great Dictator (1940) were in the vanguard of this small but important movement. Lubitsch and Chaplin were willing to put Jews on the screen in sympathetic and anti-fascist roles.

Of course Chaplin was a very independent-minded filmmaker who made the films he wanted to make and would brook no interference from anyone. He was able to finance his films himself, so he was not forced to rely on the studio system.

Neither of these two films was a great success in the United States when initially released. It was only in later years that their significance and quality were recognized by critics and fans alike.

Postwar Period

Biographies became popular in Hollywood during and after the war, and many of the central characters in these films were Jewish–Al Jolson in *The Jolson Story* (1946), George Gershwin in *Rhapsody in Blue* (1945), and Jerome Kern in *Till Clouds Roll By* (1947). But the Jewishness of the main characters was usually downplayed. Their Americanism was emphasized. So except for the beginning of *The Jolson Story*, there are very few signs of Jewishness in these films. And what signs there were, were very subtle.

In *Rhapsody in Blue*, Gershwin's father is lying on his deathbed when he comes for a last visit, and very softly in the background, you can hear "Ofn Pripichik" being played, a Yiddish song that would be used much more prominently some fifty years later in *Schindler's List* (1993).

The most powerful Jewish films of the 1940s were *Gentleman's Agreement* (1947) and *Crossfire* (1947). *Gentleman's Agreement* was produced by the most non-Jewish studio in Hollywood, Twentieth Century Fox. In fact, several Jewish producers had the opportunity to produce *Gentleman's Agreement* but turned it down. Only Elia Kazan, a non-Jew, had the courage to make this film that focused on the gentile anti-Semitism that pervaded American society.

Crossfire was an engrossing murder mystery where the victim, a Jew, was killed by an anti-Semitic bully. A non-Jew, Edward Dmytryk, directed this landmark film, and it was produced by one of the smaller and less important studios, RKO.

Despite their impact on audiences, *Gentleman's Agreement* and *Crossfire* had little lasting effect on the film industry. Jewish filmmakers almost totally ignored the two seminal events of twentieth century Jewish history–the Holocaust and the establishment of the State of Israel.

In the late 1940s and early 1950s, concern about the spread of Communism in the United States and abroad enabled the House Un-American Activities Committee and Senator Joe McCarthy to gain inordinate power. Seeking to placate McCarthy and his minions, and to offset possible losses at the box office, Hollywood blacklisted a score of alleged Communist members of the film community, several of whom were Jewish.

This tension made the Jewish moguls more insecure than before and led to an even greater search for assimilation.

The 1950s saw little change in the way Jews were presented in the movies. Producers, seeking to keep a low profile, took no chances and only allowed safe, uncontroversial Jews to appear on screen.

They escaped to old cliches and stereotypes, such as a remake of *The Jazz Singer* (1953) and biblical films like *The Ten Commandments* (1956), *Solomon and Sheba* (1959), and *Ben Hur* (1959), where Jewishness could be hidden beneath the sanctity of the Old Testament or through the use of the term "Hebrew" or "Israelite."

The Times are a Changing

The end of the 1950s saw the beginning of a revolution in American society. Racial segregation was beginning to crack, and the country's major cities were in the midst of a mass exodus of the middle class to the suburbs.

The time that had passed since the end of World War II was also having an effect on American Jewish perceptions of the Holocaust and the creation of the State of Israel, and on the role of Jews in America.

It was almost as if American Jewry had needed time to catch its collective breath before it could think about the enormous events of the 1940s. Putting it differently, American Jews, like many Holocaust survivors, needed time to put things in perspective before they could deal with the enormity of what they had experienced.

Add to this the growing strength and importance of the Jewish community in America and the growing role of Israel in the Jewish world, and we see an increasing confidence among American Jews and a growing feeling of Jewish identity.

By this time, Jews had also become important figures in the relatively new world of television, and in fact, television was quickly becoming an integral part of the film industry.

It would be a while before all this would take shape. In the early 1950s the film industry looked on TV as the mortal enemy, but eventually it would come to recognize television as a junior partner in the entertainment field, and indeed would enter and soon dominate it.

Gradually, the Jews' fear of having too high a profile in the early 1950s became a growing self-confidence in the late 1950s and early 1960s that would result in profound changes in Hollywood.

Most of the Jewish moguls were gone by the end of the 1950s, or on their way out. And a new breed of Jew, brimming with self-confidence, armed with a slew of university degrees, or backed with considerable financial and creative resources, was about to take over the industry.

But it was a rough ride to arrive at this point, and it would still be some time before Jews could feel comfortable in putting their own people up on the big screen. And the dangers of assimilation would persist to the present day.

Whereas in 1956 *The Benny Goodman Story* would push the protagonist's Jewish roots into the background, and would offer no explanation or comment when his mother calls his engagement to a non-Jewish woman a "knife in my heart." There were also a few important films about anti-Semitism like *The Diary of Anne Frank* (1959) and *Me and the Colonel* (1958). But there were still too many films like *Compulsion* (1959), where the names of the main characters were changed to keep the audience from knowing that they were Jewish.

But the times were really changing in the 1960s. Segregation was ending and civil rights became America's main focus for several years. Most of this was a direct result of work done by thousands of young people. Then came the war in Vietnam, drugs, free love, and the revolt of the young.

And everywhere change was taking place you would find young Jewish men and women.

Just as black Americans promulgated the idea that "Black is Beautiful," a growing number of young Jews began looking for their own identity and their own roots.

This was further enhanced by the events of May and June 1967. For several long tortuous days it appeared that Israel was in danger of being invaded by the Arab armies and of being pushed into the sea. Horrific memories of the Holocaust haunted American Jews and Jewish communities around the world.

Protests and marches in support of Israel swept through the United States and through Jewish communities everywhere.

Led by the younger generation, Jews all over the world took to the streets and demonstrated their support for the Jewish state.

And when the war did erupt on June 5, 1967, Jews everywhere basked in the glory of Israel's overwhelming military victory. To be a Jew was no longer to be inferior or subservient to anyone else. This newfound pride made itself felt in the movies.

Hollywood had been undergoing enormous changes throughout the 1960s. With the disappearance of the studio system, there was more freedom to experiment and to express individual points of view. And while the changes began in the early sixties, they accelerated in the last few years of the decade.

Films that focused on unabashedly Jewish characters and Jewish humor began to be produced. *I Love You, Alice B. Toklas* (1968) dealt with a Jewish lawyer seduced by the hippie culture. *The Producers* (1968) introduced the zany Jewish comedy of Mel Brooks to a large public, and *Goodbye, Columbus* (1969) dared to show Jewish characters with major flaws.

The 1960s also witnessed the first major attempts to confront the horrors of the Holocaust. *Judgment at Nuremberg* (1961) showed the crimes committed by the Nazis, and *The Pawnbroker* (1965) dealt with the survivors of the Holocaust and their problems adjusting to a normal life after the war.

The 1960s also saw Hollywood's first serious look at Israel. When Leon Uris began to research his book *Exodus*, he did so at the behest of a major studio which was interested in producing a film about Israel. The studio later got cold feet, but the book was so overwhelmingly successful that it was finally turned into a movie epic.

For the first time, a major Hollywood film showed Jews who were unafraid and uncowed by a hostile environment. It showed Jewish protagonists of heroic proportions.

Exodus (1960) was followed by *Judith* (1965) and *Cast a Giant Shadow* (1966). The last two films were less successful than the first, but all of them championed the Jewish warrior who refused to bend his neck to his enemies.

With all the changes going on in Hollywood, even films set in America began to change their tone, and Jewish characters began to appear more frequently on the silver screen.

Films like *Funny Girl* (1968) reveled in the Jewishness of the main character, and *Tobruk* (1966) featured the heroism of a group of Palestinian Jews battling the Nazis in North Africa.

And then we reach the 1970s, an era that saw great advances in the Jewish presence on screen, but it was progress with mixed results.

In the 1970s more movies featuring Jewish characters were made than ever before. Many Hollywood producers lost some of their fear about portraying Jews on screen, although there were still some who felt uncomfortable about showing the good or bad qualities of their people.

And there were many Hollywood producers who truly favored assimilation and could see no difference between Jews and gentiles. To some extent this was due to the increasing rate of intermarriage in Hollywood and the entire entertainment world. Hollywood was in the vanguard of this tendency, with many, if not most Jews, marrying non-Jewish partners.

But, as mentioned earlier, many Hollywood producers became less self-conscious about their heritage in the 1970s, and more Jewish producers and directors were prepared to put their Jewishness on the screen. Jewish filmmakers like Woody Allen, Paul Mazursky, and Mel Brooks achieved increasing success, prominence, and clout.

It was the 1970s that saw major productions of such Jewish-flavored films as *Fiddler on the Roof* (1971), *Cabaret* (1972), *The Frisco Kid* (1979), *Hester Street* (1975), *Lies My Father Told Me* (1975), *The Boys from Brazil* (1975), and *The Man in the Glass Booth* (1975), to name just a few.

Even films not completely centered on Jewish issues would often contain an undeniably Jewish character: *The Way We Were* (1973), *Save the Tiger* (1975), *The Heartbreak Kid* (1972), *Annie Hall* (1977), *Next Stop, Greenwich Village* (1976) and so on.

Being Jewish became "in." Jewish characters filled the screens, although sometimes it was necessary to look closely to identify the character as Jewish, as in *Harry & Tonto* (1974). And sometimes the films pushed assimilationist values, as in *Willie & Phil* (1980).

But Jewish-oriented films and films with Jewish characters were no longer hidden under a gentile veneer. As Jewish involvement in the greater American community increased, and as new blood took the reins of power in Hollywood, more Jews appeared on screen.

And some of the new movies were critical of sacred institutions like the State of Israel. *Eyewitness* (1981) and *Children of Rage* (1975) were terrible films, but they were also anti-Israel, and the fact that they were produced showed a growing willingness in some Hollywood circles to be more critical and not to follow the line advocated by most American Jews.

The Movies Go Home

The 1980s saw the beginning of a worldwide technological revolution that shook up the entire film industry. Video cassettes became a practical and popular method of viewing films.

At the beginning of the 1980s video cassettes were expensive, selling for about $100 each, and video cassette recorders (VCRs) were selling in the $1,200 to $1,500 range.

But as is the case with most technological advances, prices came down and the revolution caught fire. Today over 80 percent of all households in North America have a VCR, and many have more than one. And although prices of video cassettes remain high when they are released for the rental market, the sell-through market has grown exponentially.

Most video cassettes today are sold to stores that rent them out to their customers. The stores pay in the area of $70 to $100 each for cassettes. Most popular films will rent for several months and then demand dies down. About six to twelve months after a film is released on video for rental purposes, it is re-released at a sell-through price, and many stores will sell these for $15 to $25 each, depending on the suggested retail price set by the studio.

In addition, a number of films, especially children's films like *The Lion King* (1994), or very popular films like *Independence Day* (1996), are released on video immediately at sell-through prices, and these titles often will sell millions of units. The studios often can make more money by going straight to sell through, and the public gets the chance to buy and own their own copy of a film they will watch over and over again.

The video market has now progressed to the point where there is a huge selection of titles available. Not only do current feature films get released on video, but so do many older, classic films–films like *The Wizard of Oz* (1939), *The Sound of Music* (1965), *Casablanca* (1942), etc. If a studio perceives a demand for a certain film and there are no problems with copyright ownership, the film will be released on video.

But that is not the end of the supply line for video programs. Video companies have released hundreds of foreign films, and there is a huge market for television films, television specials, and mini-series, as well as certain television programs. Video companies have been very successful in releasing episodes of the *I Love Lucy* television show, the various *Star Trek series*, and many others.

If people will buy it, it will appear on video, seems to be the main principle here.

The video market has matured to such a stage that many studios produce special "direct to video" films and programs. Here Disney has been very successful with direct to video films as its sequels to *Aladdin*, all of which have sold millions of cassettes.

Video now brings in twice as much money as films do when they play in the theaters.

What all this has accomplished is to expand the marketplace for films. Today's movies begin in the theater and make whatever they can there, then go on to video, pay-per-view television, pay-TV, and finally network television. The result is more money for the studios, but it has also allowed for a greater diversity and variety in film production. Films don't have to break even or make a profit strictly from their theatrical run. Ancillary markets (video, TV, etc.) are so lucrative now that these areas can pick up a lot of the slack from the theatrical market.

As a result, producers can be more innovative, more creative, and can focus in on niche markets. This has led to a more diversified range of product and growing and more interesting sources of production.

In the long run, these developments have produced many more films centered around Jewish concerns and Jewish interests.

All this has been heightened by a greater awareness of Jewish identity. The Holocaust is no longer sacrosanct. A growing number of theatrical and made-for-television films and mini-series have been produced about the Holocaust. It's almost as if the TV miniseries *Holocaust* (1978) broke through a dam and all the pent-up feelings and emotions rushed to the surface. And through this flood of films, the Holocaust has become part of the mainstream of Western culture, brought to the forefront of the consciousness of the Western world.

Holocaust films have varied in quality from the mediocre, such as *War and Love* (1984) and *The Wall* (1982), to the longwinded, such as *QB VII* (1974), *The Winds of War* (1983), and *War and Remembrance* (1988), to the excellent, such as *Triumph of the Spirit* (1989) and *Schindler's List* (1993).

At the same time American Jews are much more aware of the importance of the State of Israel to the survival of the Jewish people, as well as of Israel's increased power and influence in the Middle East. Israel's comeback from near-defeat during the 1973 Yom Kippur War, its audacity and success at Entebbe, and the growing partnership between the United States and Israel all have made films about Israel more acceptable in the United States.

Israel has become a symbol for military success and pride, which has led to such films as *Delta Force* (1986), *The Little Drummer Girl* (1984), *Last Winter* (1984), and such television films as *Steal the Sky* (1988), *A Woman Named Golda* (1982), and *Masada* (1981).

The new self-confidence of Jewish-American producers has shown itself in numerous ways. Steven Spielberg produced the first "Jewish Christmas film" in *An American Tail* (1986), the story of a family of Eastern European Jewish mice immigrating to the United States.

Neil Diamond reinforced this trend with his remake of *The Jazz Singer* (1980), a more satisfactory version than the Jolson original, although it still accepts the Jew marrying out of his religion.

Such films as *Crossing Delancey* (1988) deal with the attraction of non-Jews, *Yentl* (1983) deals with Jewish feminism, *The Infiltrator* (1995) looks at the new Nazis in Germany, *Scandal in a Small Town* (1988) deals with anti-Semitism in the American classroom, *School Ties* (1992) deals with anti-Semitism in a private high school, while *Skokie* (1981) looks at the clash between hate-mongering and free speech, and *Zebrahead* (1992) deals with Jews seeking to meld into another culture.

Despite all the gains achieved by Jews in Hollywood, conditions are not idyllic. Fears and uncertainties still haunt film producers and audiences alike.

Producers are afraid that if they make a film too Jewish they will alienate part of the audience and the film will be considered too ethnic. While there are audiences for niche films, most producers try to make their films accessible to as large an audience as possible.

This may be why the producers of *Dirty Dancing* (1987) expunged many of the Jewish elements from its main characters. There was little doubt that Baby, the main character, played by Jennifer Grey, was Jewish. Her surname and her mannerisms bespoke Jewish. But there is no reference to that in the film. The fact that the dancers are not

Jewish is the real reason her family doesn't want her to get too close to them. This is never made clear in the film.

In *Avalon* (1990), the family is obviously Jewish, but there is almost no reference to this in the film, except for a short scene at a cemetery.

Films like *Roommates* (1995) and *Before and After* (1996), although based on books written by Jewish writers and featuring Jewish characters, had the Jewish elements removed when adapted for the screen.

At the same time, Jewish is "in" in some quarters of Hollywood. So much so that black film star Eddie Murphy got into the Jewish act by doing a Jewish shtick in the barber shop scenes of *Coming to America* (1988).

And Yiddish slang has become so commonplace that in *City Hall* (1996) the characters discuss the use of certain expressions on screen. Unfortunately, their pronunciation is excruciatingly painful to anyone who knows Yiddish.

Even the film *Georgia* (1996), about an alcoholic and strung-out singer trying to emulate her successful sister, has a scene where the band plays a Jewish simcha and does one of the worse renditions of "Hava Nagila" ever put on film.

In *The King of Comedy* (1982), one of the characters points out that it would be "better to be King for a night than shmuck for a lifetime."

Video has served to democratize the film business. The studio system that churned out films in volume and straitjacketed the creators has crumbled and is no more than a memory.

The new system allows producers to use their imagination and unfetter their creativity. The only real chains on producers today is the bottom line.

In addition, more smaller, independent films are being produced, because with the new revenue streams, backers are more likely to recoup their investments.

It is difficult to see how Steven Spielberg could have obtained support for *Schindler's List* under the studio system. Even in the 1990s, he received financial backing for his dream project only after the unprecedented success of *Jurassic Park* (1993). Not wanting to offend their top-money-earning filmmaker, Universal agreed to finance *Schindler's List.* They tried to convince Spielberg that the film would be a flop and that the theme was too serious to draw a significant audience. And they were very nervous about Spielberg's insistence on shooting the film in black and white.

Because of his clout in Hollywood, Spielberg got everything he wanted. And the film grossed almost $100 million in domestic box office and over $200 million overseas. The film was a hit!

It is unlikely that we'll see very many such hits in the future. But as long as producers, directors, writers, and actors keep their goals in sight and work to realize their dreams, the Jew will remain flickering on the screen and on home entertainment units. Hopefully the image will be true and responsible to the real world.

Conclusion

This Guide looks at the many feature films, telefilms, and TV mini-series available on video that contain Jewish content or are important in presenting the Jewish persona to the public. Based on the information provided, readers will be able to decide which videos to rent or purchase, and will know where to find them.

As mentioned earlier, video has freed up the film world. It is no longer necessary to wait for a film festival or for a revival in order to view a particular film. Nor is it necessary to wait until a television network or station shows a rerun of a program, film, or mini-series. We can often drive down to the local video store and find what we want there. As a result, we can watch what we want when we want. We can now control our viewing, and we can do it in the comfort of our own homes and at any hour of the night or day.

The only problem comes when we can't find what we want at the video store. Most video stores stock the same titles. We may have to aggressively seek out stores that carry the titles we want. Sometimes this means finding specialty stores or large superstores that carry thousands of titles, or it may mean going directly to a distributor.

Or it may mean tracking down community-funded video libraries. Doing this may take a little work, but it will be worthwhile in the long run.

---

1. Lester D. Friedman, *The Jewish Image in American Film* (Secaucus, N.J.: Citadel Press, 1987), p. 35.
2. *Ibid.*
3. *Ibid.*

1

THE FILMS

TITLE: **A LA MODE**

YEAR PRODUCED: 1994

DIRECTOR: Remy Duchemin

CAST: Ken Higelin, Jean Yanne, François Hauteserre, Florence Darel

COUNTRY OF ORIGIN: France

LANGUAGE: French with English subtitles

RUNNING TIME: 82 minutes

VIDEO: Miramax/Alliance

DESCRIPTION:

Light comedy about an orphan who is apprenticed to a Jewish tailor in Paris and becomes a high-fashion sensation in the 1960s. Entertaining and humorous film with lots of charm.

TITLE: **AARON'S MAGIC VILLAGE (AARON & THE BOOK OF WONDERS)**

YEAR PRODUCED: 1997

DIRECTOR: Albert Hanan Kaminski

CAST: Fyvush Finkel, Tovah Feldshuh

COUNTRY OF ORIGIN: United States, Hungary, France

LANGUAGE: English

RUNNING TIME: 78 minutes

VIDEO: Columbia Tristar Home Video/Alliance

DESCRIPTION:

Animated film based on some of the short stories of Isaac Bashevis Singer. The story follows young Aaron and his pet goat, Zlateh, as they arrive in the village of Chelm.

A sorcerer creates a Golem (a clay monster found in Yiddish literature and folk lore) but requires the magical "Book of Marvels," which is kept in Chelm, in order to give the Golem life. Aaron and the villagers battle to outwit the Sorcerer and his Golem.

Music was composed by Michel Legrand with lyrics by Sheldon Harnick, of *Fiddler on the Roof* fame. In Canada this video was released under the title *Aaron & the Book of Wonders*.

TITLE: **ABRAHAM**

YEAR PRODUCED: 1994

DIRECTOR: Joseph Sargent

CAST: Richard Harris, Barbara Hershey, Maximilian Schell, Vittorio Gassman

COUNTRY OF ORIGIN: United States

LANGUAGE: English

RUNNING TIME: 150 minutes

VIDEO: Turner/Malofilm

DESCRIPTION:

Excellent biblical epic made for cable television tells the story of Abraham, father of the Jewish people.

Relying only upon their faith, Abraham (Harris) and Sarah (Hershey) leave home and struggle through the wilderness to the Promised Land. Many challenges face Abraham, including the ultimate test, his willingness to sacrifice his favorite son, Isaac. A powerful film that won a number of awards and received a huge audience when telecast on cable.

TITLE: **ABOUT THE JEWS OF YEMEN: A VANISHING CULTURE**

YEAR PRODUCED: 1986

DIRECTOR: Dr. Johanna Spector

COUNTRY OF ORIGIN: United States

LANGUAGE: English

RUNNING TIME: 77 minutes

VIDEO: Ergo

DESCRIPTION:

Documentary that captures the rich culture developed by the Jews in Yemen over their 2000 years of history in that country. Describes traditional Yemenite celebrations including pre-wedding ceremony.

TITLE: **ACTOR (THE PAUL MUNI STORY)**

YEAR PRODUCED: 1978

DIRECTOR: Norman Lloyd

CAST: Herschel Bernardi, Georgia Brown, Harold Gould, Michael Kidd, Howard Duff, Jeff Lynas

COUNTRY OF ORIGIN: United States

LANGUAGE: English

RUNNING TIME: 105 minutes

VIDEO: Live (USA)

DESCRIPTION:

This television film was supposed to be a musical biography of American actor Paul Muni. In reality it is the story of the immigrant experience.

A family of Jewish vagabond actors who can't make ends meet in the Austro-Hungarian Empire of the late 1890s immigrate to the United States. The father, Favel Weisenfreund, can't get into the Jewish actors' union, so he takes his family to Cleveland, and then after a few years they move on to Chicago.

The youngest son, Muni, falls in love with the acting profession and succeeds where his father couldn't. He goes on to become a star on the Yiddish stage in New York and eventually signs a Hollywood film contract and becomes one of the greatest screen actors of his generation—Paul Muni.

This production was made for television and was recorded on video. While it did not have the big budget a film would have received, it is highly entertaining, and Herschel Bernardi is terrific as Favel; his acting, singing and dancing are the backbone of the production. Music and lyrics by Jerome Laurence and Robert E. Lee, who also did *Mame* on Broadway. New English lyrics were written for two traditional Yiddish songs, "Chiri Bim" and "Raisins and Almonds."

TITLE: **ADAM'S RIB**

YEAR PRODUCED: 1991

DIRECTOR: Viatcheslav Krichtofovitch

CAST: Inna Tchourikova, Sveltana Riabova, Macha Goloubkina, Andrei Toloubeiev, Elena Bogdanova, Andrei Kasianov

COUNTRY OF ORIGIN: Russia

LANGUAGE: Russian with English subtitles

RUNNING TIME: 75 minutes

VIDEO: Malofilm

DESCRIPTION:

Three generations of Russian women live together in a tiny Moscow apartment. The mother cares for the bedridden invalid grandmother while looking after her two daughters. The girls are by two different husbands, and the younger one has just learned that she is pregnant.

Tension and conflict fill the apartment, and the film shows the anti-Semitism and difficulties that still exist for Russian Jews. The father of the younger daughter is named Goldberg. The grandmother forced the girl to change her name so no one would know her father is Jewish. At one point the mother throws a party and invites her current boyfriend and both of her ex-husbands. When the younger girl's father comes in, he asks if the boyfriend has any problem with the fact that he is Jewish. The film makes it obvious that prejudice is still alive and thriving in Russia.

TITLE: **ALAN & NAOMI**

YEAR PRODUCED: 1992

DIRECTOR: Sterling Van Wagenen

CAST: Lukas Haas, Vanessa Zaoui, Michael Gross, Amy Aquino

COUNTRY OF ORIGIN: United States

LANGUAGE: English

RUNNING TIME: 96 minutes

VIDEO: Columbia

DESCRIPTION:

A Jewish girl from France arrives in Brooklyn after having witnessed her father's murder by the Nazis during World War II. A 14-year-old boy (Haas) who lives nearby is pressured by his parents to befriend her and try to break her out of her catatonic state. The boy acquiesces and slowly succeeds in drawing her out. Interesting Holocaust-related film.

TITLE: **ALMONDS AND RAISINS**
YEAR PRODUCED: 1984
DIRECTOR: Russ Karel
COUNTRY OF ORIGIN: United States
LANGUAGE: English
RUNNING TIME: 90 minutes
VIDEO: Ergo

DESCRIPTION:
A fascinating history of Yiddish cinema that features many film clips and interviews with participants of the vanished era. Narrated by Orson Wells.

TITLE: **THE AMBASSADOR**
YEAR PRODUCED: 1984
DIRECTOR: J. Lee Thompson
CAST: Robert Mitchum, Ellen Burstyn, Rock Hudson
COUNTRY OF ORIGIN: United States
LANGUAGE: English
RUNNING TIME: 97 minutes
VIDEO: MGM

DESCRIPTION:
An American ambassador, Robert Mitchum, is sent to the Middle East to help bring about peace. In the meantime his wife is having an affair with a PLO leader. Hudson, the ambassador's security officer, learns about the wife's affair and must deal with the problems created when terrorists blame the ambassador for making matters worse. This was Rock Hudson's last film.

AMERICAN
MATCHMAKER

TITLE: **AMERICAN MATCHMAKER (AMERICAN SHADCHEN)**

YEAR PRODUCED: 1940

DIRECTOR: Edgar G. Ulmer

CAST: Leo Fuchs, Judith Abarbanel, Yudel Dubinsky

COUNTRY OF ORIGIN: United States

LANGUAGE: Yiddish with English subtitles

RUNNING TIME: 87 minutes

VIDEO: Ergo

DESCRIPTION:

A movie star (Fuchs), who has been unlucky in love and has had several broken engagements, becomes a matchmaker and falls in love with a woman client.

This musical comedy updates the matchmaking business and even delves into modern psychoanalysis.

TITLE: **AMERICAN POP**

YEAR PRODUCED: 1981

DIRECTOR: Ralph Bakshi

CAST: Ron Thompson, Marya Small, Jerry Holland, Lisa Jane Persky, Roz Kelly

COUNTRY OF ORIGIN: United States

LANGUAGE: English

RUNNING TIME: 97 minutes

VIDEO: Columbia

DESCRIPTION:

Fascinating animated film follows the odyssey of a Jewish refugee family that arrives in America around the turn of the century and through their integration and assimilation. It showcases the changing American music styles of the 20th century.

At least one member of the family in each generation becomes a musician and by the time the film concludes, the youngest descendent is completely unaware of his Jewish roots.

A quick lesson in the disappearance of the Jew in American society.

AN AMERICAN TAIL

TITLE: **AN AMERICAN TAIL**

YEAR PRODUCED: 1986

DIRECTOR: Don Bluth

CAST: Animated film featuring the voices of Dom DeLuise, Madeline Kahn, Nehemiah Persoff, Christopher Plummer

COUNTRY OF ORIGIN: United States

LANGUAGE: English

RUNNING TIME: 81 minutes

VIDEO: MCA

DESCRIPTION:

This film, which deals with the Jewish immigrant experience in America more effectively than most live-action films, was released in theaters just before Christmas in 1986 and has since become a classic. Fievel Mousekewitz, a little boy mouse, travels to America with his family in search of a life free from persecution. In Russia, Jewish mice, like Jewish humans, are subject to religious and ethnic oppression. The place where the Mousekewitzes live is burned down during a pogrom. Fievel is lost at sea during the voyage across the Atlantic, and is washed up on shore in New York harbor. He vows to find his family, and eventually does. The animation is excellent, the voices suit the characters perfectly, and the music is delightful.

It is also a pleasure to see that the names of the characters haven't been changed or anglicized. The pronunciation may be difficult for some viewers, and the names may be harder to remember, but the producers decided to stay with authentic names rather than pander to their audience. A film that stands up well to several viewings.

TITLE: **AMONGST FRIENDS**

YEAR PRODUCED: 1993

DIRECTOR: Rob Weiss

CAST: Joseph Lindsey, Patrick McGaw, Steve Parlavecchio, Mira Sorvino

COUNTRY OF ORIGIN: United States

LANGUAGE: English

RUNNING TIME: 88 minutes

VIDEO: New Line (Columbia)

DESCRIPTION:

Story of three young Jewish suburbanites coming of age and flirting with a life of crime.

These guys live in the wealthy suburbs of Long Island. Their parents have made a lot of money, but they get into crime and violence for the thrills and for the prestige it brings on the street. They don't care much about others, as long as they get the money they need to carry on their lifestyle and feed their drug habits.

TITLE: **ANGEL OF DEATH**

YEAR PRODUCED: 1986

DIRECTOR: Jess Franco

CAST: Chris Mitchum, Fernando Rey, Susan Andrews

COUNTRY OF ORIGIN: United States

LANGUAGE: English

RUNNING TIME: 92 minutes

VIDEO: Starmaker Entertainment

DESCRIPTION:

Terrible film about a bunch of Nazi hunters trying to find the "Angel of Death," Dr. Josef Mengele, in South America.

TITLE: **ANGRY HARVEST**

YEAR PRODUCED: 1985

DIRECTOR: Angnieszka Holland

CAST: Armin Mueller-Stahl, Elisabeth Trissenaar, Wojciech Pszoniak

COUNTRY OF ORIGIN: Germany

LANGUAGE: German with English subtitles

RUNNING TIME: 102 minutes

VIDEO: Ingram International Films

DESCRIPTION:

A Polish farmer hides a young Jewish woman during the Nazi occupation of Poland. A serious relationship develops between them.

Nominated for an Academy Award as Best Foreign Film.

TITLE: **ANNE FRANK REMEMBERED**

YEAR PRODUCED: 1995

DIRECTOR: Jon Blair

COUNTRY OF ORIGIN: United States

LANGUAGE: English

RUNNING TIME: 122 minutes

VIDEO: Sony Classics/Malofilm

DESCRIPTION:

Excellent documentary that details the background of the Franks, their months in hiding, and the arrest and death of Anne and her family. This film adds a significant amount to what we already knew about Anne Frank. The producers tracked down relatives and friends, and even interviewed people who were with Anne in the camps. Documents all the events surrounding Anne, right up to her death and her father's efforts to have her diary published. The hero of the film turns out to be Miep Gies, the employee of Anne's father who helped the family hide and who found and preserved the diary after the Franks were arrested. This film won the Academy Award for feature-length documentaries.

TITLE: **ANNIE HALL**

YEAR PRODUCED: 1977

DIRECTOR: Woody Allen

CAST: Woody Allen, Diane Keaton, Tony Roberts, Paul Simon, Shelley Duvall, Carol Kane, Colleen Dewhurst, Christopher Walken

COUNTRY OF ORIGIN: United States

LANGUAGE: English

RUNNING TIME: 94 minutes

VIDEO: Fox

DESCRIPTION:

In some ways Allen's best film. Based on his own autobiographical material.

All of Allen's films have a personal base and some Jewish elements from his background. Allen seems to have perfected the Jewish "nebish" role. He always appears as the small, neurotic New York Jewish intellectual who tries to think his way out of tight spots. He is always comparing the joys of living in New York City to the drawbacks of Los Angeles.

The film is sandwiched between two jokes, at the beginning and at the end. Allen plays Alvy Singer, a paranoid, guilt-ridden Jew whose sexual hangups are a result of his fantasies about childhood and death. He blames all the world's problems on Jewishness: New York's fiscal problems, for instance, are due to the federal government's refusal to send financial assistance to the city because so many Jews live there. Allen's relationship with his dream girl, Diane Keaton, is doomed to failure because of the cultural and religious differences between them, as pointed out in the scene where he visits Keaton's family and compares her cold, aloof gentile relatives with his own warm though warring clan. Besides, how can he have a successful relationship with someone who orders pastrami on white bread with mayo and lettuce? The culture shock is too great. And it is through the Keaton character that he learns to accept his own unique qualities.

Won Academy Awards for Best Picture, Best Actress (Keaton), Best Director, and Best Original Screenplay. Received nomination for Best Actor (Allen).

TITLE: **ANTONIA AND JANE**
YEAR PRODUCED: 1991
DIRECTOR: Beeban Kidron
CAST: Imelda Staunton, Saskia Reeves
COUNTRY OF ORIGIN: Britain
LANGUAGE: English
RUNNING TIME: 77 minutes
VIDEO: Paramount

DESCRIPTION:
Enjoyable film, originally produced for British television, about two lifelong friends. One is plain, dumpy, and Jewish; the other, glamorous, attractive, successful, and not Jewish. Each thinks that the other's life is more interesting. Each envies the other.

The two friends, unbeknownst to each other, are receiving help from the same therapist. In a series of humorous flashbacks each tells about her life and her relationship to the other. At one point Antonia took Jane's boyfriend away and married him. In the end, both realize that their relationship is more important than anything else, and they remain friends.

TITLE: **THE APPRENTICESHIP OF DUDDY KRAVITZ**

YEAR PRODUCED: 1974

DIRECTOR: Ted Kotcheff

CAST: Richard Dreyfuss, Micheline Lanctot, Jack Warden, Denholm Elliott, Randy Quaid

COUNTRY OF ORIGIN: Canada

LANGUAGE: English

RUNNING TIME: 121 minutes

VIDEO: Paramount

DESCRIPTION:

Based on Mordecai Richler's novel about a Jewish boy in Montreal, right after World War II, who is determined to make his mark in the world and become rich.

A very fine film that points out the lengths to which people will go in order to succeed. One of the funniest scenes in film history has to be the showing of the bar mitzvah movie when Elliott unveils his "arty" production.

An interesting and memorable film.

TITLE: **THE ARCHITECTURE OF DOOM**

YEAR PRODUCED: 1989

DIRECTOR: Peter Cohen

CAST: James Mason, Ben Cross, Maximilian Schell, Irene Papas

COUNTRY OF ORIGIN: Sweden

LANGUAGE: Swedish with English Subtitles

RUNNING TIME: 119 minutes

VIDEO: Facets/CHV

DESCRIPTION:

Absorbing documentary from the point of view that Hitler's failed artistic ambitions may have led to World War II and his insistence on exterminating the Jews.

TITLE: **THE ASSIGNMENT**

YEAR PRODUCED: 1997

DIRECTOR: Christian Duguay

CAST: Aidunn Quinn, Donald Sutherland, Ben Kingsley

COUNTRY OF ORIGIN: United States

LANGUAGE: English

RUNNING TIME: 115 minutes

VIDEO: Motion International, Columbia Tristar Home Video

DESCRIPTION:

Action film that details the attempt by Israeli and American secret agents to track down the international terrorist, Carlos the Jackal.

A CIA operative (Sutherland) recruits an American naval officer (Quinn) who happens to be a perfect double for Carlos. With the assistance of Mossad commander Amos (Kingsley), they train the American to take on the role of Carlos, and they hope to persuade the KGB to conclude that Carlos has become a liability and get rid of him. The plot doesn't always make a lot of sense but the action is great.

TITLE: **THE ASSISI UNDERGROUND**

YEAR PRODUCED: 1984

DIRECTOR: Alexander Ramati

CAST: James Mason, Ben Cross, Maximilian Schell, Irene Papas

COUNTRY OF ORIGIN: France

LANGUAGE: English

RUNNING TIME: 115 minutes

VIDEO: MGM

DESCRIPTION:

Another true story of the Holocaust. This time the setting is in the small Italian town of Assisi. The town's Jews are slated for execution by the occupying Nazi forces when the Catholic Church steps in to rescue them.

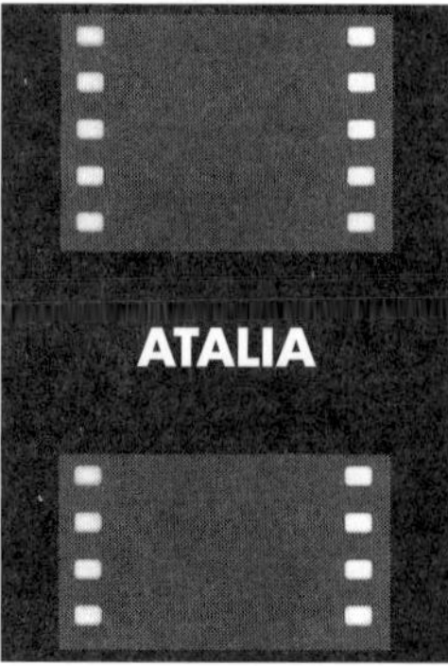

TITLE: **ATALIA**

YEAR PRODUCED: 1984

DIRECTOR: Akiva Tevet

CAST: Michal Bat-Adam, Yeftach Katzur, Dan Turen

COUNTRY OF ORIGIN: Israel

LANGUAGE: Hebrew with English subtitles

RUNNING TIME: 90 minutes

VIDEO: Ergo

DESCRIPTION:

Love between a war widow who lives on a kibbutz and a younger man creates a number of social problems. Set against the backdrop of the Yom Kippur War.

TITLE: **THE ATTIC: THE HIDING OF ANNE FRANK**

YEAR PRODUCED: 1988

DIRECTOR: John Erman

CAST: Mary Steenburgen, Paul Scofield, Lisa Jacobs

COUNTRY OF ORIGIN: United States

LANGUAGE: English

RUNNING TIME: 95 minutes

VIDEO: Cabin Fever

DESCRIPTION:

The story of Anne Frank as told from the point of view of Miep Gies, the courageous Dutch woman who tried to protect the Frank family from the Nazis.

Mary Steenburgen is outstanding as Gies in this beautifully produced television film. Certainly worth seeing, if only to learn another aspect of this heartrending story.

TITLE: **AU REVOIR LES ENFANTS**

YEAR PRODUCED: 1987

DIRECTOR: Louis Malle

CAST: Gaspard Manesse, Raphael Fejto, Francine Racette, Stanislas Carre de Malberg, Philippe Morier-Genoud, François Berleand

COUNTRY OF ORIGIN: France

LANGUAGE: French with English subtitles

RUNNING TIME: 103 minutes

VIDEO: Orion

DESCRIPTION:

Highly acclaimed drama that is partly based on Malle's own experiences during World War II.

The time is 1944. The setting is a Catholic boarding school for boys in German-occupied France. Three new boys enroll at the school. The newcomers seem to be a little withdrawn and somewhat different from the others. The oldest of the new boys, Jean Bonnet, becomes friends with Julien Quentin. They share a number of adventures, including getting lost in the forest, and a bond develops between them.

Julien learns that Jean's name is not really Bonnet, but Kippelstein, but he knows little about Jews and the problems they face in Nazi-occupied France. In the end, the headmaster is denounced and the Germans arrive to arrest him and the Jewish boys. The film ends with the three boys and the headmaster being taken away to a death camp.

Excellent film with many moving moments. This is considered one of Malle's best works.

TITLE: **AUDITIONS (ACTORS)**

YEAR PRODUCED: 1995

CAST: Yael Hadar, Rami Hoiberger, Aki Avni, Nevo Kimchi, Yoav Hite, Ayala Asherov, Tali Atzmon

DIRECTOR: Ron Ninio

COUNTRY OF ORIGIN: Israel

LANGUAGE: Hebrew with English subtitles

RUNNING TIME: 92 minutes

VIDEO: Sisu Home Entertainment/CHV Communications

DESCRIPTION:

Story about a group of young actors struggling to learn their art and make their mark in the theatrical world in Israel.

TITLE: **AUSTERIA**

YEAR PRODUCED: 1988

CAST: Ewa Domanska, Liliana Glabczynska, Franciszek Pieczka, Wojciech Pszoniak

DIRECTOR: Jerzy Kawalcrowicz

COUNTRY OF ORIGIN: Poland

LANGUAGE: Polish with English subtitles

RUNNING TIME: 110 minutes

VIDEO: Facets

DESCRIPTION:

Drama centering on a group of Orthodox Polish Jews who flee from the Cossack army in 1914. They take refuge at an inn run by an elderly.

TITLE: **AVALON**

YEAR PRODUCED: 1990

DIRECTOR: Barry Levinson

CAST: Armin Mueller-Stahl, Aidan Quinn, Elizabeth Perkins, Joan Plowright, Lou Jacobi, Leo Fuchs, Elijah Wood, Eve Gordon, Kevin Pollak

COUNTRY OF ORIGIN: United States

LANGUAGE: English

RUNNING TIME: 126 minutes

VIDEO: Columbia

DESCRIPTION:

Gentle, charming film about a Jewish immigrant in Baltimore. As time passes, especially into the 1950s and 1960s, the family slowly flies apart. Some members move into the suburbs, where the television takes over the living room and becomes the center of family activities.

A moving look at the Americanization of the Jewish family with wonderful performances by the entire cast.

TITLE: **BACHELOR GIRL**

YEAR PRODUCED: 1987

DIRECTOR: Rivka Hartman

CAST: Lyn Pierse, Kim Gyngell, Jan Friedl, Bruce Spence, Doug Tremlett, Ruth Yaffe

COUNTRY OF ORIGIN: Australia

LANGUAGE: English

RUNNING TIME: 83 minutes

VIDEO: Cineplex-Odeon (MCA)

DESCRIPTION:

Comedy about an unmarried Jewish career woman. Dot Bloom is a script writer for an Australian soap opera and has to deal with members of her family, who are trying to get her married off.
A lot of the humor turns on her family's Jewish traits and their anxiety that she not become an old maid.

BEACHES

TITLE: **BEACHES**

YEAR PRODUCED: 1988

DIRECTOR: Garry Marshall

CAST: Bette Midler, Barbara Hershey, John Heard, Spalding Gray, Lainie Kazan, Mayim Bialik

COUNTRY OF ORIGIN: United States

LANGUAGE: English

RUNNING TIME: 123 minutes

VIDEO: Touchstone

DESCRIPTION:

This is a Bette Midler film all the way—she acts, she tells jokes, and she sings. Boy does she sing! The soundtrack is terrific, and Midler is in top form for every song. The story is another matter. If you don't mind the cliches and the tearjerker of an ending, and if you're a Midler fan, you'll love this film. Midler plays C. C. Bloom, a Jewish pop star who seems to have been predestined to be a hit. Her personal life is a little more cluttered and a lot less successful. A series of flashbacks fill in Bloom's background. Her mother pushed her to become a performer, and she didn't object at all. She wanted to go on stage.

At the age of 12 C. C. meets WASP Hillary (Hershey) in Atlantic City, and the two opposites become lifetime friends. There are ups and downs in their relationship, but each can always count on the other when a crisis occurs. Over the next 30 years the two friends live, love, and make their way through life. At the end, C. C. is there to take care of Hillary when she needs it, and all the handkerchiefs come out. Midler takes this film and makes it her own. And she does an incredible job, putting her in the rare company of only a few stars who can carry a picture all by themselves. If you want to see and hear Midler at her best, this is the film to see.

TITLE: **BECAUSE OF THAT WAR**

YEAR PRODUCED: 1988

DIRECTOR: Orna Ben-Dor Niv

COUNTRY OF ORIGIN: Israel

LANGUAGE: Hebrew with English Subtitles

RUNNING TIME: 90 minutes

VIDEO: New Yorker, Sisu/CHV

DESCRIPTION:

Documentary featuring Yehuda Poliker, one of the leading rock performers in Israel.

Poliker's family came from Salonika and Poliker knew very little about his family's history during the Holocaust. This film chronicles Poliker's journey of self-discovery.

TITLE: **BEN GURION: AN APPOINTMENT WITH DESTINY**

YEAR PRODUCED: 1968

DIRECTOR: David Perlov

COUNTRY OF ORIGIN: United States

LANGUAGE: English

RUNNING TIME: 103 minutes

VIDEO: Ergo

DESCRIPTION:

Docu-drama that traces the life of Israel's first Prime Minister, David Ben Gurion, from his childhood in Russia, through his arrival in Palestine and his leadership of the Jewish community in Palestine/Israel. The film shows Ben Gurion taking his walks in the desert and recreates highlights of the historical events associated with him.

TITLE: **THE BENNY GOODMAN STORY**

YEAR PRODUCED: 1955

DIRECTOR: Valentino Davies

CAST: Steve Allen, Donna Reed, Herbert Anderson, Berta Gersten, Robert F. Simon, Gene Krupa, Lionel Hampton, Teddy Wilson

COUNTRY OF ORIGIN: United States

LANGUAGE: English

RUNNING TIME: 116 minutes

VIDEO: MCA

DESCRIPTION:

Typical Hollywood biography of the famous band leader and musician. Some mention of Goodman's Jewish background is made, including the mother's comment that it is "like a knife in my heart" when Goodman announces his engagement to a non-Jewish girl.

Great music, including "And the Angels Sing" and "Sing, Sing, Sing."

TITLE: **BEST BOY**

YEAR PRODUCED: 1979

DIRECTOR: Ira Wohl

COUNTRY OF ORIGIN: United States

LANGUAGE: English

RUNNING TIME: 111 minutes

VIDEO: National Center for Jewish Films

DESCRIPTION:

Documentary about the director's 52-year-old retarded cousin, Philly. Wohl followed Philly around for three years, filming his attempts to become independent. The film shows Philly's efforts to learn new skills and become capable of living on his own in a group home. A wonderful and moving film that won an Academy Award for Best Documentary.

TITLE: **BEYOND THE WALLS**

YEAR PRODUCED: 1985

DIRECTOR: Uri Barbash

CAST: Amon Zadok, Mohammed Bakri, Assaf Dayan

COUNTRY OF ORIGIN: Israel

LANGUAGE: Available in Hebrew with English subtitles or in dubbed versions

RUNNING TIME: 103 minutes

VIDEO: Warner

DESCRIPTION:

Gripping Israeli drama that pleads for brotherhood.

In an Israeli prison, a Jewish convict battles against the leader of the Palestinian inmates. By the end of the film each man recognizes that the other is a human being, and that unless they unite in opposition to the cruel prison authorities, they will both suffer the consequences. One of the better films to come out of Israel.

TITLE: **BILOXI BLUES**

YEAR PRODUCED: 1988

DIRECTOR: Mike Nichols

CAST: Matthew Broderick, Christopher Walken, Matt Mulhern, Casey Siemaszko, Penelope Ann Miller

COUNTRY OF ORIGIN: United States

LANGUAGE: English

RUNNING TIME: 105 minutes

VIDEO: MCA

DESCRIPTION:

The second in the Neil Simon trilogy gives us the further adventures in growing up of Brooklynite Eugene Jerome.

The time is the latter days of World War II. Eugene has been drafted and is on his way to Biloxi, Mississippi, for basic training. Through him we experience all the turmoil and problems encountered by young men, especially young Jewish men, when they have to leave home and make it on their own in the larger society.

THE BIRDCAGE

TITLE: **THE BIRDCAGE**

YEAR PRODUCED: 1996

DIRECTOR: Mike Nichols

CAST: Robin Williams, Gene Hackman, Nathan Lane, Dianne Wiest, Dan Futterman, Hank Azaria

COUNTRY OF ORIGIN: United States

LANGUAGE: English

RUNNING TIME: 118 minutes

VIDEO: MGM

DESCRIPTION:

In this Americanized version of *La Cage aux Folles*, Robin Williams and Nathan Lane play long-time partners Armand and Albert. They share a relationship that has included the raising of Armand's son, Val, into a caring, mature, and heterosexual young man.

When Val announces his engagement to the daughter of a conservative U.S. Senator and that his fiancée and her family are coming over for dinner, Armand wants to make the best impression possible.

This hilarious comedy makes it obvious that Armand and Albert are Jewish. The fact that Armand's last name is Goldman is only one of many clues. At the end, we see the two young people being married. Val is wearing a yarmulke and the ceremony is being jointly conducted by a rabbi and a minister.

TITLE: **BLACK SUNDAY**

YEAR PRODUCED: 1977

DIRECTOR: John Frankenheimer

CAST: Robert Shaw, Bruce Dern, Marthe Keller, Fritz Weaver

COUNTRY OF ORIGIN: United States

LANGUAGE: English

RUNNING TIME: 143 minutes

VIDEO: Paramount

DESCRIPTION:

Arab terrorist group attempts to blow up the Goodyear blimp over the Super Bowl stadium in order to kill the 80,000 football fans, including the President of the United States, watching the game.

Shaw plays an Israeli commando who discovers the plot and pursues the terrorists to the United States in an attempt to prevent the tragedy.

Terrific photography and nonstop action. Shows Israelis as strong, powerful force committed to stopping international terrorism.

TITLE: **BLAZING SADDLES**

YEAR PRODUCED: 1974

DIRECTOR: Mel Brooks

CAST: Cleavon Little, Gene Wilder, Harvey Korman, Madeline Kahn, Slim Pickens, Alex Karras, Mel Brooks, Dom DeLuise

COUNTRY OF ORIGIN: United States

LANGUAGE: English

RUNNING TIME: 90 minutes

VIDEO: Warner

DESCRIPTION:

Wild romp on the prairie as Brooks's bizarre Jewish humor runs rampant.

Stirred up a great deal of controversy when first released. Everything from farting around the campfire to an Indian speaking Yiddish contributes to this wacky film. It doesn't all work, but there are enough jokes that do to make this a very popular and very successful film.

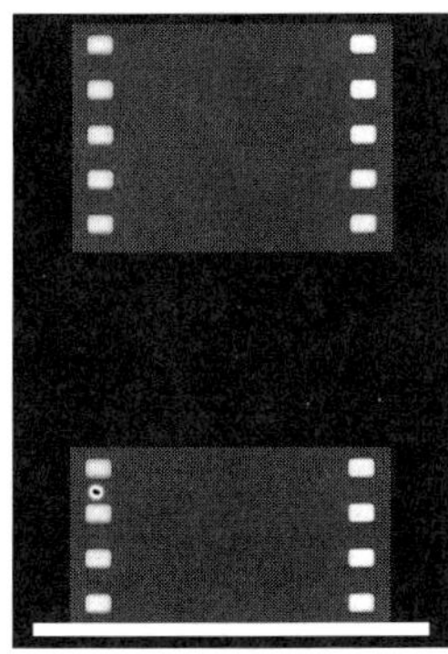

TITLE: **BLAZING SAND**

YEAR PRODUCED: 1960

DIRECTOR: Raphael Nussbaum

CAST: Daliah Lavi, Gert Gunter Hoffmann, Oded Kotler, Uri Zohar

COUNTRY OF ORIGIN: United States, Germany, Israel

LANGUAGE: English

RUNNING TIME: 98 minutes

VIDEO: Facets

DESCRIPTION:

One of the early "B" movies made in Israel, this film tells the story of five young people who find some ancient Biblical scrolls in the desert near the Jordanian border.

TITLE: **BLIND MAN'S BLUFF**

YEAR PRODUCED: 1993

DIRECTOR: Aner Preminger

COUNTRY OF ORIGIN: Israel

LANGUAGE: Hebrew with English subtitles

RUNNING TIME: 93 minutes

VIDEO: National Center for Jewish Film

DESCRIPTION:

Story of a young woman pianist who tries to find herself despite pressures and expectations from all sides—her parents, her former boyfriend, her music, and her own desires.

TITLE: **BLOOD MONEY: NAZI GOLD**

YEAR PRODUCED: 1987

DIRECTOR: Gaelen Ross

COUNTRY OF ORIGIN: United States

LANGUAGE: English

RUNNING TIME: 100 minutes

VIDEO: Ergo

DESCRIPTION:

Story of how Jews desperate to provide for their families' future, deposited their worldly assets in Swiss banks. Those that did survive have been unable to retrieve their money.

TITLE: **THE BLUM AFFAIR**

YEAR PRODUCED: 1948

DIRECTOR: Erich Engel

CAST: Hans-Christian Blech, Gisela Trowe, Kurt Ehrhardt, Paul Bildt, Klaus Becker

COUNTRY OF ORIGIN: Germany

LANGUAGE: German with English subtitles

RUNNING TIME: 109 minutes

VIDEO: Nostalgia Family Video, Facets, Applause Productions

DESCRIPTION:

A Jewish man is framed for a murder by corrupt and anti-Semitic circles in Germany after World War I.

TITLE: **THE BOAT IS FULL**

YEAR PRODUCED: 1981

DIRECTOR: Markus Imhoof

CAST: Tina Engel, Curt Bois, Renate Steiger, Mathias Gnaedinger

COUNTRY OF ORIGIN: Switzerland

LANGUAGE: German with English subtitles

RUNNING TIME: 104 minutes

VIDEO: Sultan/CHV

DESCRIPTION:

Group of Jewish refugees seek asylum in Switzerland during World War II.

Excellent production which leaves a number of moral questions unanswered, especially when the Swiss must decide whether to return the Jews to Germany and how to treat German army deserters who are also seeking asylum. This may have been one of the first times Switzerland's purported neutrality during World War II was questioned.

TITLE: **BORDER STREET (ULICA GRANICZA)**

YEAR PRODUCED: 1948

DIRECTOR: Alexander Ford

CAST: J. Leszczynski, M. Broniewski, J. Zlotnick, with introduction by Quentin Reynolds

COUNTRY OF ORIGIN: Poland

LANGUAGE: Polish with English subtitles

RUNNING TIME: 110 minutes

VIDEO: IHF

DESCRIPTION:

Follows a group of Poles from just before the Nazi invasion until the Warsaw Ghetto Uprising. The main characters are all from the same neighborhood; they include Jews and non-Jews, working people and professionals.

It is interesting that this Polish film, produced only three years after the end of World War II, is so open in its depiction of Polish anti-Semitism and the suffering of the Jews. The Yiddish song "Es Brent" is used as a theme through part of the narrative.

Border Street won a prize at the Venice Film Festival and was a forerunner of the Holocaust films of the 1980s and 1990s.

TITLE: **BORN IN BERLIN**

YEAR PRODUCED: 1991

DIRECTOR: Nomi Ben Natan and Leora Kamenetzky

COUNTRY OF ORIGIN: Israel

LANGUAGE: German, English, Swedish, and Hebrew with English subtitles

RUNNING TIME: 85 minutes

VIDEO: National Center for Jewish Films

DESCRIPTION:

Documentary about three girls who grow up in 1930s Berlin, survive the Holocaust, and are forced to build new lives elsewhere after the war. Many years later all three finally find a new home in Israel.

TITLE: **THE BOXER AND DEATH**

YEAR PRODUCED: 1963

DIRECTOR: Peter Solan

CAST: Stefan Kvietik

COUNTRY OF ORIGIN: Czechoslovakia

LANGUAGE: Czech with English subtitles

RUNNING TIME: 107 or 120 minutes, depending on source.

VIDEO: Discount Video Tapes, Nostalgia Family Video, Facets

DESCRIPTION:

Commander of a Nazi concentration camp is an enthusiastic boxing fan and takes an interest in one of his prisoners.

TITLE: **BOY TAKES GIRL**

YEAR PRODUCED: 1983

DIRECTOR: Michal Bat-Adam

CAST: Gabi Eldor, Hillel Neeman, Dina Limon

COUNTRY OF ORIGIN: Israel

LANGUAGE: Hebrew with English subtitles

RUNNING TIME: 93 minutes

VIDEO: MGM

DESCRIPTION:

A little Israeli girl has difficulty adjusting to being placed on a kibbutz for the summer.

TITLE: **THE BOYS FROM BRAZIL**

YEAR PRODUCED: 1978

DIRECTOR: Franklin J. Schaffner

CAST: Gregory Peck, Laurence Olivier, James Mason, Lilli Palmer, Uta Hagen, Steve Guttenberg, Denholm Elliott, John Rubenstein

COUNTRY OF ORIGIN: United States

LANGUAGE: English

RUNNING TIME: 123 minutes

VIDEO: Fox

DESCRIPTION:

Thriller about Nazi Josef Mengele trying to revive the Third Reich by cloning a number of copies of Adolf Hitler and the attempts by a Jewish Nazi hunter to find him before he can succeed with his mad plan. Nominated for Academy Awards for Best Actor (Olivier), Best Film Editing, and Best Original Score.

TITLE: **BRIGHTON BEACH MEMOIRS**

YEAR PRODUCED: 1986

DIRECTOR: Gene Saks

CAST: Jonathan Silverman, Blythe Danner, Bob Dishy, Judith Ivey

COUNTRY OF ORIGIN: United States

LANGUAGE: English

RUNNING TIME: 110 minutes

VIDEO: MCA

DESCRIPTION:

The first part of Neil Simon's autobiographical trilogy, based on the successful Broadway play.

This is a comedy that looks at a 15-year-old Jewish boy growing up in the Brooklyn of the late 1930s. His major concerns are baseball and girls. And in a home crowded with seven people, growing up can be both difficult and funny.

Jonathan Silverman, making his first film appearance in *Brighton Beach Memoirs*, brings charm and humor to his character.

TITLE: **A BRIVELE DER MAMEN (A LETTER TO MOTHER)**

YEAR PRODUCED: 1938

DIRECTOR: Joseph Green

CAST: Lucy Gehrman, Misha Gehrman, Edmund Zayenda

COUNTRY OF ORIGIN: United States

LANGUAGE: Yiddish with English subtitles

RUNNING TIME: 106 minutes

VIDEO: National Center for Jewish Films, Ergo

DESCRIPTION:

Story of a mother's attempt to keep her family together despite poverty, war, and migration. A real tearjerker of a melodrama.

TITLE: **BROADWAY BOUND**

YEAR PRODUCED: 1992

DIRECTOR: Paul Bogart

CAST: Jonathan Silverman, Anne Bancroft, Hume Cronyn, Corey Parker, Jerry Orbach, Michele Lee

COUNTRY OF ORIGIN: United States

LANGUAGE: English

RUNNING TIME: 90 minutes

VIDEO: ABC Video/Astral

DESCRIPTION:

Third and last entry in the Neil Simon autobiographical trilogy, after *Brighton Beach Memoirs* and *Biloxi Blues.*

This time out, Eugene Jerome and his brother Stan are struggling to become comedy writers. It is 1948, and they have begun to make inroads writing sketches for radio by basing their pieces on their own family.

Produced for television, this film shows Jerome's progression to an almost independent adult who can finally make a living and gets ready to move out and live on his own.

TITLE: **BROKEN GLASS**

YEAR PRODUCED: 1996

DIRECTOR: David Thacker

CAST: Mandy Patinkin, Henry Goodman, Margot Leicester, Elizabeth Montgomery

COUNTRY OF ORIGIN: United States

LANGUAGE: English

RUNNING TIME: 100 minutes

VIDEO: Anchor Bay Entertainment

DESCRIPTION:

Drama of Sylvia Gellburg (Leicester), a Brooklyn housewife suffering paralysis from the waist down after she learns of the anti-Semitic outbreaks in Germany following Krystallnacht. The neighborhood physician, Dr. Harry Hyman (Patinkin), makes an emergency house call and realizes this is a case of hysterical paralysis. As he probes Sylvia's mind, we learn about each of the characters as their personal lives and the horrors of Germany intermix.

TITLE: **BROTHERHOOD OF THE ROSE**

YEAR PRODUCED: 1989

DIRECTOR: Marvin J. Chomsky

CAST: Robert Mitchum, Peter Strauss, Connie Sellecca, David Morse

COUNTRY OF ORIGIN: United States

LANGUAGE: English

RUNNING TIME: 103 minutes

VIDEO: Vidmark

DESCRIPTION:

TV film based on the novel by David Morell, who also wrote *First Blood* (Rambo).

In this story, Saul (Strauss) and Chris (Morse) were raised as brothers and trained to be killers by a CIA operative. When their control officer betrays them, the two operatives run for their lives. Saul is Jewish, and he hooks up with an Israeli agent (Sellecca) to defeat the forces pursuing them.

TITLE: **BRUSSELS TRANSIT**

YEAR PRODUCED: 1980

DIRECTOR: Samy Szingerbaum

COUNTRY OF ORIGIN: United States

LANGUAGE: Yiddish with English subtitles

RUNNING TIME: 80 minutes

VIDEO: Ingram International Films

DESCRIPTION:

Yiddish film about a Jewish family's resettlement in Belgium after Word War II. The family, based on the director's, never fully adjusts to life in the new country.

Done in a semi-documentary style, but gradually takes on a more dramatic form. Ends abruptly with no real conclusion, leaving many questions unanswered. Not a very satisfying film for this reason.

TITLE: **BUT WHERE IS DANIEL WAX?**

YEAR PRODUCED: 1974

DIRECTOR: Avram Heffner

CAST: Lior Yaeni, Michael Lipkin, Esther Zevko

COUNTRY OF ORIGIN: Israel

LANGUAGE: Hebrew with English subtitles

RUNNING TIME: 95 minutes

VIDEO: Ergo

DESCRIPTION:

At a high school reunion, two men meet and discuss the popular hero of their class.

TITLE: **CABARET**

YEAR PRODUCED: 1972

DIRECTOR: Bob Fosse

CAST: Liza Minnelli, Joel Grey, Michael York, Helmut Griem, Fritz Wepper, Marisa Berenson

COUNTRY OF ORIGIN: United States

LANGUAGE: English

RUNNING TIME: 128 minutes

VIDEO: Fox

DESCRIPTION:

Once in a while all the elements come together to produce a truly great film. This was the case with Cabaret.

The film adaptation is vastly superior to the Broadway show. Several songs from the show were discarded, and new and better material was added. Bob Fosse did a magnificent job in staging this film, and Liza Minnelli and Joel Grey are superb. In fact, all of the actors do excellent work.

The story revolves around a small-time American singer in 1930s Berlin. Germany is undergoing a great deal of change under the Nazi regime, and hate permeates the atmosphere. The cabaret where Minnelli works, and especially the emcee, represents the evil that is taking place and foreshadows even worse times. Nazis are lurking everywhere. Violence is escalating. And through it all strides Minnelli, exuding humor and love for all.

The juxtaposition of songs and Nazi violence highlights the ascending spiral of evil. The presentation of the song "Tomorrow Belongs to Me," initially sung by a beautiful, cherubic teenage boy, is heartrending, especially when the camera pulls back and the adults join in what is clearly a Nazi song. Cabaret does not deal directly with the annihilation of Germany's Jews, but nonetheless is one of the great Holocaust films.

Won Academy Awards for Best Actress (Minnelli), Best Art Direction/Set Decoration, Best Cinematography, Best Director, Best Film Editing, Best Sound, Best Supporting Actor (Grey), and Best Score. Nominated for Best Adapted Screenplay and Best Picture.

TITLE: **CAFE AU LAIT**

YEAR PRODUCED: 1993

DIRECTOR: Mathieu Kassovitz

CAST: Julie Mauduech, Hubert Kounde, Mathieu Kassovitz

COUNTRY OF ORIGIN: France

LANGUAGE: French with English subtitles

RUNNING TIME: 94 minutes

VIDEO: New Yorker

DESCRIPTION:

Young Parisian woman (Mauduech) becomes pregnant but is not certain who the father is, the black law student (Kounde) or the Jewish bicycle courier (Kassovitz). Comedy that looks at race relationships.

TITLE: **A CALL TO REMEMBER**

YEAR PRODUCED: 1997

DIRECTOR: Jack Bender

ACTORS: Blythe Danner, Joe Mantegna, David Lascher

COUNTRY OF ORIGIN: United States

LANGUAGE: English

RUNNING TIME: 111 minutes

VIDEO: Universal Pictures Home Video

DESCRIPTION:

Moving drama about the after effects of the Holocaust. Paula (Blythe Danner) and David (Joe Mantegna) are two survivors who lost their families in the Holocaust, met shortly afterwards, married and started a new life in the United States.

They have two sons, with whom they share little about their experiences, until Paula receives a call informing her that a son she thought had been lost in the Holocaust, was alive and was on his way to see her.

The results are dramatic, as both adults prepare for this meeting and attempt to prepare their sons for it. Excellent performances mark this superior made-for-cable film.

TITLE: **THE CANTOR'S SON (DEM KHAZN'S ZINDL)**

YEAR PRODUCED: 1937

DIRECTOR: Ilya Motyleff and Sidney Goldin

CAST: Moishe Oysher, Florence Weiss, Judith Abarbanel

COUNTRY OF ORIGIN: United States

LANGUAGE: Yiddish with English subtitles

RUNNING TIME: 90 minutes

VIDEO: Ergo

DESCRIPTION:

Story based on the life of its star, Moishe Oysher.

A youngster leaves his European hometown and eventually arrives in America, where he works as a janitor. In time his great talent is discovered, and he gains fame as a singer.

Moishe Oysher was an actor, but his reputation was based on his magnificent voice. He was one of the great cantors of the twentieth century.

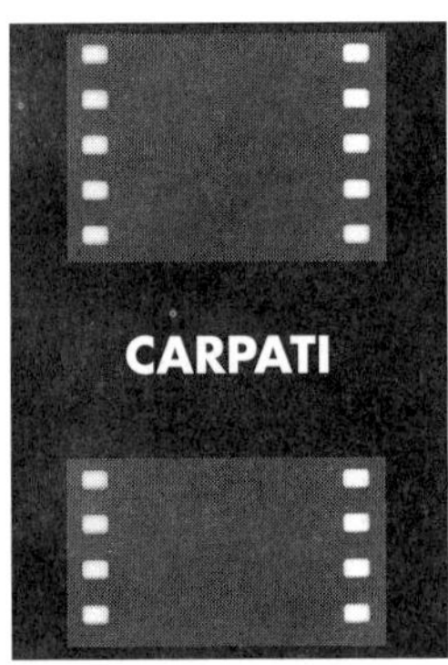

TITLE: **CARPATI**

YEAR PRODUCED: 1996

DIRECTOR: Yale Strom

COUNTRY OF ORIGIN: United States

LANGUAGE: Russian and Yiddish with English Subtitles and English narration

RUNNING TIME: 80 minutes

VIDEO: New Yorker

DESCRIPTION:

Documentary focusing on Zev Goldinger who lives in the Carpathian mountains of South East Europe. Although he lives only 50 miles from his birth place, Zev has not been there since his deportation to Auschwitz during World War II. Zev returns to his home town to revive his memories and to present a torah scroll to the town's synagogue. This film is filled with Jewish and Gypsy music and is narrated by Leonard Nimoy.

TITLE: **CAST A GIANT SHADOW**

YEAR PRODUCED: 1966

DIRECTOR: Melville Shavelson

ACTORS: Kirk Douglas, Senta Berger, Angie Dickinson, James Donald, Stathis Giallelis, Luther Adler, Frank Sinatra, Yul Brynner, John Wayne

COUNTRY OF ORIGIN: United States

LANGUAGE: English

RUNNING TIME: 139 minutes

VIDEO: Fox

DESCRIPTION:

True story of Colonel David Marcus, a lawyer and West Point graduate who served in the U.S. Army during World War II. In late 1947 he went to Palestine to help the underground organize an army to defend the Jewish state after it declared its independence. Marcus took part in several important battles that secured the road to Jerusalem through Arab territory.

Action film with excellent battle scenes. Some may appear too fantastic to be real, but were based on fact. The only questionable aspect of the film is the love interest, which supposedly was fictionalized.

Marcus was accidentally killed by one of his own men just before a truce went into effect and was laid to rest at West Point, the only soldier buried there who died under a foreign flag. His gravestone says: "Colonel David Marcus—A Soldier for All Humanity."

His casket was accompanied from Israel by the future Israeli chief of staff and politician, Moshe Dayan. In the film Yul Brynner was originally supposed to portray Dayan, but when a lawsuit was threatened, the producers had him take off the eye patch and changed the name of his character.

TITLE: **CATSKILL HONEYMOON**
YEAR PRODUCED: 1949
DIRECTOR: Josef Berne
CAST: Michal Michalesko, Jan Bart, Bas Sheva, Max and Rose Bozyk, Bobby Colt, the Feder Sisters, Henrietta Jacobson, Julius Adler, Irving Grossman, Dinah Goldberg
COUNTRY OF ORIGIN: United States
LANGUAGE: English and Yiddish no subtitles
RUNNING TIME: 93 minutes
VIDEO: National Center for Jewish Films

DESCRIPTION:
A hotel in the Catskills helps valued customers celebrate their fiftieth wedding anniversary by putting on a variety show. Lots of music and fun for all.

TITLE: **CEMETERY CLUB**
YEAR PRODUCED: 1993
DIRECTOR: Bill Duke
CAST: Ellen Burstyn, Olympia Dukakis, Diane Ladd, Danny Aiello
COUNTRY OF ORIGIN: United States
LANGUAGE: English
RUNNING TIME: 114 minutes
VIDEO: Touchstone

DESCRIPTION:
A funny and touching story about three Jewish widows who have been lifelong friends and now share the loss of their husbands.

The friends meet once a week and seemingly accept the fact that they may spend the rest of their lives alone without mates, until Ben Katz (Aiello) walks into the life of Esther Moskowitz (Burstyn). Esther enters into a passionate affair with Ben; although the relationship runs into problems, it teaches her and her friends that their happiest days have only just begun. An honest and realistic story that should appeal to everyone.

CHARIOTS OF FIRE

TITLE: **CHARIOTS OF FIRE**

YEAR PRODUCED: 1981

DIRECTOR: Hugh Hudson

CAST: Ben Cross, Ian Charleson, Nigel Havers, Cheryl Campbell, Alice Krige, Ian Holm, Sir John Gielgud, Patrick Magee, Nigel Davenport, Brad Davis, Peter Egan

COUNTRY OF ORIGIN: Britain

LANGUAGE: English

RUNNING TIME: 124 minutes

VIDEO: Warner

DESCRIPTION:

Story of two sprinters who competed in the 1924 Olympics. Harold Abraham is Jewish and seems driven by his desire to show that Jews are as capable as anyone else; Eric Liddell is a Christian who views his running as an offering to God.

Although the film spends a lot of time on both characters, it conveys a sense that Liddell is a better person because he runs for the joy of running and refuses to give up his beliefs in order to win. An example of this is when Liddell refuses to run in the 100 meters at the Olympics because it is held on a Sunday.

The film won Academy Awards for Best Picture, Best Original Screenplay, Best Costume Design, and Best Score, and was nominated for Best Director and Best Supporting Actor (Holm).

TITLE: **CHARLIE GRANT'S WAR**

YEAR PRODUCED: 1980

DIRECTOR: Martin Lavut

CAST: R. H. Thompson, Joan Orenstein, Jan Rubes, Douglas Campbell

COUNTRY OF ORIGIN: Canada

LANGUAGE: English

RUNNING TIME: 130 minutes

VIDEO: Quintex/CBC

DESCRIPTION:

True story of a Canadian diamond merchant who saved more than 600 Jews from Hitler's death camps. Produced for Canadian television by the Canadian Broadcasting Corporation.

Charlie Grant is the son of a wealthy Canadian family. He arrives in Vienna in the 1930s and is quickly robbed of all his money. He meets a Jewish couple who introduce him to some influential people, one of whom offers Charlie a job with his firm.

Charlie quickly amasses a small fortune in the diamond business. When the Nazis occupy Austria, he refuses to get involved, but when one of his Jewish friends is beaten up, Charlie decides to help as many Jews as possible to escape.

TITLE: **CHILDREN OF RAGE**
YEAR PRODUCED: 1975
DIRECTOR: Arthur Allan Seidelman
CAST: Cyril Cusack, Simon Ward
COUNTRY OF ORIGIN: United States
LANGUAGE: English
RUNNING TIME: 99 minutes
VIDEO: Academy

DESCRIPTION:
A look at the Palestinian-Israeli conflict and at terrorism from the viewpoint of an Israeli pacifist doctor. Not very sympathetic to the Israeli side.

TITLE: **THE CHOSEN**
YEAR PRODUCED: 1981
DIRECTOR: Jeremy Paul Kagan
CAST: Maximilian Schell, Rod Steiger, Robby Benson, Barry Miller, Ron Rifkin
COUNTRY OF ORIGIN: United States
LANGUAGE: English
RUNNING TIME: 107 minutes
VIDEO: Fox

DESCRIPTION:
This film, based on the acclaimed novel by Chaim Potok, is probably the best depiction of Jewish religious life in America ever produced for the screen.

The story revolves around two teenage Jewish boys. Danny Saunders comes from a Hasidic family. His father is the leader of the sect and expects Danny to follow in his footsteps. Reuven Malter comes from a traditional but more secular family. His father is a devoted Zionist who works diligently for the establishment of a Jewish state in Palestine.

The time is 1944, and the two boys meet in a neighborhood baseball game. Reuven is injured when struck in the eye by a ball hit by Danny. This leads to a strange friendship where

Reuven learns about the customs and traditions of the Hasidim and Danny confides to Reuven that he secretly wants to study Freud.

The film takes a careful and honest look at the differences between two segments of Jewish society and lovingly presents both as alternative lifestyles for committed Jews. Even the ending, with Danny going off to study psychology and Reuven deciding to become a rabbi, is an affirmation of their religion, customs, and traditions.

A wonderful film that the entire family can view and appreciate, with some remarkable performances, especially by Steiger.

TITLE: **CHRONICLE OF THE UPRISING IN THE WARSAW GHETTO ACCORDING TO MAREK EDELMAN**

YEAR PRODUCED: 1994

DIRECTOR: Jolanta Dylewska

COUNTRY OF ORIGIN: Poland

LANGUAGE: Polish with English subtitles

RUNNING TIME: 70 minutes

VIDEO: National Center for Jewish Film

DESCRIPTION:

Documentary with Marek Edelman, a Holocaust survivor, who gives a day by day account of the uprising and subsequent survival, with archival material used to illustrate the commentary.

Edelman is one of about 50 Jews who escaped from the Ghetto via the sewer system that served Warsaw.

TITLE: **COLD DAYS**
YEAR PRODUCED: 1966
DIRECTOR: Andras Kovacs
COUNTRY OF ORIGIN: Hungary
LANGUAGE: Hungarian with English subtitles
RUNNING TIME: 102 minutes
VIDEO: Facets

DESCRIPTION:
Revolves around the 1942 massacre of Jews and Serbs and the memories of four men awaiting trial after the war for this crime.

TITLE: **COMMISSAR**
YEAR PRODUCED: 1968
DIRECTOR: Alexander Askolov
CAST: Nonna Mordyukova, Rolan Bykov
COUNTRY OF ORIGIN: U.S.S.R.
LANGUAGE: Russian with English subtitles
RUNNING TIME: 105 minutes
VIDEO: Kino

DESCRIPTION:
Female soldier becomes pregnant during Russian Civil War in 1922. She is left with a Jewish family to wait out her pregnancy. Shows how women were treated as inferiors, just like members of minority races and groups, such as the Jews. Film was originally banned in the Soviet Union and received an American release in the late 1980s.

TITLE: **COMPULSION**

YEAR PRODUCED: 1959

DIRECTOR: Richard Fleischer

CAST: Orson Welles, Diane Varsi, Dean Stockwell, Bradford Dillman, E. G. Marshall, Martin Milner

COUNTRY OF ORIGIN: United States

LANGUAGE: English

RUNNING TIME: 103 minutes

VIDEO: Fox

DESCRIPTION:

Film version of Leopold-Loeb murder case of 1920s, with the names of the characters changed and little mention of their Jewish origins.

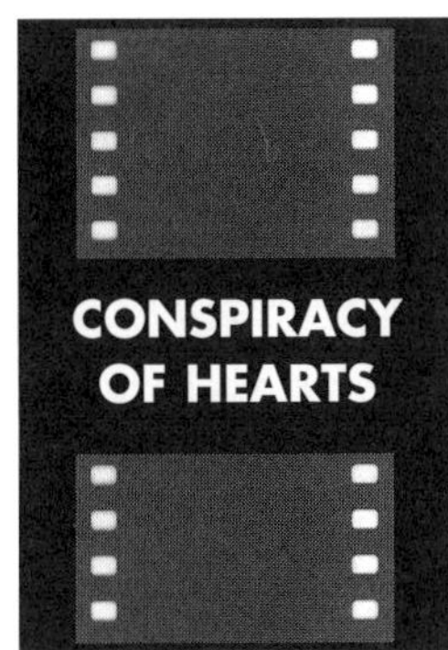

TITLE: **CONSPIRACY OF HEARTS**

YEAR PRODUCED: 1960

DIRECTOR: Ralph Thomas

CAST: Lilli Palmer, Yvonne Mitchell, Sylvia Syms, Ronald Lewis

COUNTRY OF ORIGIN: Great Britain

LANGUAGE: English

RUNNING TIME: 113 minutes

VIDEO: Learning Corporation of America

DESCRIPTION:

Nuns hide Jewish children in their Italian convent during World War II.

TITLE: **CRIMES AND MISDEMEANORS**

YEAR PRODUCED: 1990

DIRECTOR: Woody Allen

CAST: Woody Allen, Martin Landau, Alan Alda, Claire Bloom, Mia Farrow, Anjelica Huston, Jerry Orbach, Sam Waterston

COUNTRY OF ORIGIN: United States

LANGUAGE: English

RUNNING TIME: 104 minutes

VIDEO: Orion

DESCRIPTION:

In some ways this Woody Allen film has many similarities to *Hannah and Her Sisters.* It presents a profusion of characters, all with their own peculiarities and problems. Add to this mix a situation that brings morality to the fore and asks many ethical questions.

The film focuses on Judah Rosenthal (Landau), a wealthy Jewish professional with a spotless reputation. Things go wrong when his mistress (Huston) realizes he will not leave his wife and threatens to expose their affair and some of his questionable business transactions.

Judah seeks advice from his brother Jack (Orbach), who suggests that the matter can be taken care of with one phone call. Should Judah have his girlfriend eliminated? Will he be able to live with this on his conscience? Add to this a failed filmmaker (Allen), a wealthy TV producer (Alda), and a pretty television producer (Farrow).

Many serious problems are raised, but all with the patented Allen touch that adds a pinch of comedy to the most serious debates about life and morality.

TITLE: **CROSSFIRE**

YEAR PRODUCED: 1947

DIRECTOR: Edward Dmytryk

CAST: Robert Young, Robert Mitchum, Robert Ryan, Gloria Grahame

COUNTRY OF ORIGIN: United States

LANGUAGE: English

RUNNING TIME: 86 minutes

VIDEO: RKO (Turner) Astral

DESCRIPTION:

Powerful look at religious bigotry. A dark atmosphere surrounds the murder of a Jewish veteran. When police investigate, they discover that he was killed by a sadistic bully out of sheer hatred and anti-Semitism. One of the first Hollywood films to tackle anti-Semitism and religious persecution, and does it with great taste and intelligence.

Nominated for five Academy Awards: Best Picture, Best Director, Best Screenplay, Best Supporting Actor, Best Supporting Actress. Probably lost because *Gentleman's Agreement* was also nominated in many of the same categories. It is unfortunate that films with similar themes were released in the same year. This film was produced by RKO, one of the smaller Hollywood studios. The larger ones were reluctant to handle it because of its Jewish subject matter.

TITLE: **CROSSFIRE**

YEAR PRODUCED: 1989

DIRECTOR: Gideon Ganani

CAST: Dan Turgeman, Sharon Hacohen

COUNTRY OF ORIGIN: Israel

LANGUAGE: Hebrew with English subtitles

RUNNING TIME: 90 minutes

VIDEO: Ergo

DESCRIPTION:

Story of a Jewish girl and an Arab man who fall in love in Palestine of 1948 and try to cope with a country on the brink of war.

TITLE: **CROSSING DELANCEY**

YEAR PRODUCED: 1988

DIRECTOR: Joan Micklin Silver

CAST: Amy Irving, Peter Riegert, Jeroen Krabbe, Reizl Bozyk, Sylvia Miles

COUNTRY OF ORIGIN: United States

LANGUAGE: English

RUNNING TIME: 97 minutes

VIDEO: Warner

DESCRIPTION:

The street we cross in this film is from the old-fashioned Jewish world of the Lower East Side to the sophisticated world of present-day Manhattan. Amy Irving is superb as the modern independent Jewish woman who has it all. She works in a book shop that brings her into contact with all the literati of the day. She is free to meet and date any man who interests her, and she has no long-term commitments.

To remedy the last point, Irving's grandmother, wonderfully played by Yiddish theater veteran Bozyk, arranges a blind date through the neighborhood matchmaker (Miles). Irving is reluctant, but goes along to please her grandmother. The match is Sam Posner (Riegert), a young man who has inherited his father's pickle store. Perhaps this is a mismatch? Not at all. Posner is intelligent and self-effacing. He realizes that a pickle man would not be an appealing suitor for a suave, sophisticated, and literate young woman, but he's willing to give it a try.

The ending is predictable. Despite Irving's misgivings, the pickle man is the perfect match. The film speaks to many of our preconceptions about people based on their occupations and also tries to tear down some of our innate prejudices about others. Besides, sometimes an apparently simple pickle man may be a better match than an effete member of the intelligentsia.

TITLE: **CUP FINAL**

YEAR PRODUCED: 1992

DIRECTOR: Eran Riklis

CAST: Moshe Ivgi, Mohammed Bakri, Suheil Haddad

COUNTRY OF ORIGIN: Israel

LANGUAGE: Hebrew with English subtitles

RUNNING TIME: 107 minutes

VIDEO: First Run (Icarus Films)

DESCRIPTION:

Israeli film set during the 1982 invasion of Lebanon.

Cohen owns a small store and is doing his reserve duty. His passion in life is soccer. He has tickets to the World Cup in Spain but finds himself involved in Israel's 1982 invasion of Lebanon instead. When his unit comes under attack, Cohen is captured by PLO commandos who decide to trade him for money or Arab prisoners. A special relationship develops between the Israeli and his captors. An unusual perspective on the Israeli-Palestinian conflict.

TITLE: **THE DAMNED**

YEAR PRODUCED: 1969

DIRECTOR: Luchino Visconti

CAST: Dirk Bogarde, Ingrid Thulin, Helmut Griem, Charlotte Rampling, Helmut Berger

COUNTRY OF ORIGIN: Italy

LANGUAGE: Italian, available dubbed into English or with English subtitles

RUNNING TIME: 154 minutes

VIDEO: Facets

DESCRIPTION:

Follows the rise of Nazism through its effects on a German family whose members are gradually overcome by greed, lust, and insanity.

TITLE: **DANGEROUS MOVES**

YEAR PRODUCED: 1984

DIRECTOR: Richard Dembo

CAST: Michel Piccoli, Liv Ullmann, Leslie Caron, Alexandre Arbatt

COUNTRY OF ORIGIN: Switzerland

LANGUAGE: French with English subtitles

RUNNING TIME: 96 minutes

VIDEO: Karl-Lorimar, Warner

DESCRIPTION:

Powerful drama built around the World Chess Championship held in Geneva, Switzerland, in 1983.

The competitors are a 52-year-old Soviet Jew who has remained undefeated for 12 years and a 35-year-old genius who defected to the West five years earlier. The competition between them is not confined to chess, but encompasses their personal and political lives. Won an Academy Award for Best Foreign Film.

TITLE: **DARK LULLABIES**

YEAR PRODUCED: 1985

DIRECTOR: Irene Angelico, Abbey Neidik

COUNTRY OF ORIGIN: Canada

LANGUAGE: English

RUNNING TIME: 82 minutes

VIDEO: National Film Board of Canada

DESCRIPTION:

Documentary describing Angelico's quest to seek out answers to important questions that haunt her.

Angelico is the daughter of Holocaust survivors, but her parents never told her about their experiences. So she undertakes a personal journey to discover what happened and why. She interviews survivors in Montreal and in Israel, and then travels to Germany to speak to her contemporaries there, including modern Neo-Nazis.

An agonizing quest to find answers.

TITLE: **DAVID**

YEAR PRODUCED: 1979

DIRECTOR: Peter Lilienthal

CAST: Mario Fischel, Walter Taub

COUNTRY OF ORIGIN: Germany

LANGUAGE: German with English subtitles

RUNNING TIME: 106 minutes

VIDEO: Kino

DESCRIPTION:

Story of a Jewish teenager growing up in Berlin during the Nazi period. He flees from one hide-out to another and then escapes to Palestine.

Highly acclaimed film.

TITLE: **DAVID AND BATHSHEBA**

YEAR PRODUCED: 1951

DIRECTOR: Henry King

CAST: Gregory Peck, Susan Hayward, Raymond Massey, Kieron Moore, Jayne Meadows

COUNTRY OF ORIGIN: United States

LANGUAGE: English

RUNNING TIME: 116 minutes

VIDEO: Fox

DESCRIPTION:

Biblical epic that retells the story of King David and his passion for Bathsheba. Nominated for three Academy Awards, including Best Story and Best Screenplay.

TITLE: **A DAY IN OCTOBER**

YEAR PRODUCED: 1992

DIRECTOR: Kenneth Madsen

CAST: D.B. Sweeney, Kelly Wolf, Tovah Feldshuh, Daniel Benzali

COUNTRY OF ORIGIN: Denmark/United States

LANGUAGE: English

RUNNING TIME: 96 minutes

VIDEO: Academy

DESCRIPTION:

Niels Jensen (Sweeney), a Danish resistance fighter, is wounded in an action against the Nazis. Sara (Wolf), a young Jewish woman, rescues him and hides him in her home. Niels and Sara fall in love, and the resistance prepares to evacuate the entire Jewish population from Denmark before the Nazis can round them up and ship them to concentration camps.

Excellent fact-based film that discusses the need to take sides when facing evil.

TITLE: **DAY OF ATONEMENT**

YEAR PRODUCED: 1992

DIRECTOR: Alexandre Arcady

CAST: Christopher Walken, Jill Clayburgh, Jennifer Beals, Roger Hanin, Richard Berry, Gerard Darmon

COUNTRY OF ORIGIN: France

LANGUAGE: English

RUNNING TIME: 127 minutes

VIDEO: Vidmark

DESCRIPTION:

Explicit violence marks this French production about three generations of Franco-Algerian Jewish gangsters.

The family don gets out of prison in 1992 and joins the family, which now lives in Miami, just in time to celebrate his grandson's bar mitzvah. The family is involved in money laundering and drug dealing, and they come up against rival gangs working the same turf.

TITLE: **DEAD END STREET**

YEAR PRODUCED: 1983

CAST: Yehoram Gaon, Anat Atzman

COUNTRY OF ORIGIN: Israel

LANGUAGE: Hebrew with English subtitles

RUNNING TIME: 86 minutes

VIDEO: Trans-World Entertainment

DESCRIPTION:

Prostitute tries to change her lifestyle but runs into difficulties. Gaon is one of Israel's biggest film and recording stars.

TITLE: **DEADLY CURRENTS**

YEAR PRODUCED: 1991

DIRECTOR: Simcha Jacobovici

COUNTRY OF ORIGIN: Canada

LANGUAGE: English

RUNNING TIME: 115 minutes

VIDEO: Cineplex-Odeon (MCA)

DESCRIPTION:

Feature-length documentary made at the height of the Intifada in the Israeli-occupied territories on the West Bank.

Uses Israelis and Palestinians to express their views and show the intractability of each side. But it is not a "talking heads" film. At one point Jacobovici accompanies an Israeli army unit patrolling an Arab town, facing the anger and hatred of the Palestinian residents. Another time, his camera joins a group of Palestinian radicals who are interrogating an accused collaborator.

This is real stuff. Nothing has been staged. The film paints a highly accurate picture of the situation as it existed at the time, with many lessons we can still heed today.

TITLE: **DESCENDING ANGEL**

YEAR PRODUCED: 1990

DIRECTOR: Jeremy Paul Kagan

CAST: George C. Scott, Dianne Lane, Eric Roberts

COUNTRY OF ORIGIN: United States

LANGUAGE: English

RUNNING TIME: 96 minutes

VIDEO: H.B.O.

DESCRIPTION:

George C. Scott plays a Romanian refugee who is now a pillar of the community. His daughter Irina (Lane) falls in love with Michael (Roberts), who begins getting insights into her father's possible activities as a wartime collaborator with the Nazis.

This is not just another war criminal story. The cast gives such good performances that it should not be overlooked.

TITLE: **DIAMONDS**

YEAR PRODUCED: 1972

DIRECTOR: Menahem Golan

CAST: Robert Shaw, Richard Roundtree, Barbara Hershey, Shelley Winters

COUNTRY OF ORIGIN: Israel

LANGUAGE: English

RUNNING TIME: 108 minutes

VIDEO: New Line

DESCRIPTION:

Israel is one of the most important countries in the world in the field of diamond cutting and polishing. This film is a thriller about a group of thieves who set their sights on the Israel Diamond Exchange.

Golan later went to Hollywood and ran a series of independent film companies before finally going bankrupt and returning to Israel in the 1990s.

TITLE: **DIAMONDS OF THE NIGHT**

YEAR PRODUCED: 1964

DIRECTOR: Jan Nemec

CAST: Ladislav Jansky, Antonin Kumbera, Ilse Bischofova

COUNTRY OF ORIGIN: Czechoslovakia

LANGUAGE: Czech with English subtitles

RUNNING TIME: 71 minutes

VIDEO: Facets

DESCRIPTION:

Two Jewish boys escape from a Nazi transport train. Czech director's first feature film.

TITLE: **THE DIARY OF ANNE FRANK**

YEAR PRODUCED: 1959

DIRECTOR: George Stevens

ACTORS: Millie Perkins, Joseph Schildkraut, Shelley Winters, Richard Beymer, Gusti Huber, Lou Jacobi, Diane Baker, Douglas Spencer, Ed Wynn

COUNTRY OF ORIGIN: United States

LANGUAGE: English

RUNNING TIME: 151 minutes

VIDEO: Fox

DESCRIPTION:

One of the first "big" pictures to deal with the Holocaust.

The story of a young girl, her family, and a few friends and acquaintances who hid in an attic for two years during the German occupation of Amsterdam. Despite the repression and the danger, Anne retained her humanity and a certain naivete. In 1944 the Nazis discovered the hiding place and arrested everyone. All of them, with the exception of Anne's father, died. When he returned to Amsterdam, he was given Anne's diary, which had been found by a family friend. The diary was later published and became one of the classics of Holocaust literature.

Nominated for nine Academy Awards and won three: Best Art Direction/Set Decoration for a Black and White Film, Best Black and White Cinematography, Best Supporting Actress (Shelley Winters).

TITLE: **DIRTY DANCING**

YEAR PRODUCED: 1987

DIRECTOR: Emile Ardolino

CAST: Patrick Swayze, Jennifer Grey, Jerry Orbach, Cynthia Rhodes

COUNTRY OF ORIGIN: United States

LANGUAGE: English

RUNNING TIME: 105 minutes

VIDEO: Vestron

DESCRIPTION:

Dirty Dancing a Jewish movie?

It's not as crazy as you may think. Let's take a look at the plot line. An innocent young girl (Grey) is visiting a Catskill resort in 1963. Her taste in entertainment differs somewhat from that of her parents' generation. So she gets turned on by the music the staff plays at their private parties.

Romance, of course, rears its ugly head. The girl, whom her family calls Baby, falls in love with the professional dance instructor, Johnny Castle (Swayze), but her parents are opposed to her getting involved with him. Why are they opposed? Is it because the father is a doctor and Johnny is lower class? Is it because Johnny's future as a dance instructor is rather limited? Nope!

The film does not make this very explicit, but the fact is that Baby is Jewish and Johnny is not. If you look closely, you will also notice that most of the waiters are Jewish college students. Being a waiter is a prestigious job in a resort. Everyone knows that the waiters are there just for the summer, earning enough money to pay for their tuition, and a waiter earns a lot of his money in tips. Baby's parents seem to have no hesitation about allowing their daughters to go out with the waiters, but they don't approve of the non-Jewish staff. As a film, *Dirty Dancing* is not particularly well made. It was produced by Vestron, a video company that went into film production in order to ensure a steady supply of product for the video branch. *Dirty Dancing* was one of their more successful efforts. Vestron also helped finance *Platoon*, but that's another story.

The producers of Dirty Dancing were not particularly concerned about quality. But they got lucky. The two leads, Jennifer Grey and Patrick Swayze, proved very charismatic, and the film became very popular—a huge hit that made a lot of money for Vestron, but not enough to stave off eventual bankruptcy.

TITLE: **DITA SAXOVA**

YEAR PRODUCED: 1967

DIRECTOR: A. Moskalyk

CAST: List not available

COUNTRY OF ORIGIN: Czechoslovakia

LANGUAGE: Czech with English subtitles

RUNNING TIME: 98 minutes

VIDEO: Facets

DESCRIPTION:

Story of a beautiful 18-year-old girl in Prague who seems strong to all around her but commits suicide.

TITLE: **THE DOOMSDAY GUN**

YEAR PRODUCED: 1994

DIRECTOR: Robert M. Young

CAST: Frank Langella, Alan Arkin, Kevin Spacey, Tony Goldwyn

COUNTRY OF ORIGIN: United States

LANGUAGE: English

RUNNING TIME: 107 minutes

VIDEO: HBO Home Video

DESCRIPTION:

Thriller about Canadian armaments genius, Gerald Bull (Langella) who developed the Supergun, the world's largest artillery piece–a gun so powerful that it could fire a shell in Iraq and hit a target in Israel.

Saddam Hussein hired Bull to build this gun and American CIA agents, Kevin Spacek and Tony Goldwyn, follow his every move. Alan Arkin plays an Israeli agent determined to stop Bull, even if it means Bull's assassination.

TITLE: **DOUBLE EDGE**

YEAR PRODUCED: 1991

DIRECTOR: Amos Kollek

CAST: Faye Dunaway, Amos Kollek, Mohammad Bakri

COUNTRY OF ORIGIN: Israel/United States

LANGUAGE: English

RUNNING TIME: 85 minutes

VIDEO: Warner

DESCRIPTION:

Produced in Israel in English.

An ambitious American reporter (Dunaway) arrives in Israel to report on the Intifada. Intent on getting a scoop and impressing her editors, she takes a pro-Palestinian slant, although an Israeli novelist friend (Kollek) tries to steer her in a straight line, pointing out the damage a one-sided story could do. She finally becomes aware of her folly when her own life is endangered.

TITLE: **DRIFTING**

YEAR PRODUCED: 1982

DIRECTOR: Amos Guttman

CAST: Jonathan Sagalle, Ami Traub, Ben Levine

COUNTRY OF ORIGIN: Israel

LANGUAGE: Hebrew with English subtitles

RUNNING TIME: 103 minutes

VIDEO: Facets

DESCRIPTION:

Israeli film about a homosexual filmmaker. Set in modern Jerusalem.

TITLE: **DRIVING MISS DAISY**

YEAR PRODUCED: 1989

DIRECTOR: Bruce Beresford

CAST: Jessica Tandy, Morgan Freeman, Dan Aykroyd, Patti Lupone, Esther Rolle

COUNTRY OF ORIGIN: United States

LANGUAGE: English

RUNNING TIME: 99 minutes

VIDEO: Warner

DESCRIPTION:

A proud, independent southern lady is finally persuaded by her son to give up driving. He hires a chauffeur and tells him that it is his job to convince the old woman to let him drive her wherever she needs to go.

Thus begins a 25-year relationship between the woman, who is white and Jewish, and the chauffeur, who is black. Slowly the two begin to see each other as human beings, as their relationship turns slowly from strictly employer-employee to true friendship.

As the years go by, the social milieu in the South begins to change. Integration and civil rights establish a new set of rules to live by. And as the times change, so do the two main characters. Jessica Tandy and Morgan Freeman give superb performances in a subtle but intellectually stimulating film.

Won Academy Awards for Best Actress (Tandy), Best Adapted Screenplay, Best Makeup, and Best Picture. Nominated for Best Actor (Freeman), Best Costume Design, Best Film Editing, and Best Supporting Actor (Aykroyd).

TITLE: **THE DUNERA BOYS**

YEAR PRODUCED: 1985

DIRECTOR: Sam Lewin

CAST: Bob Hoskins, Joe Spano, Warren Mitchell, Joseph Furst, Moshe Kedem

COUNTRY OF ORIGIN: Australia

LANGUAGE: English

RUNNING TIME: 150 minutes

VIDEO: Prism

DESCRIPTION:

A true story that is stranger than fiction.

Just before World War II broke out, many German and Austrian Jews managed to make their way to England in search of a refuge. The British, afraid these refugees were German informers and spies, arrested them and shipped them overseas to be held in POW camps, often with real German POWs. The group dealt with in this film were sent to Australia, although other groups wound up in Canada. The Australian camp guards and officers quickly realized that these people were no threat to the Allies but were unable to obtain their release.

We follow the adventures and tribulations of these wrongfully imprisoned men and rejoice with them when they are finally released and allowed to enlist in the Allied armies.

Excellent film with a great performance by Bob Hoskins. Originally a miniseries produced for Australian television.

TITLE: **THE DYBBUK**
YEAR PRODUCED: 1937
DIRECTOR: Michal Waszynski
CAST: Leon Liebgold, Lili Liliana, Max Bozyk, Abraham Morevsky, Dina Halpern
COUNTRY OF ORIGIN: Poland
LANGUAGE: Yiddish with English subtitles
RUNNING TIME: 123 minutes
VIDEO: Facets, National Center for Jewish Film, IHF, Ergo

DESCRIPTION:
Classic Yiddish tale of a young man and woman whose fathers agree, before they are born, to have them marry each other. When they grow up they meet and fall in love, but the girl's father breaks his promise and arranges for her to marry someone else. The young man dies, and his wandering soul returns to possess the bride, necessitating an exorcism.

Probably the greatest film ever produced in Yiddish.

TITLE: **EAGLES ATTACK AT DAWN**

YEAR PRODUCED: 1974

DIRECTOR: Manahem Golan

CAST: Rick Jason, Peter Brown, Yehoram Gaon, Joseph Shiloa

COUNTRY OF ORIGIN: Israel

LANGUAGE: English

RUNNING TIME: 96 minutes

VIDEO: VidAmerica

DESCRIPTION:

After an Israeli soldier escapes from a Syrian prison, he vows to return to exact revenge.

TITLE: **EAST AND WEST**

YEAR PRODUCED: 1923

DIRECTOR: Sidney Goldin and Ivan Abramson

CAST: Molly Picon, Jacob Kalish, Sidney Goldin

COUNTRY OF ORIGIN: Austria

LANGUAGE: Silent film with Yiddish and English intertitles

RUNNING TIME: 85 minutes

VIDEO: National Center for Jewish Film

DESCRIPTION:

New York Jew returns to his hometown in Galicia with his daughter for a family wedding. Daughter falls in love with a young yeshiva student.

TITLE: **ECHOES OF CONFLICT**

YEAR PRODUCED: 1989

DIRECTOR: Amit Goren, Gur Heller, Jorge Johanan Weller

CAST: Gur Heller, Johanan Weller

COUNTRY OF ORIGIN: Israel

LANGUAGE: Hebrew with English subtitles

RUNNING TIME: 91 minutes

VIDEO: Kino

DESCRIPTION:

Three disturbing dramas by young Israeli directors that deal with how the Israeli-Palestinian conflict affects every aspect of life in Israel.

TITLE: **THE EDDIE CANTOR STORY**

YEAR PRODUCED: 1953

DIRECTOR: Alfred E. Green

CAST: Keefe Brasselle, Marilyn Erskine, Aline MacMahon, Arthur Franz, Alex Gerry, Greta Granstedt, Gerald Mohr, William Forrest, Jackie Barnett, Richard Monda, Marie Windsor, Douglas Evans, Will Rogers Jr.

COUNTRY OF ORIGIN: United States

LANGUAGE: English

RUNNING TIME: 117 minutes

VIDEO: Warner

DESCRIPTION:

Musical biography of American entertainer Eddie Cantor. Follows Cantor's career from his early days to the time this film was made. Has lots of great music, and could have been very entertaining if not for the exaggerated mannerisms of Keefe Brasselle in the lead role.

TITLE: **THE EIGHTY-FIRST BLOW**

YEAR PRODUCED: 1974

COUNTRY OF ORIGIN: Israel

LANGUAGE: Hebrew and Yiddish with English subtitles

RUNNING TIME: 115 minutes

VIDEO: Ergo

DESCRIPTION:

Compilation of testimony, rare film footage, and stills shot by the Nazis that covers the evidence from witnesses used in the trial of Adolf Eichmann.

TITLE: **ELI ELI**

YEAR PRODUCED: 1940

DIRECTOR: Joseph Seiden

CAST: Esther Field, Lazar Fried, Muni Serebroff

COUNTRY OF ORIGIN: United States

LANGUAGE: Yiddish with English subtitles

RUNNING TIME: 85 minutes

VIDEO: Facets, Audio Forum

DESCRIPTION:

Yiddish film about a family that is split apart when their farm fails. Songs by Sholom Secunda, one of the greatest Yiddish composers in America.

TITLE: **THE END OF INNOCENCE**

YEAR PRODUCED: 1990

DIRECTOR: Dyan Cannon

CAST: Dyan Cannon, John Heard, George Coe, Lola Mason, Rebecca Schaeffer

COUNTRY OF ORIGIN: United States

LANGUAGE: English

RUNNING TIME: 102 minutes

VIDEO: Paramount

DESCRIPTION:

Story of Jewish woman's road to a nervous breakdown.

Autobiographical film written and directed by Dyan Cannon. Cast is excellent, but Cannon might have been wiser to bring in an outside writer to assist her.

Rebecca Schaeffer gives a fine performance as the young Cannon; she was murdered in Los Angeles shortly after she completed work on this film.

TITLE: **ENEMIES: A LOVE STORY**

YEAR PRODUCED: 1989

DIRECTOR: Paul Mazursky

CAST: Anjelica Huston, Ron Silver, Lena Olin, Margaret Sophie Stein

COUNTRY OF ORIGIN: United States

LANGUAGE: English

RUNNING TIME: 121 minutes

VIDEO: Media

DESCRIPTION:

Ever wish you could be married to more than one woman at a time? Forget it! This film proves it would be one big hassle. Herman (Silver) is a Holocaust survivor. His life was saved by Yadwiga (Stein), his family's servant in Poland, who hid him in a barn. After the war he marries her, and the two of them emigrate to the United States.

But Herman's heart is someplace else. He is really in love with Masha (Olin), a passionate woman who excites him and is eager to live in the present. Unfortunately, Masha gets pregnant, and wanting to do what's right, Herman marries her too. So Herman has a busy life. But then his first wife, Tamara (Huston), shows up. Herman was sure Tamara had perished in the camps. Not only did she survive, she has tracked Herman down.

This is a story about a man full of human emotion who tries to please everyone at once. His difficulties are of his own making and result from his own character. And he knows it, but sometimes you are your own worst enemy. This film casts a somewhat different light on Holocaust survivors.

TITLE: **ESCAPE FROM SOBIBOR**
YEAR PRODUCED: 1987
DIRECTOR: Jack Gold
CAST: Alan Arkin, Rutger Hauer, Joanna Pacula,
Hartmut Becker,
Jack Shepperd
COUNTRY OF ORIGIN: United States
LANGUAGE: English
RUNNING TIME: 120 minutes
VIDEO: Live/MCA

DESCRIPTION:
Television film that packs quite a wallop as it describes the largest successful escape ever staged from a Nazi concentration camp.

This true story centers on Lt. Sasha Pechersky (Hauer), a Russian prisoner of war. Sent to the extermination camp at Sobibor, he realizes that action must be taken if any of the inmates are to survive. He organizes those who were lucky enough not to be killed off immediately, and they plan and execute an escape; in the process they manage to kill a few of their tormentors. Well-acted film with excellent performances by Hauer and Arkin.

TITLE: **ESCAPE TO THE SUN**

YEAR PRODUCED: 1972

DIRECTOR: Menahem Golan

CAST: Laurence Harvey, Josephine Chaplin, John Ireland, Jack Hawkins, Lila Kedrova, Clive Revill

COUNTRY OF ORIGIN: Israel

LANGUAGE: English

RUNNING TIME: 94 minutes

VIDEO: IVE (International Video Entertainment)

DESCRIPTION:

A group of Russian-Jewish university students plan to escape from the Soviet Union and emigrate to Israel. Made at the height of the worldwide campaign to obtain the release of Soviet Jews who wished to go to Israel, but the film leaves a lot to be desired and the storyline is often confusing.

TITLE: **ESTHER AND THE KING**

YEAR PRODUCED: 1960

DIRECTOR: Raoul Walsh

CAST: Joan Collins, Richard Egan

COUNTRY OF ORIGIN: United States/Italy

LANGUAGE: English

RUNNING TIME: 109 minutes

VIDEO: Fox

DESCRIPTION:

Poor production of the story of Esther and the king of Persia that is the basis for the Megilla of Esther read every year in synagogues around the world at Purim.

TITLE: **EUROPA, EUROPA**

YEAR PRODUCED: 1991

DIRECTOR: Agnieszka Holland

CAST: Marco Hofschneider, Rene Hofschneider, Julie Delpy

COUNTRY OF ORIGIN: Germany/France

LANGUAGE: German and Russian with English subtitles

RUNNING TIME: 115 minutes

VIDEO: Orion/Alliance

DESCRIPTION:

A truly great Holocaust film whose story is so incredible that it is difficult to believe—but it is true.

Solomon Perel is a Jewish youngster barely into his teens when World War II breaks out. He and his brother flee from a Polish ghetto and escape to the east. After they are separated, Solomon is picked up by some Russian soldiers who send him to an orphanage.

When the orphanage is bombed, Solomon winds up with a German army unit. He passes himself off as an Aryan and becomes the unit's interpreter and mascot. He is later sent to become a member of the Hitler Jugend. When the Russians occupy Eastern Europe, Solomon is turned over to a concentration camp survivor to be executed, but his brother, now a Red Army soldier, recognizes him and saves him.

A beautiful film with many humorous moments and a number of thought-provoking scenes. Became controversial when Germany refused to nominate it for Best Foreign Film at the Academy Awards.

TITLE: **EVERY TIME WE SAY GOODBYE**

YEAR PRODUCED: 1986

DIRECTOR: Moshe Mizrahi

CAST: Tom Hanks, Cristina Marsillach, Benedict Taylor, Anat Atzmon, Gila Almagor

COUNTRY OF ORIGIN: United States

LANGUAGE: English

RUNNING TIME: 97 minutes

VIDEO: Vestron

DESCRIPTION:

Tom Hanks in a dramatic role, playing an American anxious to join the fight against the Nazis during World War II. He enlists in the Royal Air Force and is recuperating from a leg wound at a Jerusalem hospital when he meets and falls hopelessly in love with a beautiful Jewish girl, Sarah. Her deeply religious Sephardic family rejects the gentile American pilot and fights to keep the two lovers apart.

TITLE: **THE EXECUTION**

YEAR PRODUCED: 1985

DIRECTOR: Paul Wendkos

CAST: Loretta Swit, Valerie Harper, Sandy Dennis, Barbara Barrie, Jessica Walter, Rip Torn

COUNTRY OF ORIGIN: United States

LANGUAGE: English

RUNNING TIME: 92 minutes

VIDEO: Prism

DESCRIPTION:

Five women friends in California accidentally come upon the sadistic Nazi doctor who abused them in a concentration camp during World War II. Determined to make sure that justice is done, they draw straws to choose one of them to execute the Nazi.

Made-for-television film.

TITLE: **EXODUS**

YEAR PRODUCED: 1960

DIRECTOR: Otto Preminger

CAST: Paul Newman, Eva Marie Saint, Ralph Richardson, Peter Lawford, Lee J. Cobb, Sal Mineo, John Derek, High Griffith, David Opatoshu, Jill Haworth, George Maharis

COUNTRY OF ORIGIN: United States

LANGUAGE: English

RUNNING TIME: 207 minutes

VIDEO: Fox

DESCRIPTION:

The first major film to detail the birth pangs of the State of Israel. Points out heroic stature of Jewish freedom fighters, whether members of the Haganah or of the more radical underground.

Filled with unforgettable scenes, such as the anti-Semitic British officer (Lawford) discussing his ability to spot a Jew while looking for a cinder in Paul Newman's eye, the raising of the Star of David on the refugee ship, the blowing up of the King David Hotel, the jailbreak from Acre prison, the evacuation of the children from Gan Dafna before the Arab attack, and the burial of a Jewish girl and an Arab leader side by side before the Jewish forces leave for battle. The acting is excellent throughout, the cinematography is stunning, and the music, stirring.

Won Academy Award for Best Original Score; nominated for Best Color Cinematography and Best Supporting Actor (Mineo). A landmark film.

TITLE: **EYEWITNESS**

YEAR PRODUCED: 1981

DIRECTOR: Peter Yates

CAST: William Hurt, Sigourney Weaver, Christopher Plummer, James Woods, Morgan Freeman

COUNTRY OF ORIGIN: United States

LANGUAGE: English

RUNNING TIME: 102 minutes

VIDEO: Fox

DESCRIPTION:

First major American film to show an Israeli in a completely negative light.

An Israeli diplomat murders a man in Vienna who threatens to expose an operation to release Jews held captive in the Soviet Union. Later on, the diplomat decides to kill an innocent man who he believes knows about the first murder.

TITLE: **FALLING OVER BACKWARDS**

YEAR PRODUCED: 1990

DIRECTOR: Mort Ransen

CAST: Saul Rubinek, Paul Soles, Julie St. Pierre

COUNTRY OF ORIGIN: Canada

LANGUAGE: English

RUNNING TIME: 104 minutes

VIDEO: Astral

DESCRIPTION:

Saul Rubinek plays a high school teacher who's just gone through a difficult divorce. In search of the good old days of his youth, he rents a house in the old neighborhood where he lived as a child, and brings his elderly father to live with him.

A comedy set in Montreal about new relationships and changing lifestyles.

TITLE: **FAMILY OF COPS**

YEAR PRODUCED: 1995

DIRECTOR: Ted Kotcheff

CAST: Charles Bronson, Barbara Williams,

Angela Featherstone, Sebastian Spence, Daniel Baldwin

COUNTRY OF ORIGIN: United States

LANGUAGE: English

RUNNING TIME: 90 minutes

VIDEO: Alliance

DESCRIPTION:

Police Inspector Paul Fein's (Bronson) youngest daughter returns home for her father's birthday and becomes involved in a homicide.

Good police drama centering on a Jewish family whose members don't hide their religious and ethnic background.

TITLE: **FAMILY OF COPS II: BREACH OF FAITH**

YEAR PRODUCED: 1997

DIRECTOR: David Greene

CAST: Charles Bronson, Barbara Williams,

Angela Featherstone, Sebastian Spence, Joe Penny

COUNTRY OF ORIGIN: United States

LANGUAGE: English

RUNNING TIME: 90 minutes

VIDEO: Alliance

DESCRIPTION:

Television drama about a Jewish police inspector, Paul Fein (Bronson), in Milwaukee, and his family. Two of his sons are cops, his oldest daughter is a public defender and his younger daughter winds up entering the Police Academy in this sequel.

These are good, solid dramas in which the main characters are comfortable with their Jewish heritage and do not see it as a hindrance to their careers or their lifestyles, and in this, presents a breath of fresh air on television.

TITLE: **FAMILY PRAYERS**

YEAR PRODUCED: 1993

DIRECTOR: Scott Rosenfelt

CAST: Joe Mantegna, Anne Archer, Paul Reiser, Allen Garfield, Conchata Ferrell, David Margulies, Tzvi Ratner-Stauber, Patti Lupone

COUNTRY OF ORIGIN: United States

LANGUAGE: English

RUNNING TIME: 109 minutes

VIDEO: Columbia

DESCRIPTION:

Coming-of-age film set in the Los Angeles of 1969. The Jacobs family is breaking up just when their son, Andrew, is about to have his bar mitzvah. The father (Mantegna) is a compulsive gambler and is driving the family into poverty. The son (Ratner-Stauber) is forced to witness the constant squabbling between his parents while preparing for his bar mitzvah and while becoming aware of the greater world outside his family circle, especially the problems in Vietnam.

The result is a film about maturation and becoming aware, with terrific performances by Ratner-Stauber and Mantegna.

TITLE: **FATE**

YEAR PRODUCED: 1990

DIRECTOR: Stuart Paul

CAST: Stuart Paul, Cheryl Lynn, Kaye Ballard, Yuda Barkan, Patrick Wright, Susannah York

COUNTRY OF ORIGIN: United States

LANGUAGE: English

RUNNING TIME: 114 minutes

VIDEO: Academy

DESCRIPTION:

A Jewish young man is determined to make his romantic fantasies come true. Light, off-beat comedy with a lot of charm.

TITLE: **FATHER**

YEAR PRODUCED: 1990

DIRECTOR: John Power

CAST: Max Von Sydow, Carol Drinkwater, Julia Blake, Steve Jacobs

COUNTRY OF ORIGIN: Australia

LANGUAGE: English

RUNNING TIME: 106 minutes

VIDEO: Monarch/Cabin Fever

DESCRIPTION:

Story is very similar to *The Music Box*, except that it takes place in Australia.

A woman by the name of Anne receives an anonymous telephone call telling her to watch a television news program. When she turns on the TV she is appalled to find a concentration camp survivor identifying her father as a Nazi war criminal.

Anne is fiercely loyal to her father, but doubts begin to creep in, and then the viewer begins to have doubts about the survivor's story.

Again the question is raised as to whether we can always accept things at face value and always believe our loved ones.

TITLE: **FESTIVAL AT THE POOLROOM (HAGIGA B'SNUKER)**

YEAR PRODUCED: 1975

DIRECTOR: Boaz Davidzon

CAST: Zeev Revach, Tuvia Tzafir, Yehuda Barkan

COUNTRY OF ORIGIN: Israel

LANGUAGE: Hebrew, no English subtitles

RUNNING TIME: 90 minutes

VIDEO: Kol Ami

DESCRIPTION:

Israeli comedy.

FICTITIOUS MARRIAGE

TITLE: **FICTITIOUS MARRIAGE**

YEAR PRODUCED: 1988

DIRECTOR: Haim Bouzaglo

CAST: Shlomo Bar-Aba, Irit Sheleg

COUNTRY OF ORIGIN: Israel

LANGUAGE: Hebrew with English subtitles

RUNNING TIME: 90 minutes

VIDEO: Ergo

DESCRIPTION:

Israeli high school teacher has a mid-life crisis and disappears from his hometown. In Tel Aviv he is mistaken for an Arab and offered a job as a laborer on a construction project.

TITLE: **FIDDLER ON THE ROOF**

YEAR PRODUCED: 1971

DIRECTOR: Norman Jewison

CAST: Topol, Norma Crane, Leonard Frey, Molly Picon, Paul Mann

COUNTRY OF ORIGIN: United States

LANGUAGE: English

RUNNING TIME: 169 minutes

VIDEO: MGM

DESCRIPTION:

Large-scale, spectacular adaptation of the hit Broadway musical. A delight to the ears and the eyes; epic film that retains its intimacy and charm.

Set in the shtetl of Anatevka, in tsarist Russia, shortly after the turn of the century. Tevya, an impoverished milk man, has five daughters and a wife to support on a meager income and relies on tradition and religion to supply the answers to his anguished existence. When tradition is challenged by the changing times, Tevya bends and changes with it, until he can bend no further. He finally makes a stand when he refuses to accept his third daughter's marriage to a non-Jew. Tevye recognizes that to bend that far would break him and everything he believes in. The sorrows and joys of Jewishness are celebrated in this outstanding film. The wedding scene always brings a tear to the eye. Note the use of the Yiddish song "Yomi, Yomi" as the villagers assemble for the wedding—the film's only use of music not written specifically for this musical.

The final scene, in which the Jews leave their shtetl, is heartbreaking. They must leave most of their possessions and take only what they can carry or put into a wagon or cart. They walk off into the unknown future, scattering in all directions—some to America, some to Palestine, and some to other parts of Europe. The only thing of value they possess is their tradition, as symbolized by the Fiddler who follows after them. Only by holding on to their traditions will they be able to build new lives in their new homes. The cast is first rate, especially Topol as Tevye and Molly Picon, the great Yiddish stage and film star, as Yente the Matchmaker. Jewish traditions and customs are depicted in great detail. An excellent job by the non-Jewish director, Norman Jewison.

TITLE: **FINALS (B'CHINOT BAGRUT)**

YEAR PRODUCED: 1983

DIRECTOR: Assi Dayan

CAST: Dan Toren, Irit Frank

COUNTRY OF ORIGIN: Israel

LANGUAGE: Hebrew with English subtitles

RUNNING TIME: 90 minutes

VIDEO: Kol Ami

DESCRIPTION:

Israeli drama.

TITLE: **THE FIXER**

YEAR PRODUCED: 1968

DIRECTOR: John Frankenheimer

CAST: Alan Bates, Dirk Bogarde, Georgia Brown, Hugh Griffith, Elizabeth Hartman, Ian Holm, David Opatoshu, David Warner

COUNTRY OF ORIGIN: United States

LANGUAGE: English

RUNNING TIME: 132 minutes

VIDEO: MGM

DESCRIPTION:

A Jewish handyman is accused of the ritual murder of a Christian child in turn-of-the-century tsarist Russia. Thrown into jail, he is tortured to make him confess, but he refuses to give in and is eventually released and vindicated.

Based on a true case, as fictionalized in a novel by Bernard Malamud. Alan Bates was nominated for a Best Actor Academy Award for this role.

TITLE: **FLAMES IN THE ASHES**

YEAR PRODUCED: 1986

DIRECTOR: Jacques Ehrlich and Haim Gouri

COUNTRY OF ORIGIN: Israel

LANGUAGE: Hebrew and Yiddish with English subtitles

RUNNING TIME: 90 minutes

VIDEO: Ergo

DESCRIPTION:

Testimony of eyewitnesses and recently found film about Jewish resistance against the Nazis during the Holocaust.

TITLE: **FLAMES OF REVOLT: THE IRGUN**

YEAR PRODUCED: 1990

DIRECTOR: Gideon Ganani

COUNTRY OF ORIGIN: Israel

LANGUAGE: English, some Hebrew with English subtitles

RUNNING TIME: 100 minutes

VIDEO: Ergo

DESCRIPTION:

Documentary that looks at the role played by the Irgun in the establishment of the State of Israel and includes interviews with participants and historians.

TITLE: **FORBIDDEN**

YEAR PRODUCED: 1984

DIRECTOR: Anthony Page

CAST: Jacqueline Bisset, Jurgen Prochnow, Irene Worth

COUNTRY OF ORIGIN: United States

LANGUAGE: English

RUNNING TIME: 114 minutes

VIDEO: United States Home Video

DESCRIPTION:

Based on a true story, this film is set in Berlin during World War II. Countess Nina Von Halder opposes the Nazi regime and helps the underground to save some of Berlin's remaining Jews. She falls in love with a Jewish intellectual and hides him in her apartment.

Film was made for cable television.

TITLE: **FORCED MARCH**

YEAR PRODUCED: 1990

DIRECTOR: Rick King

CAST: Chris Sarandon, Renee Soutendijk, Josef Sommer

COUNTRY OF ORIGIN: United States

LANGUAGE: English

RUNNING TIME: 104 minutes

VIDEO: SGE Home Video/MCA

DESCRIPTION:

Benjamin Kline (Sarandon), a successful television actor, takes on the film role of Miklos Radnoti, a Hungarian Jewish poet killed by the Nazis. The more he gets into the role, the more he becomes obsessed with it and the less able he is to separate it from real life.

Somewhat confusing film that is made more complicated than is necessary.

TITLE: **FREUD LEAVING HOME**

YEAR PRODUCED: 1991

DIRECTOR: Sasanne Bier

CAST: Ghita Norby, Gunilla Roor, Palle Granditsky, Philip Zanden, Jessica Zanden, Peter Andersson, Stina Ekblad

COUNTRY OF ORIGIN: Sweden

LANGUAGE: Swedish with English subtitles

RUNNING TIME: 100 minutes

VIDEO: Kino/CHV

DESCRIPTION:

Follows the problems of a Jewish family in Sweden. The parents are Holocaust survivors and are preparing to mark the mother's sixtieth birthday. The adult children return home for the celebration, including an observant daughter from Israel and a gay son from the United States. Rounding out the family is a beautiful and fun-loving 25-year-old daughter. When the mother becomes ill, the children's problems begin to surface and must finally be confronted.

TITLE: **FRIENDSHIP IN VIENNA**

YEAR PRODUCED: 1988

DIRECTOR: Arthur Allan Seidelman

CAST: Jane Alexander, Edward Asner, Stephen Macht, Jenny Lewis, Kamie Harper

COUNTRY OF ORIGIN: United States

LANGUAGE: English

RUNNING TIME: 100 minutes

VIDEO: Disney

DESCRIPTION:

Made specifically for the Disney cable channel, this film deals with two schoolgirls in 1938 Vienna. Inge (Lewis) is Jewish and Lise (Harper) is not. When they are forbidden to see each other, they continue their friendship in secret. After Germany occupies Austria, Inge and her family escape to the United States with the help of Lise.

Well-written, well-acted, heartwarming.

TITLE: **THE FRISCO KID**

YEAR PRODUCED: 1979

DIRECTOR: Robert Aldrich

CAST: Gene Wilder, Harrison Ford, Leo Fuchs, Penny Peyser

COUNTRY OF ORIGIN: United States

LANGUAGE: English

RUNNING TIME: 119 minutes

VIDEO: Warner

DESCRIPTION:

I guess there were some Jews in the Old West, although I doubt that they were as incompetent as Avram Belinski (Wilder).

Rabbi Belinski is sent from a Polish yeshiva to take over a synagogue in San Francisco. Unfortunately, he misses his connection in Philadelphia and sets out overland with a couple of newfound companions, who rob him of all his possessions and throw him out of the wagon. Eventually Belinski is befriended by a bandit (Ford), who realizes that the rabbi is a tenderfoot who can't take care of himself in the harsh conditions of the West, and shepherds him to San Francisco.

One of the funniest scenes is when Belinski comes across a community of Amish and thinks they are landsmen (countrymen). Many people have criticized this film, but I found it to contain some hilarious bits.

TITLE: **THE FRONT**

YEAR PRODUCED: 1976

DIRECTOR: Martin Ritt

CAST: Woody Allen, Zero Mostel, Herschel Bernardi, Danny Aiello

COUNTRY OF ORIGIN: United States

LANGUAGE: English

RUNNING TIME: 94 minutes

VIDEO: Columbia

DESCRIPTION:

Story of the blacklist resulting from the investigation conducted by the House Un-American Activities Committee in the 1950s.

Woody Allen plays a small-time Jewish bookie who becomes a front for television writers who cannot submit their work to the networks. During the course of the film, he develops from a man with little or no interest in politics to a strong opponent of HUAC. By the end, he is ready to support his friends and stand up for what he believes is right.

Many of the creative personnel behind this film were victims of the HUAC purge. The film received an Academy Award nomination for Best Original Screenplay.

TITLE: **FUNNY GIRL**
YEAR PRODUCED: 1968
DIRECTOR: William Wyler
CAST: Barbra Streisand, Omar Sharif, Kay Medford, Anne Francis, Walter Pidgeon
COUNTRY OF ORIGIN: United States
LANGUAGE: English
RUNNING TIME: 150 minutes
VIDEO: Columbia

DESCRIPTION:
Story of singer-comedienne Fanny Brice, her rise to stardom on Broadway, and her less-than-successful romance with gambler Nick Arnstein.

For once Hollywood got it right. The film does not gloss over Brice's personal problems, but makes them an integral part of the story. There is no attempt to play down her Jewish background. The early part of the film seems to revel in it. Excellent performance by Streisand, who also originated the role on Broadway. In her first film, she won an Academy Award for Best Actress. Brice would have been proud of her.

Outstanding score by Bcb Merrill and Jule Styne, augmented by several songs originally sung by Brice. Terrific musical, with great performances by all. In addition to Streisand's Academy Award, film was nominated for Best Cinematography, Best Film Editing, Best Picture, Best Song, Best Sound, Best Supporting Actress (Medford), and Best Score.

TITLE: **FUNNY LADY**
YEAR PRODUCED: 1974
DIRECTOR: Herbert Ross
CAST: Barbra Streisand, James Caan, Roddy McDowall, Ben Vereen, Carole Wells, Omar Sharif
COUNTRY OF ORIGIN: United States
LANGUAGE: English
RUNNING TIME: 136 minutes
VIDEO: Columbia

DESCRIPTION:
Sequel to *Funny Girl* showing Fanny Brice at the peak of her career and her marriage to showman Billy Rose. Great musical scenes provide the highlights of this film.

TITLE: **GABY: A TRUE STORY**
YEAR PRODUCED: 1987
DIRECTOR: Luis Mandoki
CAST: Rachel Levin, Liv Ullmann, Robert Loggia
COUNTRY OF ORIGIN: United States
LANGUAGE: English
RUNNING TIME: 115 minutes
VIDEO: Columbia

DESCRIPTION:
Astonishing true story of Gaby Bremmer (Levin), a Jewish woman born with cerebral palsy, and her struggle to overcome her condition.

Gaby, whose parents are refugees from Nazi Germany, is raised in Mexico. In her battle to overcome her illness, she enters school, falls in love, and graduates from university. She becomes an acclaimed writer and devotes a great deal of time and energy as an advocate for the rights of the disabled.

Although the Jewish content is minimal, except that the main character is Jewish, the film is exceptional, but some scenes may be difficult to view.

TITLE: **THE GARDEN OF THE FINZI-CONTINIS**

YEAR PRODUCED: 1971

DIRECTOR: Vittorio De Sica

CAST: Dominique Sanda, Helmut Berger

COUNTRY OF ORIGIN: Italy

LANGUAGE: Italian with English subtitles

RUNNING TIME: 94 minutes

VIDEO: Lorimar, Warner

DESCRIPTION:

Haunting drama about an aristocratic Jewish family in Italy before and during World War II. They ignore the storm clouds surrounding them until it is too late and they are shipped off to a concentration camp.

Based on a true story.

Made Sanda a world star and won an Academy Award for Best Foreign Film.

TITLE: **A GENERATION**

YEAR PRODUCED: 1954

DIRECTOR: Andrzej Wajda

CAST: Tadeusz Lomnicki, Ursula Modrzynska, Zbigniew Cybulski, Roman Polanski

COUNTRY OF ORIGIN: Poland

LANGUAGE: Polish with English subtitles

RUNNING TIME: 90 minutes

VIDEO: Facets

DESCRIPTION:

Wajda's first feature film as a director is set in 1942 in occupied Warsaw. A young man escapes from the ghetto and joins the Polish resistance. He falls in love with the leader of the local group and begins to fight for his freedom.

TITLE: **GENGHIS COHN**

YEAR PRODUCED: 1994

DIRECTOR: Elijah Moshinsky

CAST: Robert Lindsay, Diana Rigg, Antony Sher

COUNTRY OF ORIGIN: Britain

LANGUAGE: English

RUNNING TIME: 80 minutes

VIDEO: A & E/SMA

DESCRIPTION:

BBC telefilm is an audacious comedy based on a novel by Romain Gary.

Otto (Lindsay), a former Nazi concentration camp commandant, seeks to escape his past by becoming police chief in a small Bavarian town. In 1958, a series of murders rocks the town. The ghost of Genghis Cohn (Sher), a Jewish comedian whom Otto ordered killed in the camps, appears and exacts revenge in his own unique manner.

TITLE: **GENTLEMAN'S AGREEMENT**

YEAR PRODUCED: 1947

DIRECTOR: Elia Kazan

CAST: Gregory Peck, Dorothy McGuire, John Garfield, Celeste Holm, Anne Revere, June Havoc, Albert Dekker, Jane Wyatt, Dean Stockwell, Sam Jaffe

COUNTRY OF ORIGIN: United States

LANGUAGE: English

RUNNING TIME: 118 minutes

VIDEO: Fox

DESCRIPTION:

One of the first films out of Hollywood to attack anti-Semitism.

Peck plays a non-Jewish writer looking for a new angle for a magazine piece on anti-Semitism. He pretends to be Jewish and discovers a deep well of bigotry that threatens to change his own life and those around him. This was a film that Hollywood did not want to make. Jewish producers turned it down, and the project did not get off the ground until it was picked up by Twentieth Century Fox, one of the few studios whose head was not Jewish.

Film was very successful and very controversial. Won Academy Awards for Best Picture, Best Director, Best Supporting Actress (Holm). Nominated for Best Actor (Peck), Best Actress (McGuire), Best Film Editing, Best Screenplay, Best Supporting Actress (Revere).

TITLE: **GETTING AWAY WITH MURDER**

YEAR PRODUCED: 1996

DIRECTOR: Harvey Miller

CAST: Dan Aykroyd, Lily Tomlin, Jack Lemmon, Bonnie Hunt

COUNTRY OF ORIGIN: United States

LANGUAGE: English

RUNNING TIME: 92 minutes

VIDEO: HBO

DESCRIPTION:

Despite being poorly written and wasting most of its excellent cast, this film does have some redeeming qualities.

The story deals with a college ethics professor (Aykroyd) who discovers that his neighbor (Lemmon) has been accused of being a war criminal. The neighbor and his daughter (Tomlin) vehemently deny it. When it appears that the charges are incorrect, Aykroyd is so ashamed of believing them that he marries the daughter. Then he discovers that the charges are true.

Aykroyd decides to kill his father-in-law and carries out the plot, only to discover that the authorities believe the old man committed suicide.

Film's only positive element is the strong case Aykroyd makes when confronting two Holocaust deniers.

TITLE: **THE GLORY BOYS**

YEAR PRODUCED: 1984

DIRECTOR: Michael Ferguson

CAST: Rod Steiger, Anthony Perkins

COUNTRY OF ORIGIN: Britain

LANGUAGE: English

RUNNING TIME: 110 minutes

VIDEO: Prism/ BFS

DESCRIPTION:

British film about Israeli scientist targeted for assassination by PLO and IRA. A little slow on the action.

TITLE: **GOD, MAN AND DEVIL**

YEAR PRODUCED: 1949

DIRECTOR: Joseph Seiden

CAST: Mikhal Mikhalesko, Gustav Berger

COUNTRY OF ORIGIN: United States

LANGUAGE: Yiddish with English subtitles

RUNNING TIME: 100 minutes

VIDEO: National Center for Jewish Film

DESCRIPTION:

Poor Torah scribe's business partner turns him into a greedy, dishonest man and he loses his religious beliefs in the process.

TITLE: **THE GOLEM**

YEAR PRODUCED: 1920

DIRECTOR: Paul Wegener and Carle Boese

CAST: Paul Wegener, Albert Steinruck, Ernst Deutsch, Syda Salmonava

COUNTRY OF ORIGIN: Germany

LANGUAGE: Silent film

RUNNING TIME: 80 minutes

VIDEO: Sinister Cinema, Moore Video, Nostalgia

DESCRIPTION:

Huge clay figure is given life by medieval rabbi in order to protect Jews of Prague ghetto. Once brought to life the Golem quickly breaks all bonds the rabbi may have over him.

Famous Jewish legend has been filmed a number of times and may be the basis for the Frankenstein story. Story is really about our responsibility for the lives we create.

TITLE: **GOOD EVENING, MR. WALLENBERG**

YEAR PRODUCED: 1992

DIRECTOR: Kjell Grede

CAST: Stellen Skarsgard

COUNTRY OF ORIGIN: Sweden

LANGUAGE: Swedish, German, and Hungarian with English subtitles

RUNNING TIME: 115 minutes

VIDEO: Fox/Lorber

DESCRIPTION:
The story of Raoul Wallenberg and his race against time to save as many Jews as possible in German-occupied Hungary.

TITLE: **GOODBYE, COLUMBUS**

YEAR PRODUCED: 1969

DIRECTOR: Larry Peerce

CAST: Richard Benjamin, Ali MacGraw, Jack Klugman, Nan Martin, Michael Myers

COUNTRY OF ORIGIN: United States

LANGUAGE: English

RUNNING TIME: 105 minutes

VIDEO: Paramount

DESCRIPTION:
Satiric comedy based on Philip Roth's bestselling novel.

Film looks at a successful Jewish family and their spoiled daughter from the viewpoint of a poor working-class librarian from the Bronx. Although all of them are Jewish, their class differences lead to many problems. MacGraw's family has made it, while Benjamin's has not. This creates a great deal of jealousy and resentment in Benjamin, which eventually leads to the end of the relationship. The only well adjusted characters are MacGraw's father, played by Klugman, and her brother, played by Myers, who steals every scene he is in. Richard Benjamin and Ali MacGraw are superb in their film debuts.

The wedding scene is a classic.

TITLE: **GOODBYE, NEW YORK**

YEAR PRODUCED: 1984

DIRECTOR: Amos Kollek

CAST: Julie Hagerty, Amos Kollek, David Topaz, Shmuel Shiloh, Aviva Ger, Jennifer Babtist

COUNTRY OF ORIGIN: Israel

LANGUAGE: English

RUNNING TIME: 90 minutes

VIDEO: Vestron

DESCRIPTION:

Comedy about New York woman who catches her husband in bed with another woman. She decides to leave the lout and grabs the first flight to Paris. Unfortunately, she sleeps through the stopover in Paris and winds up in Israel, without any money or luggage.

She meets an Israeli soldier on leave and decides to make the best of a bad situation. She stays on a kibbutz for a while, has a short-lived affair, and finally winds up in Jerusalem.

The film has some good humorous moments.

TITLE: **THE GOVERNESS**

YEAR PRODUCED: 1998

DIRECTOR: Sandra Goldbacher

CAST: Minnie Driver, Tom Wilkinson, Florence Hoath, Jonathan Rhys Meyers

COUNTRY OF ORIGIN: Great Britain

LANGUAGE: English

RUNNING TIME: 114 minutes

VIDEO: Behaviour (Malo)

DESCRIPTION:

Story of a Sephardic woman, Rosina, in early Victorian England. When Rosina's father dies suddenly, leaving the family in debt, she is forced to find work and decides to pose as a Gentile and accepts a position as a governess on a remote island in Scotland.

Rosina has an affair with the father and becomes interested in his research into photography. The film stretches credibility and includes quite a bit of nudity, but tells an interesting story about an adventurous woman challenging the world and living her life on her own terms.

TITLE: **THE GREAT DICTATOR**

YEAR PRODUCED: 1940

DIRECTOR: Charles Chaplin

CAST: Charles Chaplin, Paulette Goddard, Jack Oakie, Billie Gilbert

COUNTRY OF ORIGIN: United States

LANGUAGE: English

RUNNING TIME: 126 minutes

VIDEO: Fox

DESCRIPTION:

One of the great anti-Nazi films and also one of the first to be produced in the United States. Chaplin uses comedy to ridicule fascism and point out its danger to the whole world.

Chaplin plays two roles—the Jewish barber facing continual religious persecution, and the lookalike dictator, Adenoid Hynkel, an obvious lampoon of Adolf Hitler.

This was Chaplin's first full-dialogue film. It was not very successful in the United States and was banned in Germany. Nominated for six Academy Awards, it was voted one of the year's Ten Best by the New York Times. Today it is considered one of the great comedies of all time, although the monologue at the close could have been cut without lessening the film's power.

TITLE: **GREEN FIELDS (GRINE FELDER)**

YEAR PRODUCED: 1937

DIRECTOR: Jacob Ben-Ami and Edgar G. Ulmer

CAST: Michael Goldstein, Herschel Bernardi, Helen Beverly

COUNTRY OF ORIGIN: United States

LANGUAGE: Yiddish with English subtitles

RUNNING TIME: 95 minutes

VIDEO: National Center for Jewish Films, Ergo

DESCRIPTION:

Romantic story based on tale of a young Hasidic scholar who leaves his yeshiva to search the countryside for common people and a meaningful existence close to the land. Some Jewish peasants take him in as a boarder and tutor for their children.

TITLE: **GREEN FIELDS**

YEAR PRODUCED: 1989

DIRECTOR: Isaac Yeshurun

COUNTRY OF ORIGIN: Israel

LANGUAGE: Hebrew with English subtitles

RUNNING TIME: 92 minutes

VIDEO: Facets

DESCRIPTION:

An Israeli family traveling to a son's army graduation gets lost in the West Bank and winds up in the middle of a battle between rock-throwing Palestinians and Israeli soldiers.

Israel's first feature film about the Intifada; focuses on the reactions of various family members and how they deal with issues raised by the Arab revolt.

TITLE: **GRETA**

YEAR PRODUCED: 1986

DIRECTOR: Krysztof Gruber

CAST: Janusz Grabowski, Agnieszka Kruszewska, Eva Borowik, Tomasz Grochoczki

COUNTRY OF ORIGIN: Poland

LANGUAGE: Polish with English subtitles

RUNNING TIME: 60 minutes

VIDEO: European Video Distributor, Ingram International Films, Facets

DESCRIPTION:

A 10-year-old boy escapes from a labor camp in occupied Poland. After meeting a German deserter, he witnesses the deserter's execution by an SS officer. Later the boy meets a girl his own age who invites him to her house. Once there, the boy finds that the SS officer is her father.

TITLE: **HAMSIN (HOT DESERT WIND)**

YEAR PRODUCED: 1983

DIRECTOR: Daniel Wachsman

CAST: Shlomo Tarshish, Yasin Shawad, Hemda Levy

COUNTRY OF ORIGIN: Israel

LANGUAGE: Hebrew with English subtitles

RUNNING TIME: 90 minutes

VIDEO: Ergo

DESCRIPTION:

Jewish landowner and Arab worker get along well until the government decides to confiscate some Arab land in the area. A confrontation occurs. Tension between Jews and Arabs rises, reaching a climax when the Jewish farmer learns that his sister is having an affair with the Arab.

Nominated for an Academy Award for Best Foreign Film.

TITLE: **HANNAH AND HER SISTERS**

YEAR PRODUCED: 1986

DIRECTOR: Woody Allen

CAST: Woody Allen, Michael Caine, Mia Farrow, Carrie Fisher, Barbara Hershey, Lloyd Nolan, Maureen O'Sullivan, Daniel Stern, Max von Sydow, Dianne Wiest

COUNTRY OF ORIGIN: United States

LANGUAGE: English

RUNNING TIME: 103 minutes

VIDEO: HBO

DESCRIPTION:

Woody Allen as the perpetual outsider, watching the world from his own perspective, commenting on what he observes and envying the participants.

Film revolves around Hannah (Farrow) and her two sisters (Hershey and Wiest). Allen was married to Hannah and is the father of their twin sons. As a result, he is a permanent member of the family and continually hangs around.

Not only is Allen the outsider, he is paranoid about death and illness, two fears that skew his outlook on the world. The film deals with the romantic entanglements of the various characters, and their personal problems. By the end Allen may have found some answers.

TITLE: **HANNA K.**

YEAR PRODUCED: 1983

DIRECTOR: Constantin Costa-Gavras

CAST: Jill Clayburgh, Jean Yanne, Gabriel Byrne, Muhammed Dukri

COUNTRY OF ORIGIN: France

LANGUAGE: English

RUNNING TIME: 108 minutes

VIDEO: MCA

DESCRIPTION:

Disappointing film to come from Costa-Gavras. Story about a woman lawyer and her relationships with a number of men, including a Palestinian Arab.

Stirred up some controversy when first released because of its pro-Palestinian bias and a circumcision scene that made the custom appear barbaric.

TITLE: **HANNA'S WAR**

YEAR PRODUCED: 1988

DIRECTOR: Menahem Golan

CAST: Maruschka Detmers, Ellen Burstyn, Anthony Andrews, Donald Pleasence, David Warner

COUNTRY OF ORIGIN: United States

LANGUAGE: English

RUNNING TIME: 148 minutes

VIDEO: Media, Cannon

DESCRIPTION:

On Mount Herzl, overlooking the city of Jerusalem, is a cemetery dedicated to Israel's fallen heroes. Buried there are the remains of a woman who gave her life for the Jewish people.

In 1939 Hanna Senesh left her native Hungary and emigrated to Palestine. She attended the agricultural school at Nahalal, but was soon swept up by world events. Hanna agreed to join the British army and parachute into occupied Europe to organize an escape route for downed Allied pilots, with the understanding that her job would also entail making contact with, and helping, the Jewish communities in Hungary and Yugoslavia. Unfortunately, she was captured by the Nazis, tortured, and executed.

Maruschka Detmers gives a powerful performance as Hanna. And Menahem Golan has provided a haunting setting for her poem "Eli, Eli," which has become a classic in memory of the

Holocaust. After Hanna completes her military training, she learns that her brother has arrived in Palestine. She rushes to the prison camp at Atlit to see him, and as they walk along the beach, she recites the poem, while in the background, a female voice can be heard singing the mournful Hebrew lyrics. A heartrending moment. Dov Seltzer, the film's music director, uses the Yiddish "Song of the Partisans" very effectively throughout the film. While this film has some faults, it is a story that should be seen by everyone.

TITLE: **HATE**

YEAR PRODUCED: 1995

DIRECTOR: Mathieu Kassavitz

CAST: Vincent Cassel, Hubert Kounde, Said Taghaoui

COUNTRY OF ORIGIN: France

LANGUAGE: French with English subtitles

RUNNING TIME: 95 minutes

VIDEO: Malofilm

DESCRIPTION:

One day in the lives of three toughs in an economically depressed area of Paris—a Jew, an Arab, and a black. They wander the city, getting into minor scrapes with the law and with others. Then they realize they don't have the money to pay for a cab back to their own part of town when public transportation closes for the night.

Despite the foul language and their violent acts, the viewer slowly becomes sympathetic to these guys. They are really misfits in society who have nowhere to go to get a helping hand.

TITLE: **THE HEARTBREAK KID**

YEAR PRODUCED: 1972

DIRECTOR: Elaine May

CAST: Charles Grodin, Cybill Shepherd, Jeannie Berlin, Eddie Albert

COUNTRY OF ORIGIN: United States

LANGUAGE: English

RUNNING TIME: 106 minutes

VIDEO: Media Home Entertainment

DESCRIPTION:

After a short courtship, a Jewish sporting goods salesman marries a girl he met at a singles bar. On their honeymoon he realizes he has made a mistake; he meets a beautiful college student from a wealthy WASP family and pursues her.

Neil Simon's script is very funny at times, but poses the eternal question: Why do Jewish boys prefer non-Jewish girls? The film contrasts the sexy allure of the blond, gentile girl with the boring, unattractive style of the Jewish girl. It also highlights the differences between the cold stand-offishness of the WASP family and the warm love of the Jewish family. At the end, the real question is whether Grodin gave up too much to attain his adolescent fantasy.

TITLE: **HEAVY METAL**

YEAR PRODUCED: 1981

DIRECTOR: Gerald Potterton

CAST: Animated feature using voices of John Candy, Joe Flaherty, Don Francks, Eugene Levy, Harold Ramis, John Vernon

COUNTRY OF ORIGIN: Canada

LANGUAGE: English

RUNNING TIME: 90 minutes

VIDEO: Columbia

DESCRIPTION:

Animated science fiction comedy made up of a series of vignettes, one of which includes a Jewish secretary being kidnapped by a robot. Film is raunchy and has an R rating.

TITLE: **THE HERITAGE**
YEAR PRODUCED: 1993
DIRECTOR: Amnon Rubinstein
CAST: Avi Toledano, Yael Abecassis, Alon Aboutboul, Levana Finkelstein
COUNTRY OF ORIGIN: Israel
LANGUAGE: Hebrew with English subtitles
RUNNING TIME: 85 minutes
VIDEO: Sisu Home Entertainment/CHV Communications

DESCRIPTION:
Two interwoven love stories set hundreds of years apart.

An Israeli man travels to Spain on a business trip and falls in love with a Spanish girl. This story is then interrupted with flashbacks to the Spanish inquisition when the man's ancestor, a Jew who was raised as a Christian, falls in love with a Marano and rescues her and her family from death. Singer/actor Avi Toledano is very credible as the main character in both stories and this appears to be one of the most ambitious Israeli films yet produced.

TITLE: **THE HERO**
YEAR PRODUCED: 1969
DIRECTOR: Richard Harris
CAST: Richard Harris, Romy Schneider, Kim Burfield, Yossi Yadin
COUNTRY OF ORIGIN: United States
LANGUAGE: English
RUNNING TIME: 97 minutes
VIDEO: Embassy, Sultan

DESCRIPTION:
A soccer player (Harris) becomes friends with a 12-year-old boy who idolizes him. When his girlfriend threatens to leave him if he doesn't get a decent job and marry her, he takes money from a gambler in return for throwing the big game. On the day of the game, he changes his mind and is determined to win, even if the gambler kills him.

Film was made in Israel, although the script leaves some ambiguity as to where it takes place.

TITLE: **HERSHALEH**

YEAR PRODUCED: 1977

DIRECTOR: Yoel Silberg

CAST: Mike Burstyn, Ariah Elias

COUNTRY OF ORIGIN: Israel

LANGUAGE: Hebrew with English subtitles

RUNNING TIME: 90 minutes

VIDEO: Kol Ami

DESCRIPTION:

Musical comedy about a recent immigrant and a gang of Israeli roughnecks who learn to get along and get things accomplished by cooperating.

TITLE: **HESTER STREET**

YEAR PRODUCED: 1974

DIRECTOR: Joan Micklin Silver

CAST: Steven Keats, Carol Kane

COUNTRY OF ORIGIN: United States

LANGUAGE: English and Yiddish with English subtitles

RUNNING TIME: 89 minutes

VIDEO: Vestron

DESCRIPTION:

When a Jewish immigrant arrives in New York to join her husband, she is shocked to discover that he has become Americanized. He has forsaken all manifestations of his Jewish past and has fallen in love with a "modern" American woman.

A wonderfully emotional film about the importance of preserving one's customs and traditions, even while adjusting to a new way of life.

Terrific performances by the lead actors. Carol Kane is especially good, considering she had no knowledge of Yiddish before she made this film.

TITLE: **HIDE AND SEEK**

YEAR PRODUCED: 1980

DIRECTOR: Dan Wolman

CAST: Gila Almagor, Doron Tavori, Chaim Hadaya

COUNTRY OF ORIGIN: Israel

LANGUAGE: Hebrew with English subtitles

RUNNING TIME: 90 minutes

VIDEO: Ergo

DESCRIPTION:

Study of adolescence in Palestine in the late 1940s and the factors that affected the first generation of Israelis.

TITLE: **HILL 24 DOESN'T ANSWER**

YEAR PRODUCED: 1955

DIRECTOR: Thorold Dickinson

CAST: Edward Mulhare, Haya Harareet, Michael Wager, Michael Shilo, Arieh Lavi

COUNTRY OF ORIGIN: Israel

LANGUAGE: English

RUNNING TIME: 102 minutes

VIDEO: Ergo

DESCRIPTION:

One of the first films produced in Israel tells the story of four soldiers defending a hill outside Jerusalem during Israel's War of Independence.

Told in flashback and includes some background on the battle for Jerusalem during Israel's first war.

TITLE: **HIS PEOPLE**

YEAR PRODUCED: 1925

DIRECTOR: Edward Sloman

COUNTRY OF ORIGIN: United States

LANGUAGE: Silent.

RUNNING TIME: 91 minutes

VIDEO: National Center for Jewish Films

DESCRIPTION:

Set on the Lower East Side of New York during the early years of the twentieth century, film looks at the conflicts between two generations of immigrants. The younger generation seeks to be more Americanized and is more willing to stray from the traditions of their parents.

In the end both generations learn to adapt and respect each other's desires, with the family still the center of love and dignity.

TITLE: **HIS WIFE'S LOVER (ZAYN VAYBS LUBOVNIK)**

YEAR PRODUCED: 1931

DIRECTOR: Sidney Goldin

CAST: Ludwig Satz, Michael Rosenberg, Isadore Cashier, Lucy Levine.

COUNTRY OF ORIGIN: United States

LANGUAGE: Yiddish with English subtitles

RUNNING TIME: 80 minutes

VIDEO: Facets, National Center for Jewish Films, Ergo

DESCRIPTION:

Yiddish comedy about an actor who disguises himself as an old man and wins the affections of a beautiful young woman, then drops his disguise and attempts to seduce her in a test of her loyalty.

TITLE: **HISTORY OF THE WORLD, PART I**

YEAR PRODUCED: 1981

DIRECTOR: Mel Brooks

CAST: Mel Brooks, Gregory Hines, Dom DeLuise, Madeline Kahn, Harvey Korman, Cloris Leachman

COUNTRY OF ORIGIN: United States

LANGUAGE: English

RUNNING TIME: 92 minutes

VIDEO: Fox

DESCRIPTION:
Mel Brooks strings together a number of skits to give us his version of world history. Some of them show how the Jews have been persecuted throughout time. While the film is a strong statement against racism, its humor is often over the top, and it is difficult for the audience to sustain interest.

TITLE: **HIT THE DUTCHMAN**

YEAR PRODUCED: 1992

DIRECTOR: Menahem Golan

CAST: Bruce Nozick, Edie Bowz, Sally Kirkland

COUNTRY OF ORIGIN: United States

LANGUAGE: English

RUNNING TIME: 116 minutes

VIDEO: Vidmark

DESCRIPTION:
Gangster film centering on 1930s mobster Dutch Schultz.

Schultz, whose real name was Arthur Fleggenheimer, emerged from the Jewish community to challenge Legs Diamond for a share of the New York territory. Using strong-arm methods, Schultz cut a swath through the world of organized crime until he met his own bloody demise.

Film was shot in Moscow and provides lots of action and excitement, with a very strong Jewish flavor, including a wonderful soundtrack. Not bad for a genre film.

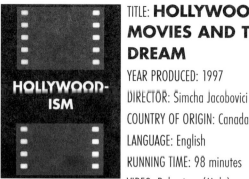

TITLE: **HOLLYWOODISM: JEWS, MOVIES AND THE AMERICAN DREAM**

YEAR PRODUCED: 1997

DIRECTOR: Simcha Jacobovici

COUNTRY OF ORIGIN: Canada

LANGUAGE: English

RUNNING TIME: 98 minutes

VIDEO: Behaviour (Malo)

DESCRIPTION:

Documentary on the men who founded Hollywood and the image of America they created. The film tells the story of a small group of Jewish immigrants who created the most influential art form of the twentieth century–the Hollywood movie.

Film uses interviews with children and grandchildren of Hollywood moguls, writers and scholars, as well as dozens of film clips. Although the film is based on Neal Gabler's best-selling book, "An Empire of Their Own: How the Jews Invented Hollywood", it is a creative work that stands on its own merits.

TITLE: **HOLOCAUST**

YEAR PRODUCED: 1978

DIRECTOR: Marvin J. Chomsky

CAST: Meryl Streep, James Woods, Michael Moriarty, Joseph Bottoms, David Warner, Sam Wanamaker

COUNTRY OF ORIGIN: United States

LANGUAGE: English

RUNNING TIME: 450 minutes

VIDEO: Worldvision

DESCRIPTION:

Made-for-television miniseries that brought the Holocaust back to the world's attention. Received huge ratings everywhere it was shown, including North America and Germany.

Follows two German families, the Weisses and the Dorfs, from 1935 to 1945. The Weiss family is Jewish; the Dorf family isn't, and the husband rises to a high position in the Nazi hierarchy. Film covers an enormous amount of ground as it tries to present the complete scope of the Holocaust. One Weiss brother, Woods, is an artist who marries a gentile woman and is incarcerated at Terezin. Another brother, Bottoms, joins the partisans and witnesses the massacre at Babi Yar, in the Soviet Union. The father is shipped back to his native Poland, where he takes part in the Warsaw Ghetto Uprising.

The acting is often superb, but this television film has been criticized for being too shallow. The criticism is probably correct. But the Holocaust was so enormous that no one film or TV miniseries can cover it properly. Nonetheless, the film raised awareness of the Holocaust all over the world, bringing the topic to the attention of millions of people who had never heard of it or had never known very much about it. Nominated for 16 Emmy Awards and won eight.

TITLE: **HOMICIDE**
YEAR PRODUCED: 1991
DIRECTOR: David Mamet
CAST: Joe Mantegna, William H. Macy
COUNTRY OF ORIGIN: United States
LANGUAGE: English
RUNNING TIME: 100 minutes
VIDEO: Columbia

DESCRIPTION:
A Jewish detective is pulled off a big drug case just before the bust goes down because of the murder of a wealthy Jewish shopkeeper. The victim's son, with a lot of clout in the department, specifically asks for Gold (Mantegna) to be assigned to the case. The son hopes that because Gold is Jewish, he will investigate the case more thoroughly than someone else might.

Gold resents the intrusion into his big case but gets caught up in an old arms conspiracy and a case involving anti-Semitism. And until Gold can better understand his own roots, he won't be able to work out a solution to the murder.

Somewhat confusing storyline but a strong cast, especially Mantegna, makes this film interesting throughout.

TITLE: **HOTEL TERMINUS: THE LIFE AND TIMES OF KLAUS BARBIE**

YEAR PRODUCED: 1987

DIRECTOR: Marcel Ophuis

COUNTRY OF ORIGIN: France

LANGUAGE: French with English subtitles

RUNNING TIME: 267 minutes

VIDEO: Video Treasures

DESCRIPTION:

Focuses on Klaus Barbie, a Nazi war criminal who was sentenced to death in absentia after World War II and would have been executed had he been found. Decades later, he was discovered living in Bolivia and brought back to France for a new trial.

Excellent documentary by the filmmaker of *The Sorrow and the Pity*.

TITLE: **THE HOUSE ON CHELOUCHE STREET**

YEAR PRODUCED: 1973

DIRECTOR: Moshe Mizrahi

CAST: Gila Almagor, Michal Bat-Adam, Shai K. Ofir

COUNTRY OF ORIGIN: Israel

LANGUAGE: Hebrew with English subtitles

RUNNING TIME: 111 minutes

VIDEO: Video Yesterday, National Center for Jewish Film

DESCRIPTION:

The struggles of a North African Jewish family in 1946 Palestine before the creation of the State of Israel. Nominated for an Academy Award for Best Foreign Film.

TITLE: **THE HOUSE ON GARIBALDI STREET**

YEAR PRODUCED: 1979

DIRECTOR: Peter Collinson

CAST: Topol, Nick Mancuso, Martin Balsam, Janet Suzman

COUNTRY OF ORIGIN: United States

LANGUAGE: English

RUNNING TIME: 96 minutes

VIDEO: Fries

DESCRIPTION:

Television film about the capture of Adolf Eichmann in Argentina and his removal to Israel. Interesting and keeps to the facts.

TITLE: **HUNGRY HEARTS**

YEAR PRODUCED: 1922

DIRECTOR: E. Mason Hopper

COUNTRY OF ORIGIN: United States

LANGUAGE: Silent film

RUNNING TIME: 80 minutes

VIDEO: National Center for Jewish Film

DESCRIPTION:

Filmed on location in the Lower East Side of New York; explores the problems and dreams of Jewish immigrants to America in the early 1900s.

TITLE: **HUNTED**

YEAR PRODUCED: 1979

COUNTRY OF ORIGIN: Germany

LANGUAGE: German with English subtitles

RUNNING TIME: 90 minutes

VIDEO: Video Gama

DESCRIPTION:

Jewish boy teams up with resistance fighter to find his mother in Germany during World War II.

TITLE: **I DON'T BUY KISSES ANYMORE**

YEAR PRODUCED: 1992

DIRECTOR: Robert Marcarelli

CAST: Jason Alexander, Nia Peeples, Lainie Kazan, Lou Jacobi, Eileen Brennan

COUNTRY OF ORIGIN: United States

LANGUAGE: English

RUNNING TIME: 112 minutes

VIDEO: Paramount

DESCRIPTION:

Amusing romantic comedy about Bernie (Alexander), a shy, overweight Jewish shoe salesman, and Theresa (Peeples), a beautiful, outgoing non-Jewish psychology student who is also an aerobics nut. They meet at a corner candy store and become friends. Then their friendship turns into love.

In his pursuit of Theresa, Bernie determines to shed some of his extra poundage and finds that a new life is possible once he slims down. Lainie Kazan plays the overprotective Jewish mother who believes that food is love. No real insights into interreligious or interethnic relationships, but a pleasant bit of entertainment.

I DON'T GIVE A DAMN

TITLE: **I DON'T GIVE A DAMN**

YEAR PRODUCED: 1988

DIRECTOR: Shmuel Imberman

CAST: Ika Sohar, Anat Waxman

COUNTRY OF ORIGIN: Israel

LANGUAGE: Hebrew with English subtitles

RUNNING TIME: 94 minutes

VIDEO: Trans-World Entertainment

DESCRIPTION:

An Israeli soldier, wounded in an engagement with Arab terrorists, returns to civilian life after undergoing a leg amputation. His bitter attitude makes things difficult for his friends and family and for himself. Eventually the love of a good woman gets him through the trauma of having to deal with life under the trying conditions created by his injuries.

First part may be a bit confusing as the subtitles don't come on for a few minutes, but this is a serious film about a topic that is not discussed much—the adjustment problems of the thousands of wounded soldiers and wounded souls that result from modern warfare.

TITLE: **I LOVE YOU, ALICE B. TOKLAS**

YEAR PRODUCED: 1968

DIRECTOR: Hy Averback

CAST: Peter Sellers, Jo Van Fleet, Leigh Taylor-Young,

COUNTRY OF ORIGIN: United States

LANGUAGE: English

RUNNING TIME: 94 minutes

VIDEO: Warner

DESCRIPTION:

A conservative, mild-mannered Jewish lawyer seems to have everything going for him—a solid career and a devoted girlfriend whom he is about to marry. Suddenly he decides to abandon it all for a free-spirited, uninhibited girl he has just met. He starts wearing beads and bell bottoms, and gets into hash and free love.

A fun comedy that could only have been made in the 60's and reflects those times perfectly, even when Seller's character discovers that the results can be devastating. Much satirizing of Jewish institutions and Jews; the funeral scene is one example, as is the wedding scene at the end. Sellers was perfect for this role.

TITLE: **I LOVE YOU... DON'T TOUCH ME**

YEAR PRODUCED: 1998

DIRECTOR: Julie Davis

CAST. Marla Schaffel, Meredith Scott Lynn, Mitchell Whitfield

COUNTRY OF ORIGIN: United States

LANGUAGE: English

RUNNING TIME: 85 minutes

VIDEO: Orion

DESCRIPTION:

Comedy abut 25 year old Katic who is looking for a relationship. Her neighbor Ben has a crush on he but she sets him up with her girlfriend Janet. When Ben and Janet hit if off immediately, Katie has second thoughts.

TITLE: **I LOVE YOU, I LOVE YOU NOT**

YEAR PRODUCED: 1997

DIRECTOR: Billy Hopkins

CAST: Jeanne Moreau, Claire Danes, Jude Law, James Van Der Beck, Robert Sean Leonard

COUNTRY OF ORIGIN: United States

LANGUAGE: English

RUNNING TIME: 92 minutes

VIDEO: Miramax

DESCRIPTION:

An adolescent (Danes) feels very close to her grandmotehr (Moreau), a survivor of Auschwitz, but is personally unaware of anti-Semitism until her girlfriend snubs her. Then the boy she falls for (Law) shows insensitivity and prejudice.

Film includes flashbacks to her grandmother's youth with Danes also playing the young grandmother.

TITLE: **I LOVE YOU, ROSA**
YEAR PRODUCED: 1972
DIRECTOR: Moshe Mizrahi
CAST: Michal Bat-Adam, Gabi Osterman, Yoseph Shiloah
COUNTRY OF ORIGIN: Israel
LANGUAGE: Dubbed into English
RUNNING TIME: 90 minutes
VIDEO: National Center for Jewish Films, Facets

DESCRIPTION:
Slow-moving, artsy film that focuses on values and traditions, set in late nineteenth century Jerusalem.

Rosa is widowed at the age of 20. Tradition decrees that she must marry her husband's brother, who at age 11 is several years away from manhood. The question is, should she adhere to tradition or marry someone else?

TITLE: **THE ILLEGALS**
YEAR PRODUCED: 1947
DIRECTOR: Meyer Levin
CAST: Tereska Torres, Yankel Mikalowitz
COUNTRY OF ORIGIN: United States
LANGUAGE: English
RUNNING TIME: 56 minutes
VIDEO: Ergo

DESCRIPTION:
A classic produced by novelist Meyer Levin shortly after the end of World War II in a semi-documentary style.

Levin joined up with the Haganah's Aliyah Bet and Bricha to accompany a group of Jewish refugees crossing the border from Eastern Europe to the DP camps in the West, over the Alps to Italy, and onto a small illegal ship on its clandestine trip across the Mediterranean to the shores of Palestine. The two lead characters, Sarah and Micah, are played by actors whose dialogue seems to have been dubbed into English. Numerous documentary makers have used clips from this film to augment their own productions.

TITLE: **I'M NOT RAPPAPORT**

YEAR PRODUCED: 1997

DIRECTOR: Herb Gardner

CAST: Walter Matthau, Ossie Davis, Amy Irving, Martha Plimpton, Craig T. Nelson

COUNTRY OF ORIGIN: United States

LANGUAGE: English

RUNNING TIME: 135 minutes

VIDEO: MCA Universal Home Video

DESCRIPTION:

Based on the award-winning play by Herb Gardner, this adaptation features a standout performance by Matthau.

If you like a film with ideas and passion, then you will enjoy this one. Matthau plays Nat Moyer, an elderly Jewish man who was raised in the socialist movement that flourished in the first half of the twentieth century in New York. He has never forgotten the lofty principles of his youth, and challenges anyone who takes advantage of the little man.

Sometimes Nat's passions push him a little too far. When he meets Midge Carter (Ossie Davis) in Central Park and learns that Midge is about to be retired from his job running an ancient boiler in an apartment building, he takes up Midge's cause and for a short time wins him a reprieve. But most of Nat's battles are behind him. The film makes no excuses for Nat's Jewishness. In fact, the opening scene takes place as a flashback to Nat's youth when he attended a union meeting where many of the members spoke Yiddish.

TITLE: **THE IMPORTED BRIDEGROOM**

YEAR PRODUCED: 1990

DIRECTOR: Pamela Berger

CAST: Eugene Troobnick, Avi Hoffman, Greta Cowan

COUNTRY OF ORIGIN: United States

LANGUAGE: English

RUNNING TIME: 93 minutes

VIDEO: Ergo

DESCRIPTION:

Turn of the century comedy about a wealthy American widower, Asriel Stroon (Troobnick), returning to his home town in Poland and "buying" himself a brilliant scholar to marry his daughter (Cowan). Unfortunately for Stroon, his daughter has her own idea about the man she will marry.

TITLE: **THE IMPOSSIBLE SPY**

YEAR PRODUCED: 1987

DIRECTOR: Jim Goddard

CAST: John Shea, Eli Wallach

COUNTRY OF ORIGIN: Britain

LANGUAGE: English

RUNNING TIME: 96 minutes

VIDEO: HBO

DESCRIPTION:

Television film that provides excellent entertainment. If you visit northern Israel, the tour guide is certain to take you up to the Golan Heights. From that vantage point you can look down and see a large part of Galilee stretched out in front of you. That was the view the Syrian artillery gunners had before the Six-Day War in 1967. They sat in their bunkers, looked down on the fertile Israeli farmland, and lobbed shells at the Jews whenever they wanted to.

And if you look closely, you will also see clumps of trees on the Heights. They were planted there by the Syrians at the suggestion of Eli Cohen to hide their gun emplacements from Israeli view. They also marked the location of the guns for the Israelis when they launched their attack in the final days of the 1967 war. Eli Cohen was one of Israel's most successful spies. He passed himself off as an Arab, won the confidence of leading members of the Syrian hierarchy, and provided Israel with detailed information. At one point, Cohen was invited to join the Syrian cabinet.

Unfortunately, Cohen became a bit sloppy and his activities were eventually uncovered. He was tortured and hanged in front of a huge crowd. His execution was shown throughout the Middle East on Syrian television. The Impossible Spy is a well-acted, well-produced rendition of his story.

TITLE: **IN THE PRESENCE OF MINE ENEMIES**

YEAR PRODUCED: 1997

DIRECTOR: Joan Micklin Silver

CAST: Armin Mueller-Stahl, Charles Dance, Elina Lowensohn, Don McKellar, Chad Lowe

COUNTRY OF ORIGIN: United States

LANGUAGE: English

RUNNING TIME: 96 minutes

VIDEO: Coscient Astral

DESCRIPTION:

Acclaimed screen writer Rod Serling first wrote this play as the final presentation of "Playhouse 90" in the early days of television.

Set in the Warsaw Ghetto in 1943, this new production was produced by the Showtime Cable Network and features Armin Mueller-Stahl as Rabbi Adam Heller. Heller tries to maintain some semblance of normalcy despite growing despair and tension inside the Ghetto.

Heller's own son suddenly reappears after being missing in action for several years and his daughter is offered an opportunity to escape from the Ghetto, with the assistance of a German soldier.

TITLE: **INDEPENDENCE DAY**

YEAR PRODUCED: 1996

DIRECTOR: Roland Emmerich

CAST: Will Smith, Bill Pullman, Jeff Goldblum, Judd Hirsch

COUNTRY OF ORIGIN: United States

LANGUAGE: English

RUNNING TIME: 145 minutes

VIDEO: Fox

DESCRIPTION:

Blockbuster hit of the summer of 1996, grossing over $300 million in the United States and Canada alone.

This story about alien invaders coming to earth to destroy all human life has a distinctly Jewish element. The chief computer nerd (Goldblum), who eventually figures out how to stop the aliens, is Jewish.

There are several scenes where Goldblum's Jewish background, and that of his father (Hirsch), come into play. When Goldblum and Smith are about to board a fighter to take out the alien mother-ship, Hirsch hands Goldblum a yarmulke and a prayer book. A nice homey touch.

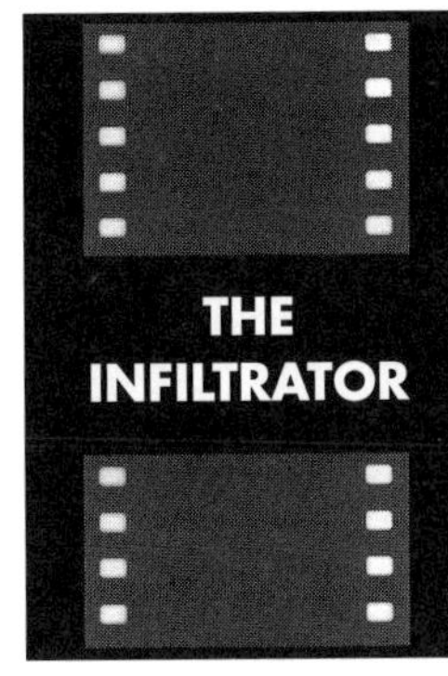

TITLE: **THE INFILTRATOR**

YEAR PRODUCED: 1994

DIRECTOR: John MacKenzie

CAST: Oliver Platt, Arlis Howard, Peter Riegert, Alan King

COUNTRY OF ORIGIN: United States

LANGUAGE: English

RUNNING TIME: 102 minutes

VIDEO: HBO

DESCRIPTION:

True story made into an exciting telefilm about an Israeli-American journalist who goes undercover to infiltrate a Nazi organization in Germany. He makes friends with some of the leaders and discovers a link between the younger generation of skinheads and the surviving Nazis who served in the Third Reich. A realistic look at modern right-wing extremism and the violence it engenders.

TITLE: **INFINITY**

YEAR PRODUCED: 1996

DIRECTOR: Matthew Broderick

CAST: Matthew Broderick, Patricia Arquette, Peter Riegert

COUNTRY OF ORIGIN: United States

LANGUAGE: English

RUNNING TIME: 119 minutes

VIDEO: CFP

DESCRIPTION:

Love story set in the 1930s and 1940s as told by world-renowned Jewish physicist Richard Feynman in the autobiography he wrote shortly before his death.

As a young man, Feynman (Broderick) fell in love with Arline Greenbaum (Arquette). She developed tuberculosis, then an incurable disease, but he married her, despite his family's opposition, and took her with him to New Mexico when he worked on the atomic bomb during World War II. Feynman took care of his beloved Arline until the very end.

TITLE: **THE INHERITORS**

YEAR PRODUCED: 1985

DIRECTOR: Walter Bannert

CAST: Nikolas Vogel, Roger Schauer, Klaus Novak, Johanna Tomek

COUNTRY OF ORIGIN: Germany

LANGUAGE: German with English subtitles

RUNNING TIME: 89 minutes

VIDEO: Sultan Entertainment

DESCRIPTION:

German boy gets involved in Nazi organization in modern Germany. Not really about Jews, but interesting study of how such groups operate.

TITLE: **INSIDE THE THIRD REICH**

YEAR PRODUCED: 1982

DIRECTOR: Marvin J. Chomsky

CAST: Derek Jacobi, Rutger Hauer, Randy Quaid, Blythe Danner, Maria Schell, John Gielgud

COUNTRY OF ORIGIN: United States

LANGUAGE: English

RUNNING TIME: 250 minutes

VIDEO: Sultan Entertainment/Embassy

DESCRIPTION:

Television miniseries detailing career of Albert Speer, one of Hitler's main advisors.

TITLE: **INTIMATE STORY**

YEAR PRODUCED: 1981

DIRECTOR: Nadav Levitan

CAST: Chava Alberstein, Alex Peleg

COUNTRY OF ORIGIN: Israel

LANGUAGE: Hebrew with English subtitles

RUNNING TIME: 95 minutes

VIDEO: Ergo

DESCRIPTION:

A childless couple on a kibbutz run into marital problems as they blame each other for their situation. Chava Alberstein is one of Israel's leading singers and recording artists. Mirrors some of the problems encountered by people living in a small, intimate society like a kibbutz.

TITLE: **IRON EAGLE 2**

YEAR PRODUCED: 1988

DIRECTOR: Sidney J. Furie

CAST: Louis Gossett Jr., Mark Humphrey, Stuart Margolin, Alan Scarfe, Maury Chaykin

COUNTRY OF ORIGIN: Canada/Israel

LANGUAGE: English

RUNNING TIME: 105 minutes

VIDEO: Live, MCA

DESCRIPTION:

Somewhat confusing story of Gossett recruiting pilots to travel to Israel and team up with Soviet fliers on a secret mission.

Only saving grace is some of the aerial photography. Much of the film was made on location in Israel, and the dogfights were photographed in the Negev, with Israeli Kfir aircraft subbing for enemy planes.

TITLE: **ISRAEL: A NATION IS BORN**

YEAR PRODUCED: 1992

DIRECTOR: Alan Rosenthal

COUNTRY OF ORIGIN: United States

LANGUAGE: English

RUNNING TIME: 260 minutes

VIDEO: Museum of Tolerance

DESCRIPTION:

Five-part documentary detailing the history of the State of Israel, narrated by and with the participation of Abba Eban. Film was intended for the Public Broadcasting System in the United States, but because of political wrangling, PBS refused to air it.

Excellent primer on the creation and growth of the State of Israel.

TITLE: **IVAN AND ABRAHAM (ME IVAN, YOU ABRAHAM)**

YEAR PRODUCED: 1993

DIRECTOR: Yolande Zauberman

CAST: Roma Alexandrovitch, Sacha Iakovlev, Vladimir Machkov, Maria Lipkina

COUNTRY OF ORIGIN: France

LANGUAGE: Yiddish with English subtitles

RUNNING TIME: 105 minutes

VIDEO: New Yorker

DESCRIPTION:

Remarkable re-creation of life in a Jewish shtetl in Poland in the 1930s.

A 9-year-old Jewish boy and a 13-year-old Christian boy run away together. The Jewish kid's sister and her boyfriend look for them.

The film is in black and white. The dialogue is in several languages, but Yiddish predominates (the Christian boy knows Yiddish because he is apprenticed to a Jewish craftsman).

Certainly one of the most unusual films in many years.

TITLE: **IVANHOE**

YEAR PRODUCED: 1952

DIRECTOR: Richard Thorpe

CAST: Robert Taylor, Elizabeth Taylor, Joan Fontaine, George Sanders, Emlyn Williams

COUNTRY OF ORIGIN: United States

LANGUAGE: English

RUNNING TIME: 107 minutes

VIDEO: MGM

DESCRIPTION:

Spectacular film, based on the novel by Sir Walter Scott, of one brave man's attempt to restore Richard the Lion-Hearted to the English throne. Elizabeth Taylor plays the beautiful Jewish girl, Rebecca.

TITLE: **IVANHOE**

YEAR PRODUCED: 1997

DIRECTOR: Stuart Orme

CAST: Steven Waddington, Ciaran Hinds, Susan Lynch, Nick Brimble

COUNTRY OF ORIGIN: Britain

LANGUAGE: English

RUNNING TIME: 300 minutes

VIDEO: A & E Home Video

DESCRIPTION:

Classic story of Ivanhoe saving King Richard the Lion-Hearted from the machinations of his evil brother, Prince John. Produced by the BBC for British television, this six-part miniseries features great production values and a stellar cast.

The Jewish moneylender, Isaac of York, and his daughter, Rebecca, are presented as sympathetic characters, with Rebecca providing a great deal of impetus for the plot. At one point she makes a speech very reminiscent of Shakespeare's Shylock.

Although a bit long, an excellent updating of an enduring tale.

TITLE: **JACOB**

YEAR PRODUCED: 1994

DIRECTOR: Peter Hill

CAST: Matthew Modine, Lara Flynn Boyle, Irene Papas, Giancarlo Giannini

COUNTRY OF ORIGIN: United States

LANGUAGE: English

RUNNING TIME: 94 minutes

VIDEO: Turner/Malofilm

DESCRIPTION:

Almost everyone knows the biblical story about Jacob that is told in this made-for-cable-television film. Jacob tricks his father into giving him the blessing meant for his older brother, Esau. When Esau threatens to kill him, Jacob flees to his uncle Laban. He meets and falls in love with Rachel, is tricked into marrying Leah, but eventually marries his true love and establishes the tribes of Israel. Well-produced film; second entry in the biblical series produced by Turner.

TITLE: **JACOB THE LIAR**

YEAR PRODUCED: 1974

DIRECTOR: Frank Beyer

CAST: Vlastimil Brodsky, Erwin Gerschonneck

COUNTRY OF ORIGIN: Germany

LANGUAGE: German with English subtitles

RUNNING TIME: 96 minutes

VIDEO: Icestorm International/Morningstar

DESCRIPTION:

Polish Jew makes up farfetched stories and tells them to his companions living in a ghetto during the Nazi occupation of Poland. Original film upon which Robin William's 1999 production was based.

TITLE: **THE JAZZ SINGER**

YEAR PRODUCED: 1927

DIRECTOR: Alan Crosland

CAST: Al Jolson, May McAvoy, Warner Oland, Eugenie Besserer, Otto Lederer, William Demarest, Roscoe Karns.

COUNTRY OF ORIGIN: United States

LANGUAGE: English

RUNNING TIME: 89 minutes

VIDEO: Fox

DESCRIPTION:

The first talkie was really a silent film with a few talking and singing sequences.

Tells the story of Jakie Rabinowitz, the ambitious son of a cantor. The father wants Jakie to follow in his footsteps. Jakie wants to be a Broadway star. He runs away, drops all outward signs of his Jewishness, and becomes the star he wanted to be. Years later Jakie's father falls ill and Jakie is asked to sing the Kol Nidre service in his place. He agrees, despite the fact that it means missing the opening of his new show.

The film seems to wallow in Jakie's rejection of Judaism, his assimilation, and his marriage to a non-Jew. It is dated and only of interest as a period piece and because of its historical significance. Its success revolutionized the film industry and ushered in the sound era.

TITLE: **THE JAZZ SINGER**

YEAR PRODUCED: 1952

DIRECTOR: Michael Curtiz

CAST: Danny Thomas, Peggy Lee, Mildred Dunnock, Eduard Franz

COUNTRY OF ORIGIN: United States

LANGUAGE: English

RUNNING TIME: 107 minutes

VIDEO: Warner

DESCRIPTION:

Best version of *The Jazz Singer* is this 1952 remake featuring Danny Thomas and Peggy Lee, both in top form.

The music is much more contemporary than in the 1927 production, but the story about a cantor's son seeking to put his name in lights on Broadway remains the same.

Interestingly, there is nothing to indicate whether Peggy Lee's character is Jewish or not. The question is simply ignored. The cantor does say Kaddish for his son, but that is because the son refuses to become the temple's next cantor, thus ending the family tradition. Instead the son wants to try his luck in show business.

A couple of beautiful songs make this version worth watching.

TITLE: **THE JAZZ SINGER**

YEAR PRODUCED: 1980

DIRECTOR: Richard Fleischer

CAST: Neil Diamond, Laurence Olivier, Lucie Arnaz, Caitlin Adams, Franklin Ajaye

COUNTRY OF ORIGIN: United States

LANGUAGE: English

RUNNING TIME: 115 minutes

VIDEO: Paramount

DESCRIPTION:

The third incarnation of *The Jazz Singer* sees a number of significant changes in tone and atmosphere. Partly this may be a result of the natural maturing of the American Jewish community in the half century since the Al Jolson version. The old tug of war between Jewish tradition and assimilation continues to pull at the leading character. In this version, Jess Robinovitch is a junior cantor, about to take over for his father in the synagogue. He is married and seems to have a full life except that he is being pulled by the lure of show business.

Jess decides to go to Los Angeles to find out whether his music has any merit and there meets Molly Bell, an attractive gentile agent. When Jess refuses to return to his wife and Jewish life, she divorces him and Jess winds up marrying Molly. Of course Jess is very successful in his musical career, but his father refuses to accept the fact that he has turned his back on Judaism. Jess too has problems dealing with this conflict; he forsakes his music, and begins drifting and searching for answers to his questions. The film comes to a climax on Yom Kippur. Jess takes over the services for Kol Nidre and then rushes over to a studio for a big TV special. This version of the story tries to show that one need not choose between traditions and career. You can have them both. Jess reconciles with his wife and with his father. And unlike the original version of The Jazz Singer, in this film his gentile wife even tries to adopt some Jewish customs. There is no rejection of Judaism or of Jewish tradition. There are just some alterations in order to accommodate them to the modern lifestyle.

TITLE: **THE JEW**

YEAR PRODUCED: 1995

DIRECTOR: Jom Tob Azulay

CAST: Filipe Pinheiro, Dina Sfat, Mario Viegas, Jose Lewgoy

COUNTRY OF ORIGIN: Portugal, Brazil

LANGUAGE: Portuguese with English subtitles

RUNNING TIME: 108 minutes

VIDEO: First Run Features/CHV

DESCRIPTION:

In eighteenth century Portugal, writer Antonio da Silva is accused of secretly being a Jew. He is imprisoned and is forced to admit being a Jew, or be executed by slow torture.

TITLE: **JEWISH LUCK**

YEAR PRODUCED: 1925

CAST: Solomon Michoels

COUNTRY OF ORIGIN: U.S.S.R.

LANGUAGE: Silent with Yiddish and English intertitles

RUNNING TIME: 100 minutes

VIDEO: National Center for Jewish Films, Kol Ami

DESCRIPTION:

Based on Sholem Aleichem's story of Menachem Mendel.

TITLE: **THE JOLLY PAUPERS (FREYLEKHE KABTSONIM)**

YEAR PRODUCED: 1937

DIRECTOR: Zygmund Turkow

CAST: Shimon Dzigan, Yisroel Shumacher, Max Bozyk, Menasha Oppenheim

COUNTRY OF ORIGIN: Poland

LANGUAGE: Yiddish with English subtitles

RUNNING TIME: 62 minutes

VIDEO: National Center for Jewish Film, Facets, Alden Films

DESCRIPTION:

Yiddish musical comedy about the efforts of two small-town Jews to win fame and fortune despite many setbacks. Interesting look at Jewish life in Poland squeezed between Polish anti-Semitism and the rising tide of Nazism.

NCJF restored the film and added new English subtitles.

TITLE: **JOLSON SINGS AGAIN**

YEAR PRODUCED: 1949

DIRECTOR: Henry Levin

CAST: Larry Parks, Barbara Hale, William Demarest, Ludwig Donath, Bill Goodwin

COUNTRY OF ORIGIN: United States

LANGUAGE: English

RUNNING TIME: 96 minutes

VIDEO: Columbia

DESCRIPTION:

Sequel to highly successful *The Jolson Story* with Larry Parks returning in the lead and Jolson again supplying the singing voice.

Begins with Jolson ending his retirement to return to his first love—singing. After early difficulties, he finds his way when he volunteers to entertain troops during World War II, and his career rebounds when *The Jolson Story* is released.

Once again, great music, and although not as good as the first film, some terrific entertainment. Again, little about Jolson's Jewish background.

Nominated for three Academy Awards—Best Writing, Best Cinematography, Best Music Scoring.

TITLE: **THE JOLSON STORY**

YEAR PRODUCED: 1946

DIRECTOR: Alfred E. Green

CAST: Larry Parks, Evelyn Keyes, William Demarest, Bill Goodwin

COUNTRY OF ORIGIN: United States

LANGUAGE: English

RUNNING TIME: 129 minutes

VIDEO: Columbia

DESCRIPTION:

Highly successful and very entertaining biographical film about one of the greatest performers in show business history. Follows Jolson from his childhood as Asa Yoelson, a cantor's talented son, to his success on Broadway and in Hollywood.

Great music sung by Jolson himself, and terrific performance by Larry Parks in the lead role.

Little emphasis on Jolson's Jewish upbringing except for a few minutes at the beginning. Won Academy Awards for Best Sound and Best Score. Nominated for Best Actor (Parks), Best Color Cinematography, Best Film Editing, and Best Supporting Actor (Demarest).

TITLE: **JONAH WHO LIVED IN THE WHALE**

YEAR PRODUCED: 1993

DIRECTOR: Robert Faenza

CAST: Jean Hugues Anglade, Juliet Aubrey

COUNTRY OF ORIGIN: Italy/France

LANGUAGE: English

RUNNING TIME: 89 minutes

VIDEO: Sullivan Entertainment

DESCRIPTION:

Four-year-old boy is uprooted from his normal life after the Nazi occupation of Amsterdam and sent to the Bergen-Belsen concentration camp. Despite the horrors, he survives with soul and imagination intact. Based on the autobiography of Dutch physicist Jona Oberski.

TITLE: **JOSEPH**

YEAR PRODUCED: 1995

DIRECTOR: Roger Young

CAST: Ben Kingsley, Paul Mercurio, Martin Landau, Alice Krige, Monica Bellucci, Dominique Sanda, Lesley Ann Warren

COUNTRY OF ORIGIN: United States

LANGUAGE: English

RUNNING TIME: 189 minutes

VIDEO: Turner/Malofilm

DESCRIPTION:

Third installment in Turner's biblical series, the story of Joseph and his brothers, with Mercurio playing the title role and Landau excellent as his father.

Made-for-cable-television miniseries running over three hours, with a great deal of time spent on Joseph's youth and the events leading up to his arrival in Egypt.

TITLE: **JOSHUA THEN AND NOW**

YEAR PRODUCED: 1985

DIRECTOR: Ted Kotcheff

CAST: James Woods, Gabrielle Lazure, Alan Arkin, Michael Sarrazin, Linda Sorenson, Alan Scarfe

COUNTRY OF ORIGIN: Canada

LANGUAGE: English

RUNNING TIME: 102 minutes

VIDEO: Fox

DESCRIPTION:

Comedy, based on a novel by Mordecai Richler, that spans 40 years in the life of a popular Jewish writer.

Facing a scandal about an alleged homosexual affair, and with his gentile wife in a mental hospital, Joshua devotes some time to self-examination, looking back at his life. His father was a small-time gangster who taught him an unusual version of the Torah and his own set of moral guidelines. His mother was a stripper, and his wife has family connections to the Canadian upper class. Although Joshua loves his wife, and they share many common beliefs, the differences between them in ethnic background, class, and wealth finally come to haunt him.

Originally shown as a television mini-series, but edited down to feature-film length. Terrific performances by Woods and Arkin.

TITLE: **JUD SUESS**

YEAR PRODUCED: 1940

DIRECTOR: Veit Harlan

CAST: Ferdinand Marian, Werner Krauss, Heinrich George, Kristina Soderbaum, Eugene Klopfer

COUNTRY OF ORIGIN: Germany

LANGUAGE: German with English subtitles

RUNNING TIME: 100 minutes

VIDEO: Nostalgia Family Video, Video City Productions, International Historic Films (IHF)

DESCRIPTION:

Infamous Nazi propaganda film designed to whip up anti-Semitism and justify anti-Jewish policies.

Film caused riots in Germany when shown there. Story tells about an unscrupulous Jew rising to power by abusing and raping Aryans.

TITLE: **JUDGMENT AT NUREMBERG**

YEAR PRODUCED: 1961

DIRECTOR: Stanley Kramer

CAST: Spencer Tracy, Burt Lancaster, Richard Widmark, Marlene Dietrich, Judy Garland, Maximilian Schell, Montgomery Clift, William Shatner

COUNTRY OF ORIGIN: United States

LANGUAGE: English

RUNNING TIME: 178 minutes

VIDEO: MGM

DESCRIPTION:

Excellent film about the Nuremberg war crimes trials and one of the American presiding judges. Raises question of what is justice and the accountability of the individual when acting under orders of a superior. One of the first Hollywood films to deal with the crimes perpetrated during the Holocaust. The acting is superb; Judy Garland's dramatic performance marked a turning point in her career.

Maximilian Schell won Academy Award for Best Actor, and film won Academy Award for Best Adapted Screenplay. Nominated for Best Actor (Tracy), Best Art Direction/Set Decoration, Best Black and White Cinematography, Best Costume Design, Best Director, Best Film Editing, Best Picture, Best Supporting Actor (Clift), Best Supporting Actress (Garland).

TITLE: **JUDITH (CONFLICT)**

YEAR PRODUCED: 1966

DIRECTOR: Daniel Mann

CAST: Sophia Loren, Peter Finch, Jack Hawkins

COUNTRY OF ORIGIN: United States

LANGUAGE: English

RUNNING TIME: 109 minutes

VIDEO: Knight Service

DESCRIPTION:

Loren plays a Holocaust survivor who goes to Palestine in search of the Nazi husband who betrayed her. The film tries to follow in the footsteps of *Exodus*, but somehow fails. How a film with Sophia Loren could be so dull is hard to understand. There are a few interesting scenes, such as the arrival of a shipload of illegal immigrants in Palestine, but they don't make up for the plot's lack of believability. Called Judith when released in theaters; name changed to *Conflict* when released on video.

TITLE: **JULIA**

YEAR PRODUCED: 1977

DIRECTOR: Fred Zinnemann

CAST: Jane Fonda, Vanessa Redgrave, Jason Robards, Maximilian Schell, Hal Holbrook, Meryl Streep

COUNTRY OF ORIGIN: United States

LANGUAGE: English

RUNNING TIME: 118 minutes

VIDEO: Fox

DESCRIPTION:

Based on a story from Lillian Hellman's Pentimento. Hellman (Fonda), a noted Jewish writer, recalls her lifelong relationship with independent-minded and politically active Julia (Redgrave), who devotes her life to political causes and opposes fascism. While traveling in Europe, Hellman is approached by one of Julia's friends to help smuggle money from one country to another.

Excellent film that won Academy Awards for Best Adapted Screenplay, Best Supporting Actor (Robards), and Best Supporting Actress (Redgrave), and received nominations for Best Actress (Fonda), Best Cinematography, Best Costume Design, Best Director, Best Film Editing, Best Picture, Best Supporting Actor (Schell), and Best Original Score.

TITLE: **A JUMPIN' NIGHT IN THE GARDEN OF EDEN**

YEAR PRODUCED: 1988

DIRECTOR: Michael Goldman

COUNTRY OF ORIGIN: United States

LANGUAGE: English

RUNNING TIME: 75 minutes

VIDEO: Ergo

DESCRIPTION:

Documentary on the Klezmer music revival. Originally shown on the Public Broadcasting System, film focuses primarily on Henry Sapoznick and Hankus Netsky, two of the prime movers in this Jewish music revival.

TITLE: **JUSTINE**

YEAR PRODUCED: 1969

DIRECTOR: George Cukor

CAST: Anouk Aimee, Michael York, Dirk Bogarde, Philippe Noiret, Michael Constantine, John Vernon, Jack Albertson

COUNTRY OF ORIGIN: United States

LANGUAGE: English

RUNNING TIME: 115 minutes

VIDEO: Fox

DESCRIPTION:

Story takes place in 1930s Egypt. A prostitute marries a banker and becomes involved in a plot to arm the Jews in Palestine to help them revolt against British rule.

TITLE: **KAPO**

YEAR PRODUCED: 1959

DIRECTOR: Gillo Pontecorvo

CAST: Susan Strasberg, Laurent Terzieff, Emmanuelle Riva, Gianno Garko

COUNTRY OF ORIGIN: Italy, France, Yugoslavia co-production

LANGUAGE: Mainly English but subtitled when other languages used.

RUNNING TIME: 116 minutes

VIDEO: Discount Video Tapes Ltd., Horizon Entertainment, Facets

DESCRIPTION:

Jewish family from Paris is rounded up and sent to a Nazi concentration camp. The 14-year-old daughter manages to become a guard, but moral conflicts bring her back to reality.

Nominated for Academy Award for Best Foreign Film.

TITLE: **KAZABLAN**

YEAR PRODUCED: 1974

DIRECTOR: Menahem Golan

CAST: Yehoram Gaon, Arie Elias, Efrat Lavie, Joseph Graber

COUNTRY OF ORIGIN: Israel

LANGUAGE: English/Hebrew with English Subtitles

RUNNING TIME: 114 minutes

VIDEO: Sisu/CHV

DESCRIPTION:

West Side Story with a Middle East twist with a terrific musical score by Dov Seltzer.

Based on a popular Israeli stage play, the movie version is a colorful adaptation that features Yehoram Gaon, the best known singer and actor in Israel.

Most of the action takes place in the run down areas of Jaffa where Moraccan-born Kaza and his gang rule the turf. Kaza falls in love with a "Polish Princess", but her parents oppose the romance until Kaza proves he is a good man who deserves "respect". The film may seem a little silly and naive now, but when it was filmed it set a new standard for Israeli films.

It was produced in two versions, each scene being filmed twice, once in Hebrew and then in English. I still prefer the Hebrew version.

TITLE: **KING DAVID**

YEAR PRODUCED: 1985

DIRECTOR: Bruce Beresford

CAST: Richard Gere, Edward Woodward, Alice Krige

COUNTRY OF ORIGIN: United States

LANGUAGE: English

RUNNING TIME: 114 minutes

VIDEO: Paramount

DESCRIPTION:

Biblical film that tries to take a more realistic look at the great king of Israel. Follows David's life from the time he was a common shepherd boy through to his craving for Bathsheba.

Received a lot of bad publicity because of the infamous scene in which Gere, as David, dances through the streets of Jerusalem dressed only in a loincloth. But it really isn't too bad a film, and there are some fine performances, great photography, and an excellent score.

TITLE: **KING FOR A DAY**

YEAR PRODUCED: 1982

DIRECTOR: Assi Dayan

CAST: Gabi Amrani, Chanan Goldblatt, Carolyn Langford

COUNTRY OF ORIGIN: Israel

LANGUAGE: Hebrew with English subtitles

RUNNING TIME: 90 minutes

VIDEO: Kol Ami

DESCRIPTION:

Israeli comedy about a hotel doorman who hasn't seen his daughter for fifteen years. He has written to her and told her he was a successul businessman. When she arrives in Israel without warning, the hotel treats the father like a walthy guest in order to back up his boasts.

TITLE: **KING OF COMEDY**

YEAR PRODUCED: 1983

DIRECTOR: Martin Scorsese

CAST: Robert DeNiro, Jerry Lewis, Sandra Bernhard, Shelley Hack, Tony Randall, Ed Herlihy

COUNTRY OF ORIGIN: United States

LANGUAGE: English

RUNNING TIME: 109 minutes

VIDEO: Columbia

DESCRIPTION:

Excellent comedy about a wannabe stand-up comic who is desperate to get on a Johnny Carson-like late-night show. The would-be comic and his Jewish girlfriend kidnap the host, and the ransom is a spot on his show. Somewhat bizarre comedy with outstanding performances by DeNiro as the wannabe comic and Lewis as the host.

Filled with Jewish humor.

TITLE: **KORCZAK**

YEAR PRODUCED: 1990

DIRECTOR: Andrzej Wajda

CAST: Wojteck Pszoniak, Ewa Dalkowsska

COUNTRY OF ORIGIN: Poland

LANGUAGE: Polish with English subtitles

RUNNING TIME: 118 minutes

VIDEO: Facets/Alliance

DESCRIPTION:

Excellent film about Janusz Korczak, a Jewish doctor, writer, and radio personality who operated an orphanage in the Warsaw Ghetto. When offered the opportunity to save himself, he refused and accompanied his children to the extermination camp.

Extremely moving film based on a true story.

TITLE: **KUNI LEMEL IN CAIRO**

YEAR PRODUCED: 1983

DIRECTOR: Yoel Silberg

CAST: Mike Burstyn, Chana Laslo, Moshe Ivgi

COUNTRY OF ORIGIN: Israel

LANGUAGE: Hebrew, English subtitles

RUNNING TIME: 90 minutes

VIDEO: Ergo

DESCRIPTION:

Third of the Kuni Lemel films. If you are a Mike Burstyn fan, you might like this one, but it is the weakest in the series.

TITLE: **KUNI LEMEL IN TEL AVIV**

YEAR PRODUCED: 1977

DIRECTOR: Yoel Silberg

CAST: Mike Burstyn, Mandy Rice-Davies

COUNTRY OF ORIGIN: Israel

LANGUAGE: Hebrew with English subtitles

RUNNING TIME: 90 minutes

VIDEO: Ergo

DESCRIPTION:

Sequel to *Shnei Kuni Lemel*, one of the best Israeli comedies of the 1960s.

Mike Burstyn again plays the schlimazel, only this time the setting has been updated to modern times. When Grandfather Kuni offers $5 million to the first of his twin grandsons to marry a Jewish girl and emigrate to Israel, the twins set off on a wild and funny race.

Not as good as the original, but Mike Burstyn is terrific.

TITLE: **LADIES' TAILOR**

YEAR PRODUCED: 1990

DIRECTOR: Leonid Gorovets

COUNTRY OF ORIGIN: U.S.S.R.

LANGUAGE: Russian with English subtitles

RUNNING TIME: 92 minutes

VIDEO: National Center for Jewish Film

DESCRIPTION:

Set in Kiev in September of 1941, this film tells the story of a Jewish family as it counts down the hours to deportation and execution at Babi Yar. Despite almost certain doom, the family still maintains some hope.

TITLE: **THE LAST ANGRY MAN**

YEAR PRODUCED: 1959

DIRECTOR: Daniel Mann

CAST: Paul Muni, David Wayne, Betsy Palmer, Luther Adler, Godfrey Cambridge, Billy Dee Williams

COUNTRY OF ORIGIN: United States

LANGUAGE: English

RUNNING TIME: 100 minutes

VIDEO: Columbia

DESCRIPTION:

Story about an old Jewish doctor in Brooklyn who is going to have a television documentary made about his life and career. The doctor gives up this opportunity for immortality when he walks out just before air time to treat a young black man who needs medical care.

One of the first films to focus on a relatively well rounded Jewish character. Shows the doctor's commitment to his calling rather than his own aggrandizement.

TITLE: **THE LAST BUTTERFLY**

YEAR PRODUCED: 1990

DIRECTOR: Karel Kachyna

CAST: Tom Courtenay, Brigitte Fossey, Freddie Jones, Ingrid Held, Milan Knazko, Josef Kemer

COUNTRY OF ORIGIN: Czechoslovakia/Britain

LANGUAGE: English

RUNNING TIME: 106 minutes

VIDEO: New Line (Columbia)

DESCRIPTION:

Fictional story of a Jewish actor (Courtenay) from France who is forced to perform in Terezin, the model camp set up by the Nazis to show Red Cross delegates how well the Jews were being treated. Powerful performance by Courtenay.

TITLE: **THE LAST KLEZMER**

YEAR PRODUCED: 1995

DIRECTOR: Yale Strom

CAST: Documentary

COUNTRY OF ORIGIN: United States

LANGUAGE: English

RUNNING TIME: 84 minutes

VIDEO: New Yorker

DESCRIPTION:

Documentary about Leopold Kozlowski, 70-year-old klezmer musician who survived the Holocaust but still mourns the relatives he lost.

Kozlowski now lives in Cracow, Poland, but embarks on a journey to the small Ukrainian town where he grew up, accompanied by Strom and a film camera. Thankfully, Kozlowski is not really the last klezmer, as klezmer music has enjoyed a rebirth in the last few years.

TITLE: **THE LAST METRO**
YEAR PRODUCED: 1980
DIRECTOR: François Truffaut
CAST: Catherine Deneuve, Gerard Depardieu, Heinz Bennent, Jean-Louis Richard, Jean Poiret
COUNTRY OF ORIGIN: France
LANGUAGE: French with English subtitles
RUNNING TIME: 135 minutes
VIDEO: Fox

DESCRIPTION:
Touching drama about a theater company in Nazi-occupied Paris. The Jewish theater director (Bennent) is forced into hiding and turns the theater over to his wife (Deneuve). In the meantime, she is attracted to the company's leading man (Depardieu), who is secretly working for the Resistance.

TITLE: **THE LAST SEA**
YEAR PRODUCED: 1980
DIRECTOR: Haim Gouri
CAST: Documentary
COUNTRY OF ORIGIN: Israel
LANGUAGE: Hebrew and Yiddish with English subtitles
RUNNING TIME: 90 minutes
VIDEO: Ergo

DESCRIPTION:
Holocaust survivors tell of making their way by truck, train, and on foot to ports from which they could sail to Palestine. The final leg of the journey was often in unseaworthy, overcrowded vessels.

TITLE: **THE LAST SEVEN MONTHS OF ANNE FRANK**

YEAR PRODUCED: 1988

DIRECTOR: Willy Lindwer

COUNTRY OF ORIGIN: United States

LANGUAGE: English

RUNNING TIME: 75 minutes

VIDEO: Ergo

DESCRIPTION:

Documentary that takes up where Anne's diary ends. It tells about the events after Anne Frank and her group in the attic were arrested. Eight women who were with the Franks at the concentration camps of Westerbork, Auschwitz and Bergen-Belsen give their testimony about the fate of the Franks in these last few days.

TITLE: **THE LAST WINTER**

YEAR PRODUCED: 1984

DIRECTOR: Riki Shelach

CAST: Kathleen Quinlan, Yona Elian, Zipora Peled, Stephen Macht

COUNTRY OF ORIGIN: United States/Israel

LANGUAGE: English

RUNNING TIME: 92 minutes

VIDEO: Columbia

DESCRIPTION:

An American woman, Kathleen Quinlan, married to an Israeli, Stephen Macht, arrives in Israel after her husband is declared missing in action during the Yom Kippur War. She identifies a face in a blurry news photo of a group of POWs as her husband. The problem is that another woman has identified the same face as that of her husband.

As the two women wait to find out whose husband the man in the photo really is, they strike up a very close friendship, although both realize that one of them is going to be bitterly disappointed.

The film poses an interesting dilemma and resolves it in a most unusual way.

TITLE: **LATE SUMMER BLUES**

YEAR PRODUCED: 1987

DIRECTOR: Renen Schorr

CAST: Dor Zweigenbom, Shahar Segal, Yoav Tsafir, Omri Dolov

COUNTRY OF ORIGIN: Israel

LANGUAGE: Hebrew with English subtitles

RUNNING TIME: 101 minutes

VIDEO: Home Vision

DESCRIPTION:

The time is 1969. The War of Attrition is raging along the Suez Canal. Every day new incidents shatter the peace the Six-Day War was supposed to guarantee.

Seven Israeli high school seniors spend the summer preparing for induction into the army. The seven make up a wide array of opinions. One expects to enter a combat unit, as did his brothers before him. Another is a pacifist who goes around painting walls with anti-war slogans and claims that he will refuse to report for military service. Another decides to get married before he has to leave for basic training. And a fourth boy, the group's unofficial historian and cinematographer, obtains a medical exemption but really intends to leave the country to study film. Whatever the members of the group do, the specter of military service affects their lives. Despite this, they have a lot of fun and engage in hijinks over the summer.

An excellent and thought-provoking film that points out the insecurities and realities of being a young person in Israel.

TITLE: **LAUGHTER THROUGH TEARS**

YEAR PRODUCED: 1928

DIRECTOR: Grigori Gricher-Cherikover

COUNTRY OF ORIGIN: U.S.S.R.

LANGUAGE: Silent film

RUNNING TIME: 92 minutes

VIDEO: National Center for Jewish Films, Jewish Book Center

DESCRIPTION:

Re-creation of life in a Russian shtetl in tsarist times, based on stories by Sholem Aleichem. National Center for Jewish Films claims that it provides a more complete and better-quality copy of this film.

TITLE: **LAURA ADLER'S LAST LOVE AFFAIR**

YEAR PRODUCED: 1990

DIRECTOR: Avram Heffner

CAST: Rita Zohar, Shulamit Adar, Menashe Warshavski

COUNTRY OF ORIGIN: Israel

LANGUAGE: Hebrew and Yiddish with English subtitles

RUNNING TIME: 96 minutes

VIDEO: Ergo

DESCRIPTION:

Interesting film about the star of a Yiddish theater group who is offered the lead in an international film at the same time she is having an affair with a complete stranger.

TITLE: **LE GOLEM: THE LEGEND OF PRAGUE**

YEAR PRODUCED: 1935

DIRECTOR: Julien Duvivier

CAST: Harry Baur

COUNTRY OF ORIGIN: Czechoslovakia

LANGUAGE: French with English subtitles

RUNNING TIME: 96 minutes

VIDEO: Ergo

DESCRIPTION:

The legend of The Golem as dramatised in the 1935 Czech film with English subtitles.

TITLE: **LEON THE PIG FARMER**

YEAR PRODUCED: 1992

DIRECTOR: Gary Sinyor

CAST: Mark Frankel, Janet Suzman, Brian Glover, Connie Booth

COUNTRY OF ORIGIN: Britain

LANGUAGE: English

RUNNING TIME: 98 minutes

VIDEO: Malofilm

DESCRIPTION:

Strange but entertaining comedy about Leon (Frankel), a Jewish young man who learns that he is the product of artificial insemination. His dad has a low sperm count, so his parents sought some assistance in producing a family.

Leon learns that his biological father is a Yorkshire pig farmer. When Leon visits him, the farmer goes overboard to make him feel at home by learning Yiddish phrases, preparing Jewish meals, and reading Portnoy's Complaint.

Some of the humor is absolutely hilarious and over the top.

TITLE: **LEPKE**

YEAR PRODUCED: 1974

DIRECTOR: Meahem Golan

CAST: Tony Curtis, Anjanette Comer, Michael Callan, Warren Berlinger, Gianni Russo, Vic Tayback, Milton Berle, Mary Wilcox

COUNTRY OF ORIGIN: United States

LANGUAGE: English

RUNNING TIME: 110 minutes

VIDEO: Warner

DESCRIPTION:

Story of 1930s Brooklyn gangster Louis "Lepke" Buchalter, chairman of Murder, Inc.

Well-produced story of one of the top Jewish mobsters of the depression era, from his childhood on the Lower East Side to his execution at Sing Sing in 1944. Tony Curtis gives a very good performance in the title role, and Milton Berle is excellent as Lepke's father-in-law.

TITLE: **LES MISÉRABLES**

YEAR PRODUCED: 1995

DIRECTOR: Claude Lelouch

CAST: Jean-Paul Belmondo, Michel Boujenah, Alessandra Martines

COUNTRY OF ORIGIN: France

LANGUAGE: French with English subtitles

RUNNING TIME: 175 minutes

VIDEO: Warner

DESCRIPTION:

Unusual mixing of Victor Hugo's novel and the story of a Jewish family which is saved during the Nazi occupation of France by a Jean Valjean–type character (Belmondo).

The story begins at the turn of the century when an innocent chauffeur is arrested and imprisoned for the death of his employer. The chauffeur's son, Roger Fortin, grows up to run a moving company. When the Germans arrive in Paris, a wealthy Jewish lawyer hires Fortin to move his family to a safer place. But no place is safe and the family winds up dispersed, with Fortin seeing to it that the lawyer's daughter survives.

There is much more to the story, but it really needs to be seen, and this may be Lelouch's finest film.

TITLE: **LES PATRIOTES**

YEAR PRODUCED: 1994

DIRECTOR: Eric Rochant

CAST: Yvan Attal, Sandrine Kiberlain, Richard Masur, Yossi Banai, Nancy Allen

COUNTRY OF ORIGIN: France

LANGUAGE: French with English subtitles, some English and some Hebrew

RUNNING TIME: 142 minutes

VIDEO: Malofilm

DESCRIPTION:

Ariel is an idealistic French Jew who travels to Israel soon after his eighteenth birthday to enlist in the Israeli secret service, the Mossad. After four years of training, he is posted to Paris in order to track down a scientist supplying vital nuclear information to Iraq. Then he is sent to Washington to help an American spy transfer important secret documents to Israel.

All of the missions described in this film are based on true espionage cases, and the film is exciting throughout as the veil of secrecy is lifted from these events.

TITLE: **LES VIOLONS DU BAL**

YEAR PRODUCED: 1974

DIRECTOR: Michael Drach

CAST: Marie-Jose Nat, Jean-Louis Trintignant

COUNTRY OF ORIGIN: France

LANGUAGE: French with English subtitles

RUNNING TIME: 110 minutes

VIDEO: Connoisseur Video Collection, Ingram International Films, Professional Media Service Corp.

DESCRIPTION:

Jewish boy and his family attempt to escape occupied France. Boy grows up to be a filmmaker obsessed with making a film about his experiences.

TITLE: **LIES MY FATHER TOLD ME**

YEAR PRODUCED: 1975

DIRECTOR: Jan Kadar

CAST: Yossi Yadin, Marilyn Lightstone, Len Birman, Jeffrey Lynas

COUNTRY OF ORIGIN: Canada

LANGUAGE: English

RUNNING TIME: 103 minutes

VIDEO: Columbia/Astral

DESCRIPTION:

Beautiful film set in the late 1920s in Montreal's Jewish immigrant neighborhood.

Six-year-old David lives with his Canadian-born parents and his immigrant grandfather, a junk peddler. The father dreams of making it by designing new inventions. The grandfather is a humble man who sticks to tradition and religion, waiting for the good times that will prevail when the Messiah comes. The boy and the grandfather develop a special relationship, and the boy loves nothing better than to accompany his grandfather on his rounds.

TITLE: **LIFE IS BEAUTIFUL**

YEAR PRODUCED: 1997

DIRECTOR: Roberto Benigni

CAST: Roberto Benigni, Nicoletta Braschi, Giustino Durano, Sergio Bustric, Marisa Paredes, Horst Buchholz, Giorgio Cantarini

COUNTRY OF ORIGIN: Italy

LANGUAGE: Italian with English subtitles

RUNNING TIME: 122 minutes

VIDEO: Miramax/Alliance

DESCRIPTION:

A marvellous comedy that consists of two parts. The first half tells the story of Guido, a Jewish waiter who falls madly in love with school teacher Dora. This part is a comic masterpiece where Benigni gets the opportunity to prove his mastery of physical comedy.

The second part takes place five years later. Guido and Dora have married and have a son, Grosue. When the Germans take over control of the town and deport the Jews to a concentration camp, Guido turns it into a game, in an effort to protect his son and to ensure that his son will survive the war. The film serves as an affirmation of life and of the will to survive, even through the horrors of the Holocaust.

TITLE: **THE LIGHT AHEAD**

YEAR PRODUCED: 1939

DIRECTOR: Edgar G. Ulmer

CAST: David Opatoshu, Isadore Cashier, Helen Beverly

COUNTRY OF ORIGIN: United States

LANGUAGE: Yiddish with English subtitles

RUNNING TIME: 94 minutes

VIDEO: National Center for Jewish Film, Ergo

DESCRIPTION:

Two lovers dream of escaping shtetl life and head for the big city of Odessa. A bookseller helps them with their plans. Based on stories by Mendele Mokher Seforim.

TITLE: **THE LITTLE DRUMMER GIRL**

YEAR PRODUCED: 1984

DIRECTOR: George Roy Hill

CAST: Diane Keaton, Yorgo Voyagis, Klaus Kinski

COUNTRY OF ORIGIN: United States

LANGUAGE: English

RUNNING TIME: 130 minutes

VIDEO: Warner

DESCRIPTION:

Diane Keaton and Klaus Kinski turn in outstanding performances in this film adaptation of the John le Carré novel. Story goes off on a number of tangents and gets a bit confusing at times. Basically, it revolves around an American actress recruited by Israeli intelligence to track down a Palestinian terrorist. Some of the confusion results from the fact that we are not always sure who is doing the recruiting and who is the target of the plot.

Although many viewers felt the film was pro-Palestinian, it shifts its loyalties from one side to the other, depending on the scene. Although critical of Israeli methods of interrogating Palestinian terrorists, it's also very unsympathetic to Arab terrorism. Moreover, it holds Israeli intelligence in very high, almost reverent, esteem. A film worth seeing if only for the terrific performances of Keaton and Kinski.

TITLE: **LITTLE ODESSA**

YEAR PRODUCED: 1994

DIRECTOR: James Gray

CAST: Tim Roth, Edward Furlong, Moira Kelly, Vanessa Redgrave, Maximilian Schell

COUNTRY OF ORIGIN: United States

LANGUAGE: English

RUNNING TIME: 99 minutes

VIDEO: New Line/Alliance

DESCRIPTION:

Story about Russian Jews and their connection to the Russian mob in the Brighton Beach section of Brooklyn.

Joshua (Roth) is a hitman for the Russian mafia. His latest assignment takes him back to his old neighborhood, where he meets his younger brother (Furlong), who tells him that their mother is dying of cancer.

Joshua tries to reconcile with his father and wants to prevent his brother from following in his footsteps, but tragedy is almost guaranteed from the opening scene.

TITLE: **THE LIVING ORPHAN**

YEAR PRODUCED: 1939

CAST: Gustav Berger, Fania Rubina

COUNTRY OF ORIGIN: United States

LANGUAGE: Yiddish with English subtitles

RUNNING TIME: 90 minutes

VIDEO: Jewish Book Center

DESCRIPTION:

Story of actor who forces his wife to give up her acting career to care for him and their child. In the end all turns out for the best and the family lives happily ever after.

TITLE: **LOAN ME YOUR WIFE**

YEAR PRODUCED: 1988

DIRECTOR: Zeev Revach

CAST: Zeev Revach, Yona Elian, Avraham More

COUNTRY OF ORIGIN: Israel

LANGUAGE: Hebrew, no English subtitles

RUNNING TIME: 90 minutes

VIDEO: Kol Ami

DESCRIPTION:

Israeli comedy.

TITLE: **LONG DAYS OF SUMMER**

YEAR PRODUCED: 1980

DIRECTOR: Dan Curtis

CAST: Dean Jones, Joan Hackett

COUNTRY OF ORIGIN: United States

LANGUAGE: English

RUNNING TIME: 105 minutes

VIDEO: Live

DESCRIPTION:

Made-for-television film, set sometime before World War II, about a Jewish lawyer who faces prejudice in the New England town where he lives.

Sequel to *When Every Day Was the Fourth of July.*

TITLE: **LONG IS THE ROAD**

YEAR PRODUCED: 1948

DIRECTOR: Herbert B. Fredersdof and Marek Goldstein

CAST: Israel Becker, Betinna Moissi, Berta Litwina, Jakob Fischer, Otto Wernicke, Paul Dahlke, Alex Bardnini

COUNTRY OF ORIGIN: Germany

LANGUAGE: Yiddish, German, and Polish with English subtitles

RUNNING TIME: 77 minutes

VIDEO: National Center for Jewish Films

DESCRIPTION:

Film made by and about Jewish displaced persons just after World War II. Filmed on location in a DP camp in Germany, the film follows a Polish Jew and his family from their life in prewar Warsaw, through the concentration camps, to a postwar DP camp.

TITLE: **THE LONG WAY HOME**

YEAR PRODUCED: 1997

DIRECTOR: Mark Jonathan Harris

COUNTRY OF ORIGIN: United States

LANGUAGE: English

RUNNING TIME: 120 Minutes

VIDEO: BWE Video/Morningstar Home Video

DESCRIPTION:

Excellent Academy Award winning documentary traces the efforts of Jewish survivors to reestablish their lives in the Displaced Persons' camps after World War II, and their attempts to get to the only place that was willing to accept them, Palestine.

TITLE: **THE LONGEST HATRED**

YEAR PRODUCED: 1991

DIRECTOR: Rex Bloomstein

COUNTRY OF ORIGIN: Great Britain

LANGUAGE: English

RUNNING TIME: 150 minutes

VIDEO: Ergo

DESCRIPTION:

An excellent and thorough television documentary history of anti-Semitism through the ages.

TITLE: **LOST IN YONKERS**

YEAR PRODUCED: 1993

DIRECTOR: Martha Coolidge

CAST: Richard Dreyfuss, Mercedes Ruehl, Irene Worth, David Strathairn

COUNTRY OF ORIGIN: United States

LANGUAGE: English

RUNNING TIME: 89 minutes

VIDEO: Columbia

DESCRIPTION:

Based on the Neil Simon play about two teenage boys brought to stay with their grandmother (Worth) in Yonkers during the early 1940s. Their mother has died, and their father intends to look for work in a southern factory.

The grandmother is a formidable personality—strict, cold, and humorless. The only relief the boys have is their Aunt Bella (Ruehl), the grandmother's fun-loving and strange younger daughter.

Ruehl and Worth give magnificent performances. Dreyfuss appears briefly as Uncle Louie, a small-time hood whose full connection with the mob is never explained, but who returns to his mother's house for a few days. During that time his charm completely captivates the two boys.

The brothers learn a lot about life from observing their grandmother and their other relatives. As the film progresses we become increasingly involved with the characters, despite their many hangups and idiosyncrasies. Although there is little or no reference to it, the characters are obviously all Jewish.

TITLE: **THE LOVER**

YEAR PRODUCED: 1990

DIRECTOR: Vera Belmont

CAST: Valerie Kaprisky, Peter Gallagher, Yves Jacques, Nick Mancuso, Stacy Keach

COUNTRY OF ORIGIN: Canada/France/Germany

LANGUAGE: English

RUNNING TIME: 141 minutes

VIDEO: Malofilm

DESCRIPTION:

Love story set in nineteenth-century Europe that entangles several men, including Franz Kafka.

TITLE: **LUNA PARK**
YEAR PRODUCED: 1991
DIRECTOR: Pavel Lounguine
CAST: Oleg Borisov, Andrei Goutine, Natalya Yegorova
COUNTRY OF ORIGIN: Russia
LANGUAGE: Russian with English subtitles
RUNNING TIME: 105 minutes
VIDEO: New Yorker

DESCRIPTION:
Andrei (Goutine) leads a group of anti-Semitic skin heads involved in beating up anyone they dislike. Then Andrei learns that his father is Jewish and he embarks on a search for his father and his past.

TITLE: **LUPO**
YEAR PRODUCED: 1970
DIRECTOR: Menahem Golan
CAST: Yuda Barkan, Gabi Armeni, Esther Greenberg
COUNTRY OF ORIGIN: Israel
LANGUAGE: Hebrew with English subtitles
RUNNING TIME: 99 minutes
VIDEO: MGM

DESCRIPTION:
Israeli comedy about a poor peddler threatened with losing his home and family and his battle with Israeli bureaucracy.

TITLE: **MADAME ROSA**

YEAR PRODUCED: 1977

DIRECTOR: Moshe Mizrahi

CAST: Simone Signoret, Claude Dauphin

COUNTRY OF ORIGIN: France

LANGUAGE: French with English subtitles

RUNNING TIME: 105 minutes

VIDEO: Vestron/CHV

DESCRIPTION:

An aging prostitute, a survivor of the Holocaust, looks after children of other ladies of the night. A beautiful relationship develops between her and an abandoned Arab boy.

TITLE: **MADMAN**

YEAR PRODUCED: 1979

DIRECTOR: Dan Cohen

CAST: Michael Beck, Sigourney Weaver, F. Murray Abraham

COUNTRY OF ORIGIN: United States

LANGUAGE: English

RUNNING TIME: 92 minutes

VIDEO: United

DESCRIPTION:

Russian immigrant joins the Israeli army and tries to get into a combat unit so he can kill Russians. While in the Soviet Union he had been imprisoned and tortured in a mental institution.

Weaver's first starring role, and one of Abraham's early appearances.

Poor film.

TITLE: **THE MAGICIAN OF LUBLIN**

YEAR PRODUCED: 1979

DIRECTOR: Menahem Golan

CAST: Alan Arkin, Valerie Perrine, Louise Fletcher, Lou Jacobi, Shelley Winters

COUNTRY OF ORIGIN: United States

LANGUAGE: English

RUNNING TIME: 105 minutes

VIDEO: HBO

DESCRIPTION:

Based on Isaac Bashevis Singer novel about a con man who travels through Poland working his schemes until he is finally shown up as a charlatan.

Poorly made but has a few interesting moments.

TITLE: **A MAJORITY OF ONE**

YEAR PRODUCED: 1961

DIRECTOR: Mervyn LeRoy

CAST: Ray Danton, Alec Guiness, Rosalind Russell

COUNTRY OF ORIGIN: United States

LANGUAGE: English

RUNNING TIME: 153 minutes

VIDEO: Warner Home Video

DESCRIPTION:

Comedy in which Russell plays Mrs. Jacoby, a Jewish widow who meets and falls in love with a Japanese widower. Because of family opposition to the match, Russell decides to give up the relationship.

TITLE: **MAMELE (LITTLE MOTHER)**

YEAR PRODUCED: 1938

DIRECTOR: Joseph Green

CAST: Molly Picon, Edmund Zayenda, Max Boxyk

COUNTRY OF ORIGIN: Poland

LANGUAGE: Yiddish with English subtitles

RUNNING TIME: 100 minutes

VIDEO: National Center for Jewish Films, Ergo

DESCRIPTION:

Molly Picon's mother dies and she is left to keep house for a family of seven.

TITLE: **THE MAN WHO CAPTURED EICHMANN**

YEAR PRODUCED: 1996

DIRECTOR: William A. Graham

CAST: Robert Duvall, Arlis Howard, Jeffrey Tambor, Jack Laufer, Nicolas Surovy, Joel Brooks, Sam Robards, Michael Tucci, Michael Laskin, Rita Zohar

COUNTRY OF ORIGIN: United States

LANGUAGE: English

RUNNING TIME: 96 minutes

VIDEO: Warner

DESCRIPTION:

A thriller produced for the Turner cable network that describes the capture of the infamous war criminal, Adolf Eichmann (Duvall). The film centers on Peter Malkin, the Mossad agent responsible for Eichmann's kidnapping.

Although this material has been put on film several times, the dialogue between Malkin and Eichmann, while Eichmann is being held in Argentina, is fascinating. Duvall gives a riveting performance and almost gets you to believe that he was a minor cog in the Nazi killing machine who simply followed orders and obeyed the laws of the Nazi regime.

A chillingly effective film.

TITLE: **MARATHON MAN**

YEAR PRODUCED: 1976

DIRECTOR: John Schlesinger

CAST: Dustin Hoffman, Laurence Olivier, Roy Scheider, William Devane, Marthe Keller

COUNTRY OF ORIGIN: United States

LANGUAGE: English

RUNNING TIME: 125 minutes

VIDEO: Paramount

DESCRIPTION:

Hoffman plays a graduate student preparing to compete in the Olympic marathon who becomes mixed up in a plot that involves an old Nazi war criminal. This is a thriller that will keep you on edge until the very end. The scene where the Nazi tortures Hoffman remains one of the most memorable in film history. Laurence Olivier received an Academy Award nomination for his supporting role.

TITLE: **MARJORIE MORNINGSTAR**

YEAR PRODUCED: 1958

DIRECTOR: Irving Rapper

CAST: Natalie Wood, Gene Kelly, Claire Trevor, Ed Wynn, Martin Balsam, Carolyn Jones

COUNTRY OF ORIGIN: United States

LANGUAGE: English

RUNNING TIME: 123 minutes

VIDEO: Republic

DESCRIPTION:

Eighteen-year-old Jewish girl leaves home to spend the summer performing in the theater at an east coast resort. She meets and falls in love with an older man who is the producer of the play and then follows him to Broadway.

The film's importance lies mainly in the fact that it was one of the first Hollywood productions to allow the characters' Jewishness to remain intact. Several scenes, including a bar mitzvah and a Passover seder, point out that their religion is an important element in their lives.

It was also one of the first films where a woman character carried most of the plot development.

TITLE: **MARRY ME, MARRY ME**

YEAR PRODUCED: 1969

DIRECTOR: Claude Berri

CAST: Claude Berri, Elisabeth Wiener, Regine, Luisa Colpeyn

COUNTRY OF ORIGIN: France

LANGUAGE: French with English subtitles

RUNNING TIME: 87 minutes

VIDEO: Available through some Blockbuster stores.

DESCRIPTION:
Delightful little slapstick comedy about love and marriage when a Jewish salesman falls in love with a Belgian woman. Great wedding scene with terrific Yiddish songs. If you ever come across a copy of the soundtrack, get it. It's worth buying.

TITLE: **MASADA**

YEAR PRODUCED: 1981

DIRECTOR: Boris Sagal

CAST: Peter O'Toole, Peter Strauss, Barbara Carrera, Anthony Quayle, David Warner

COUNTRY OF ORIGIN: United States

LANGUAGE: English

RUNNING TIME: 131 minutes

VIDEO: MCA

DESCRIPTION:
Television mini-Series dramatization of the siege of Masada in the first century. The TV series was telecast over an eight-hour period, so a great deal of editing was required to pare it for this video version. The result is a bit confusing at times, and important segments have been moved about or removed altogether.

During its first telecast, the series began and ended with a contemporary scene showing Israeli soldiers ascending Masada to be sworn in atop the fortress. This moving bit of modern history set the perfect tone for the flashback which told the story of Masada. It was cut from later telecasts and from the video, eliminating an important tie between the Jews of present-day Israel and first-century Judea.

TITLE: **MAX AND HELEN**

YEAR PRODUCED: 1990

DIRECTOR: Philip Saville

CAST: Treat Williams, Alice Krige, Martin Landau

COUNTRY OF ORIGIN: United States/Britain

LANGUAGE: English

RUNNING TIME: 94 minutes

VIDEO: Turner

DESCRIPTION:

Sometimes fact is stranger than fiction. This is one such case. Max (Williams) and Helen (Krige) were lovers before the war. When the Nazis conquer Poland, they are sent to a work camp. Max escapes to the Soviet zone but winds up being exiled to Siberia. Many years after the war, Max is finally released. But he is not a happy man. He can never forget his first love. Eventually, Simon Wiesenthal (Landau) helps him reunite with Helen.

A highly moving film with a surprise ending. It is worth renting the video just to see what happens when Max and Helen meet.

TITLE: **ME AND THE COLONEL**

YEAR PRODUCED: 1958

DIRECTOR: Peter Glenville

CAST: Danny Kaye, Curt Jurgens, Nicole Maurey, Francoise Rosay

COUNTRY OF ORIGIN: United States

LANGUAGE: English

RUNNING TIME: 109 minutes

VIDEO: Columbia

DESCRIPTION:

Satiric comedy based on a play by Franz Werfel.

Kaye plays Jacobowsky, a Jewish refugee from Poland. With the Germans about to occupy Paris, he is seeking a way out of the city. He finds an automobile, but an anti-Semitic Polish army officer needs it for his own escape. The two antagonists are forced to share the car and spend time together as they make their way south, to unoccupied France.

By the end of the film, the refugee has won the officer's grudging admiration, especially after Jacobowsky refuses to abandon the Polish officer, even though he could probably move faster and easier on his own.

TITLE: **MENDEL**

YEAR PRODUCED: 1997

DIRECTOR: Alexander Rosler

CAST: Thomas Jungling Sorenson

COUNTRY OF ORIGIN: Norway, Denmark, Germany

LANGUAGE: Norwegian with English subtitles

RUNNING TIME: 98 minutes

VIDEO: First Run Features/CHV

DESCRIPTION:

Story of a Jewish refugee family that arrives in Norway in the 1950's. Youngest son, Mendel, observes life and wonders why his parent's generation didn't fight back during the Holocaust.

TITLE: **MINA TENANBAUM**

YEAR PRODUCED: 1994

DIRECTOR: Martine Dugowson

CAST: Romane Bohringer, Elsa Zylberstein

COUNTRY OF ORIGIN: France

LANGUAGE: French with English subtitles

RUNNING TIME: 128 minutes

VIDEO: New Yorker

DESCRIPTION:

Story of the 25-year friendship between two Jewish Parisian women, Mina and Ethel. They meet as children at ballet class and continually get together on a park bench to discuss their lives and loves, until both fall in love with the same man.

Excellent performances enhance this film.

TITLE: **MINDBENDER**
YEAR PRODUCED: 1995
DIRECTOR: Ken Russell
CAST: Ishai Golan, Terrence Stamp
COUNTRY OF ORIGIN: United States
LANGUAGE: English
RUNNING TIME: 92 minutes
VIDEO: Republic/Astral

DESCRIPTION:
Biographical film about Israeli mentalist Uri Geller. Focuses on his early years, and his first attempts to build an act around his ability to bend metal spoons and fix broken watches. Ends with an appearance by the real Uri Geller.

TITLE: **MIRACLE AT MIDNIGHT**
YEAR PRODUCED: 1998
DIRECTOR: Ken Cameron
CAST: Sam Waterston, Mia Farrow, Justin Whalin
COUNTRY OF ORIGIN: United States
LANGUAGE: English
RUNNING TIME: 89 minutes
VIDEO: Disney

DESCRIPTION:
The courageous story of the rescue of most of the Jewish population in Denmark in 1943.

When the Danish resistance learned that the Nazis planned to round up and deport the Jews, they set in motion one of the largest rescue operations of the war and saved the lives of almost all of Denmark's Jews.

This film, which was produced for the Disney television program, is available on video, but only directly from Disney.

TITLE: **MIRACLE AT MOREAUX**

YEAR PRODUCED: 1986

DIRECTOR: Paul Shapiro

CAST: Loretta Swit, Marsha Moreau, Robert Joy, Ken Pogue, Robert Kosoy, Talya Rubin

COUNTRY OF ORIGIN: United States

LANGUAGE: English

RUNNING TIME: 58 minutes

VIDEO: Public Media Video, Home Vision Cinema, Ignatius Press

DESCRIPTION:

Three Jewish children find sanctuary with a nun during the Nazi occupation of France.

Originally a PBS television program.

TITLE: **MIRELE EFROS**

YEAR PRODUCED: 1939

DIRECTOR: Josef Berne

CAST: Berta Gersten

COUNTRY OF ORIGIN: United States

LANGUAGE: Yiddish with English subtitles

RUNNING TIME: 80 minutes

VIDEO: National Center for Jewish Films, Ergo

DESCRIPTION:

Although Mirele is a widow, she has worked hard and become a successful businesswoman. She chooses a woman for her eldest son and then has major disagreements with her.

The film is based on the difficulties the two women have.

TITLE: **MISS ROSE WHITE**

YEAR PRODUCED: 1992

DIRECTOR: Joseph Sargent

CAST: Kyra Sedgwick, Amanda Plummer, Penny Fuller, Maximilian Schell, Maureen Stapleton

COUNTRY OF ORIGIN: United States

LANGUAGE: English

RUNNING TIME: 95 minutes

VIDEO: Republic/Malofilm

DESCRIPTION:

Television movie about a Jewish immigrant (Sedgwick) to the United States who tries to fit into American society as quickly as possible.

She changes her name from Rayzel Weiss to Rose White and has a promising future at a large Manhattan department store. Suddenly she learns that her long-lost sister Luisa (Plummer) survived the Holocaust and is on her way to America. Luisa's arrival opens a Pandora's box of secrets and guilt which Rose has suppressed.

Excellent Hallmark Hall of Fame production that raises many questions about the desire and need to assimilate and hide one's roots.

TITLE: **MR. EMMANUEL**

YEAR PRODUCED: 1944

CAST: Felix Aylmer, Greta Gynt, Walter Rilla, Jean Simmons

COUNTRY OF ORIGIN: United States

LANGUAGE: English

RUNNING TIME: 97 minutes

VIDEO: Learning Corporation of America

DESCRIPTION:

Elderly Jewish man leaves his English home in 1935 to look for the mother of a German refugee boy and suffers cruel treatment in Germany.

TITLE: **MR. HALPERN & MR. JOHNSON**

YEAR PRODUCED: 1983

DIRECTOR: Alvin Rakoff

CAST: Laurence Olivier, Jackie Gleason

COUNTRY OF ORIGIN: United States

LANGUAGE: English

RUNNING TIME: 57 minutes

VIDEO: United States Home Video

DESCRIPTION:

Gleason attends the funeral of a Jewish friend who had been his lover many years before and meets the woman's husband.

Originally filmed as a television program.

TITLE: **MR. KLEIN**

YEAR PRODUCED: 1977

DIRECTOR: Joseph Losey

CAST: Alain Delon, Jeanne Moreau, Michael Lonsdale

COUNTRY OF ORIGIN: France

LANGUAGE: French with English subtitles

RUNNING TIME: 122 minutes

VIDEO: Columbia

DESCRIPTION:

Catholic art dealer who takes advantage of Jews in need of cash during the War is mistaken for a Jew with the same surname.

TITLE: **MR. SATURDAY NIGHT**

YEAR PRODUCED: 1992

DIRECTOR: Billy Crystal

CAST: Billy Crystal, David Paymer, Julie Warner, Helen Hunt, Jerry Orbach, Ron Silver

COUNTRY OF ORIGIN: United States

LANGUAGE: English

RUNNING TIME: 118 minutes

VIDEO: New Line (Columbia)

DESCRIPTION:

Billy Crystal produced, directed, co-wrote, and starred in this nostalgic, sorrowful look at a Jewish comic who could have been a big star but always managed to snatch defeat out of the jaws of victory.

The story is told in a series of flashbacks as a 70-year-old failure recalls his comic roots and fantasizes as to what might have been. What we discover is that Buddy (Crystal) did everything a successful comic should do. He played to his family at an early age, he trained in the Catskills, and he even had a Saturday night television show. But whenever things were going well, something in his personality always managed to blow it for him.

A better film than the box office returns would indicate; immersed in Jewish atmosphere.

TITLE: **MOSES**

YEAR PRODUCED: 1975

DIRECTOR: Gianfranco De Sosio

CAST: Burt Lancaster, Anthony Quayle, Ingrid Thulin, Irene Papas, Laurent Terzieff

COUNTRY OF ORIGIN: Britain/Italy

LANGUAGE: English

RUNNING TIME: 141 minutes

VIDEO: Fox

DESCRIPTION:

Edited version of 6-hour television mini-Series.

Cast is impressive, especially Burt Lancaster in the title role. An attempt to make the story more realistic does not always work.

TITLE: **MOSES**

YEAR PRODUCED: 1996

DIRECTOR: Roger Young

CAST: Ben Kingsley

COUNTRY OF ORIGIN: United States

LANGUAGE: English

RUNNING TIME: 184 minutes

VIDEO: Turner Home Video/Malofilm Video

DESCRIPTION:

Another in the Turner cable TV series of Bible films.

This time Ben Kingsley takes on the role of Moses, the man who brought the Jews out of Egypt and led them to the Promised Land, and who gave the Jews, and the rest of the world, the backbone of our judicial and moral system, the Ten Commandments.

Not as spectacular as the Cecil B. DeMille version, but interesting in its own way.

TITLE: **MOTEL THE OPERATOR**

YEAR PRODUCED: 1939

CAST: Chaim Tauber, Seymour Rechzeit, Yetta Zwerling

COUNTRY OF ORIGIN: United States

LANGUAGE: Yiddish with English subtitles

RUNNING TIME: 89 minutes

VIDEO: Jewish Book Center

DESCRIPTION:

The battle between labor and management in turn-of-the-century American Jewish community.

TITLE: **MOTHER NIGHT**

YEAR PRODUCED: 1996

DIRECTOR: Keith Gordon

CAST: Nick Nolte, Sheryl Lee, Alan Arkin, John Goodman, Kirsten Dunst, Arye Gross, David Strathairn

COUNTRY OF ORIGIN: United States

LANGUAGE: English

RUNNING TIME: 113 minutes

VIDEO: Miramax/Alliance

DESCRIPTION:

Engrossing film that raises serious questions of morality and human behavior.

Howard Campbell (Nolte), an American who grew up in Germany, is a successful German playwright married to a leading German actress. On the eve of World War II he is recruited by American intelligence, and as a cover does a series of radio broadcasts denouncing the United States and the Jews. Only three people know about the arrangement–Campbell himself, the agent who recruited him, and President Roosevelt. After the war Campbell returns to the United States. He leads a nondescript life for several years, but winds up in an Israeli prison charged with war crimes.

Did Campbell only pretend to be a Nazi and an anti-Semite, or did he become what he pretended to be? At times he himself doesn't seem to know where reality begins and pretense ends. Compelling film with a great performance by Nolte.

TITLE: **MOTHERS OF TODAY (HAYNTIKE MAMES)**

YEAR PRODUCED: 1939

DIRECTOR: Henry Lynn

CAST: Esther Field

COUNTRY OF ORIGIN: United States

LANGUAGE: Yiddish with English subtitles

RUNNING TIME: 90 minutes

VIDEO: Ergo

DESCRIPTION:

Yiddish melodrama about a cantor whose son runs off with an immoral woman and disappoints his parents.

TITLE: **THE MURDER OF MARY PHAGAN**

YEAR PRODUCED: 1987

DIRECTOR: Billy Hale

CAST: Jack Lemmon, Peter Gallagher, Richard Jordan, Robert Prosky, Paul Dooley, Rebecca Miller, Kathryn Walker, Charles S. Dutton, Kevin Spacey, Wendy J. Cooke

COUNTRY OF ORIGIN: United States

LANGUAGE: English

RUNNING TIME: 251 minutes

VIDEO: Orion

DESCRIPTION:

Television mini-series about the infamous Leo Frank lynching.

Frank was a Jewish factory manager in Atlanta. In 1913 a female worker was found murdered. Frank was arrested and convicted on very flimsy evidence. When the case was reopened by Georgia Governor John Slaton, a mob rioted in the streets and Frank was lynched. His name was not cleared until the 1970s.

Excellent re-creation of a landmark case in American history.

TITLE: **THE MURDERERS AMONG US: THE SIMON WIESENTHAL STORY**

YEAR PRODUCED: 1989

DIRECTOR: Brian Gibson

CAST: Ben Kingsley, Craig T. Nelson, Renee Soutendijk

COUNTRY OF ORIGIN: United States

LANGUAGE: English

RUNNING TIME: 159 minutes

VIDEO: HBO

DESCRIPTION:

Simon Wiesenthal's name has become synonymous with Nazi hunting and the famous documentation center in Vienna. But Wiesenthal was not always like this, as we find out in this made-for-cable-television film. Wiesenthal is a Holocaust survivor!

After he is liberated from Mauthausen death camp, Wiesenthal joins the American war crimes unit and helps document the Nazi atrocities. This gives him a reason to continue living, and after the Nuremberg trials, Wiesenthal opens his own documentation center.

Ben Kingsley is magnificent in this demanding role that reveals the motives behind Wiesenthal's unremitting urge to find and prosecute every war criminal he can find.

TITLE: **MUSIC BOX**

YEAR PRODUCED: 1989

DIRECTOR: Constantin Costa-Gavras

CAST: Jessica Lange, Armin Mueller-Stahl, Frederic Forrest, Donald Moffat, Lukas Haas

COUNTRY OF ORIGIN: United States

LANGUAGE: English

RUNNING TIME: 126 minutes

VIDEO: Live/MCA

DESCRIPTION:

The topic of war criminals has often been in the news in recent years. This film tries to deal with the subject in a slightly different way.

Jessica Lange plays an attorney whose father is accused of committing war crimes in Hungary during World War II. Everyone who knows the old man finds it difficult to believe the accusations. They know him only as a kind elderly gentleman who would not hurt anyone.

Suddenly, the daughter finds evidence that the charges may be true—that her father may indeed have been the monster he is accused of having been. She is faced with a moral dilemma. Will she make the evidence public and thus do irreparable damage to her loving father, or will she thwart justice and suppress the evidence?

Jessica Lange, as the daughter, is excellent, and Mueller-Stahl gives his usual strong performance.

TITLE: **MY FAVORITE YEAR**

YEAR PRODUCED: 1982

DIRECTOR: Richard Benjamin

CAST: Peter O'Toole, Jessica Harper, Joseph Bologna, Mark Linn-Baker, Lainie Kazan,

COUNTRY OF ORIGIN: United States

LANGUAGE: English

RUNNING TIME: 92 minutes

VIDEO: MGM

DESCRIPTION:

One of the best comedies of the early eighties.

A junior scriptwriter on a television comedy show is assigned to babysit the week's guest star, an over-the-hill matinee idol, to ensure that he shows up on time and in a sober condition.

The film is full of Jewish comedy, highlighted by a scene in which the scriptwriter brings the actor to his Brooklyn home for dinner.

TITLE: **MY KNEES WERE JUMPING: REMEMBERING THE KINDER-TRANSPORTS**

YEAR PRODUCED: 1996

DIRECTOR: Melissa Hacker

COUNTRY OF ORIGIN: United States

LANGUAGE: English

RUNNING TIME: 90 minutes

VIDEO: National Center for Jewish Film

DESCRIPTION:

Joanne Woodward narrates this documentary about a rescue mission by British Jews and Quakers that saved almost 10,000 children from Germany, Austria, Czechoslovakia and Poland between December 1938 and August 1939, most of whom were Jewish.

The director's mother was one of the rescued children.

TITLE: **MY MICHAEL**

YEAR PRODUCED: 1975

DIRECTOR: Dan Wolman

CAST: Oded Kotler, Efrat Lavie

COUNTRY OF ORIGIN: Israel

LANGUAGE: Hebrew with English subtitles

RUNNING TIME: 95 minutes

VIDEO: Ergo

DESCRIPTION:

Michael and Hanna are a young married couple living in divided Jerusalem in the late 1950s. Hanna is unhappy with her petit-bourgeois life.

TITLE: **MY MOTHER'S COURAGE**

YEAR PRODUCED: 1996

DIRECTOR: Michael Verhoeven

CAST: Pauline Collins, Natalie Morse, Herbert Sasse, Ulrich Tukur

COUNTRY OF ORIGIN: Germany

LANGUAGE: German with English subtitles

RUNNING TIME: 88 minutes

VIDEO: National Center for Jewish Film

DESCRIPTION:

Elsa Tabori (Collins), is a Budapest housewife who is arrested by Hungarian police in 1944 and is placed on board a train bound for the concentration camps. Believing that she has done nothing wrong, she convinces a German officer (Tukur) that her arrest was a mistake. He accompanies her back to Budapest and she returns to her family.

TITLE: **NADIA**

YEAR PRODUCED: 1987

DIRECTOR: Amnon Rubinstein

CAST: Hana Azulai-Hasfary, Yuval Banai, Meir Banai

COUNTRY OF ORIGIN: Israel

LANGUAGE: Hebrew with English subtitles

RUNNING TIME: 90 minutes

VIDEO: Ergo

DESCRIPTION:

Teenage Israeli Arab girl enrolls in a Jewish high school and faces prejudice and antagonism from both Jews and Arabs.

TITLE: **THE NASTY GIRL**

YEAR PRODUCED: 1989

DIRECTOR: Michael Verhoeven

CAST: Lena Stoltz, Monika Baumgartner, Michael Gahr

COUNTRY OF ORIGIN: Germany

LANGUAGE: German with English subtitles

RUNNING TIME: 94 minutes

VIDEO: H.B.O. / Cineplex-Odeon, MCA

DESCRIPTION:

True story of a German student who enters an essay contest about the role her hometown played during World War II. Researching the topic, she runs into a series of roadblocks. She's harassed and even attacked—all in an attempt to keep her from learning the truth. Eventually, she is forced to leave town.

Excellent performance by Stoltz, with wonderfully deft directing by Verhoeven.

TITLE: **NEIGHBORS**

YEAR PRODUCED: 1938

CAST: Helen Gross, Eugene Bodo

COUNTRY OF ORIGIN: Poland

LANGUAGE: Yiddish with English subtitles

RUNNING TIME: 72 minutes

VIDEO: Jewish Book Center

DESCRIPTION:

Comedy about two families with the same last name living in the same apartment building. Set in prewar Poland.

TITLE: **NEVER FORGET**

YEAR PRODUCED: 1991

DIRECTOR: Joseph Sargent

CAST: Leonard Nimoy, Blythe Danner, Dabney Coleman

COUNTRY OF ORIGIN: United States

LANGUAGE: English

RUNNING TIME: 94 minutes

VIDEO: Turner

DESCRIPTION:

Film produced for cable television tells the true story of Holocaust survivor Mel Mermelstein (Nimoy). When a neo-Nazi group challenges anyone to prove in court that the Holocaust really took place, Mermelstein takes on the task and is successful. Interesting for its treatment of the subject and because Holocaust deniers have rarely been challenged in court.

TITLE: **NEWLAND (ERETZ HADASHA)**

YEAR PRODUCED: 1994

DIRECTOR: Orna Ben-Dor Niv

CAST: Etti Ankri, Ania Bukstein, Rami Danon, Michael Phelman, Shuli Rand, Asher Tzafati

COUNTRY OF ORIGIN: Israel

LANGUAGE: Hebrew with English subtitles

RUNNING TIME: 107 minutes

VIDEO: Sisu Home Entertainment/CHV Communications

DESCRIPTION:

Drama about a young sister and brother who arrive in Israel after World War II and are placed in a transit camp. The children search for their family amongst the new immigrants that flooded into Israel at that time.

TITLE: **NEXT STOP, GREENWICH VILLAGE**

YEAR PRODUCED: 1976

DIRECTOR: Paul Mazursky

CAST: Lenny Baker, Shelley Winters, Ellen Greene, Christopher Walken, Lou Jacobi, Jeff Goldblum

COUNTRY OF ORIGIN: United States

LANGUAGE: English

RUNNING TIME: 109 minutes

VIDEO: Fox

DESCRIPTION:

Tender yet hilarious coming-of-age story. Twenty-two-year-old Larry Lapinsky moves from his parents' home in Brooklyn to Greenwich Village in order to achieve independence and seek fame and fortune as an actor. He is also leaving to get away from his domineering mother, played beautifully by Shelley Winters. In the Village Lapinsky meets up with various free spirits, finds himself a part-time job in a delicatessen, and pursues his chosen career. He also now has a place where he and his girlfriend can get together. Eventually he has a screen test, wins a part in a Hollywood film, and prepares to leave for Los Angeles.

But before all this can happen, he must pass through a series of crises and deal with his mother's guilt trips. Among other things, a friend commits suicide, his girlfriend gets pregnant and has an abortion, his girlfriend cheats on him, etc. But the bottom line is that he has to deal with his mother, who represents his Jewishness. He has to learn not to be ashamed of her and of his background. In the opening scene we see Larry packing to move out of his parents' house. He takes his yarmulke off and puts it in a drawer. Later, on the subway into Manhattan, he puts on a beret. He seems to be rejecting his background and replacing it with something more modern. Or is he just replacing one form of tradition with another, just as today a more traditional youngster might wear a baseball cap instead of a yarmulke?

In the same way his mother is always showing up, not letting him cut the ties with her, and not letting him forget who he is and where he comes from. She tries to explain this at the end by telling him that his grandmother stole across the Polish border in a hay wagon, but she is not very successful in putting her feelings into words. Jewishness pervades this film, and in the end, when Larry leaves for the Coast to pursue his film career, we know that he will never forget where he comes from. As he walks away from his parents' house, a musician on the street is playing "Ofn Pripichik," a Yiddish song about children learning the letters of the alphabet. Larry may go wherever he chooses, but his tradition will always follow him.

TITLE: **THE NIGHTMARE YEARS**
YEAR PRODUCED: 1989
DIRECTOR: Anthony Page
CAST: Sam Waterston, Marthe Keller, Kurtwood Smith
COUNTRY OF ORIGIN: United States
LANGUAGE: English
RUNNING TIME: 237 minutes
VIDEO: Turner/Malofilm

DESCRIPTION:
Not a Jewish film per se, this television mini-Series follows journalist William Shirer through the late 1930s as he covers the rise of the Third Reich for the American media, providing a perceptive look at the events that led up to the Second World War.

Shirer later wrote a major history of the Nazi era, *The Rise and Fall of the Third Reich.*

TITLE: **NOA AT SEVENTEEN**

YEAR PRODUCED: 1982

DIRECTOR: Isaac Yeshurum

CAST: Dalia Shimko, Idit Zur, Shmuel Shilo

COUNTRY OF ORIGIN: Israel

LANGUAGE: Hebrew with English subtitles

RUNNING TIME: 86 minutes

VIDEO. Ergo

DESCRIPTION:

A look at Israel's socialist movement and the debate in the 1950s between individual and societal mores in the kibbutz movement. The question is also whether Israeli socialism should follow Moscow's lead unquestioningly.

Coming-of-age story set amidst ideological battles and Noa's desire for individuality and the right to ask questions. Echoes of this debate continued until the 1967 Six-Day War, when most Israeli socialists realized that Moscow was following a Russia-first policy and would always support the Arabs unconditionally because it was better for the Soviet Union on the world political scene.

TITLE: **NOT IN THIS TOWN**

YEAR PRODUCED: 1997

DIRECTOR: Donald Wrye

CAST: Kathy Baker, Adam Arkin, Ed Bagley Jr., Max Gail, Bradford Tatum

COUNTRY OF ORIGIN: United States

LANGUAGE: English

RUNNING TIME: 95 minutes

VIDEO: Universal Pictures Home Video

DESCRIPTION:

Film made for cable television tells the true story of one woman's fight against prejudice in Billings, Montana.

When hate leaflets are distributed in town, Tammy Schnitzer (Baker) enlists the support of the police chief and rallies the community to oppose the hatemongers.

TTITLE: **NOT LIKE SHEEP TO THE SLAUGHTER: THE STORY OF THE BIALYSTOK GHETTO**

YEAR PRODUCED: 1990

DIRECTOR: Adah Ushpiz

COUNTRY OF ORIGIN: Israel

LANGUAGE: Hebrew with English subtitles

RUNNING TIME: 150 minutes

VIDEO: Ergo

DESCRIPTION:

Documentary about the small group of resistance fighters who attempted to stop the Nazi plan to destroy the Bialystok Ghetto. Includes testimony from witnesses and survivors.

ITLE: **NOT QUITE PARADISE**

YEAR PRODUCED: 1986

DIRECTOR: Lewis Gilbert

CAST: Sam Robards, Joanna Pacula, Libby Morris

COUNTRY OF ORIGIN: Britain

LANGUAGE: English

RUNNING TIME: 106 minutes

VIDEO: New World

DESCRIPTION:

A group of volunteers arrive at an Israeli kibbutz. Most of them are British except for an American medical student (Robards), who meets and falls in love with a kibbutz girl (Pacula).

The film revolves around the love story, and things are kept on a light note for most of the first half. Then a couple of British youngsters burn down one of the settlement's buildings and some volunteers out on an excursion are kidnapped by Arab terrorists. Most films of this kind would have had the American hero grab a gun and rush off to rescue the hostages. Thankfully that does not happen here. Instead, the heroics are left to Israeli commandos who take care of the terrorists and free the hostages. The volunteers can then carry on with their lives.

Not Quite Paradise has also been released under the title *Not Quite Jerusalem* and is an entertaining comedy for anyone interested in Israel.

TITLE: **THE ODESSA FILE**

YEAR PRODUCED: 1974

DIRECTOR: Ronald Neame

CAST: Jon Voight, Maximilian Schell, Mary Tamm

COUNTRY OF ORIGIN: Britain

LANGUAGE: English

RUNNING TIME: 130 minutes

VIDEO: GoodTimes

DESCRIPTION:

Adapted from a Frederick Forsyth novel. Journalist finds diary left behind by elderly Jewish man who committed suicide. Diary tells of the unspeakable crimes, torture, and mass murder perpetrated by SS Captain Eduard Roschmann, commandant of a death camp at Riga, Latvia. Journalist begins manhunt to track down Roschmann, and winds up in the heart of a powerful secret organization of former SS members called ODESSA.

Thriller with some fascinating moments and great performances by Voight and Schell. Music by Andrew Lloyd Webber.

TITLE: **OLIVER**

YEAR PRODUCED: 1968

DIRECTOR: Carol Reed

CAST: Ron Moody, Oliver Reed, Shani Wallis, Mark Lester, Jack Wild, Harry Secombe, Hugh Griffith, Sheila White

COUNTRY OF ORIGIN: Britain

LANGUAGE: English

RUNNING TIME: 153 minutes

VIDEO: Columbia

DESCRIPTION:

Superb musical adaptation of Charles Dickens's *Oliver Twist*, about a boy who escapes from an orphanage and is drawn into a gang of young thieves.

Lionel Bart's score is terrific, with haunting hints of Bart's Jewish origins.

Won six Academy Awards: Best Art Direction/Set Decoration, Best Director, Best Picture, Best Sound, Best Score, and a special award for Choreography. Nominated for Best Actor (Moody), Best Adapted Screenplay, Best Cinematography, Best Costume Design, Best Film Editing, Best Supporting Actor (Wild).

TITLE: **ON MY WAY TO FATHER'S LAND**

YEAR PRODUCED: 1995

DIRECTOR: Aner Preminger

COUNTRY OF ORIGIN: Israel

LANGUAGE: Hebrew with English subtitles

RUNNING TIME: 98 minutes

VIDEO: National Center for Jewish Film

DESCRIPTION:

Documentary about an Israeli's efforts to learn about his father's life, from his father's childhood days in Vienna, to his struggles as an immigrant to Palestine and his establishment of the Hebrew Communist Party.

TITLE: **ONCE UPON A TIME IN AMERICA**

YEAR PRODUCED: 1984

DIRECTOR: Sergio Leone

CAST: Robert DeNiro, James Woods, Elizabeth McGovern, Treat Williams, Tuesday Weld, Burt Young, Joe Pesci, Danny Aiello

COUNTRY OF ORIGIN: United States

LANGUAGE: English

RUNNING TIME: 225 minutes

VIDEO: Warner

DESCRIPTION:

Epic story of five Jewish men growing up in Brooklyn during the 1920s and becoming powerful mob figures. Lots of violence, but a powerful film with a tremendous cast.

The video version comes in several different lengths. It is only in the longer versions that the whole story unfolds as Leone intended.

TITLE: **ONE OF US (EHAD MISHELANU)**

YEAR PRODUCED: 1989

DIRECTOR: Uri Barabash

CAST: Alon Abutbul, Sharon Alexander, Arnon Tzadok

COUNTRY OF ORIGIN: Israel

LANGUAGE: Hebrew, no English subtitles

RUNNING TIME: 110 minutes

VIDEO: Kol Ami

DESCRIPTION:

Drama about the moral dilemma facing Israeli soldiers. Palestinian terrorists attack an Israeli camp and all but one are killed in the ensuing battle. The survivor dies while in captivity, and an investigation is undertaken to determine whether there was any wrongdoing in his death.

TITLE: **THE ONLY WAY**

YEAR PRODUCED: 1970

CAST: Jane Seymour, Martin Potter

COUNTRY OF ORIGIN: United States

LANGUAGE: English

RUNNING TIME: 86 minutes

VIDEO: Video Communications

DESCRIPTION:

The plight of Denmark's Jews during the Nazi occupation, and how the Danes rescued them just before the Jews were to be rounded up.

OPERATION THUNDERBOLT

TITLE: **OPERATION THUNDERBOLT (OPERATION JONATHAN)**

YEAR PRODUCED: 1977

DIRECTOR: Menahem Golan

CAST: Yehoram Gaon, Klaus Kinski, Assaf Dayan, Shai K. Ophir, Sybil Danning

COUNTRY OF ORIGIN: Israel

LANGUAGE: English / Hebrew with English subtitles

RUNNING TIME: 120 minutes

VIDEO: MGM, Sisu / CHV

DESCRIPTION:

Best of the films about the Israeli raid on Entebbe. Shows how the terrorists singled out the Jewish passengers and attempted to use them to obtain the release of comrades imprisoned in Israel and Europe. Emphasizes the meticulous planning of the operation and the courage of the Israeli commandos who flew halfway across Africa to rescue 104 passengers hijacked by Arab terrorists.

The Israeli government and military cooperated in the production of this film. Very realistic about the techniques and methods of the Israeli commandos; some of the hijacked passengers served as extras.

Each scene was filmed twice–once in English and once in Hebrew. *Operation Thunderbolt* is the English version and *Operation Jonathan* is the Hebrew version and comes with English subtitles.

TITLE: **THE OPPERMANNS (THE OPPERMANN FAMILY)**

YEAR PRODUCED: 1982

DIRECTOR: Egon Monk

COUNTRY OF ORIGIN: Germany

LANGUAGE: German with English subtitles

RUNNING TIME: 238 minutes

VIDEO: Facets, Applause Productions

DESCRIPTION:

German television mini-Series about a Jewish family trying to survive in Berlin after Hitler comes to power.

TITLE: **THE OUTSIDE CHANCE OF MAXIMILIAN GLICK**

YEAR PRODUCED: 1988

DIRECTOR: Allan A. Goldstein

CAST: Saul Rubinek, Jan Rubes, Noam Zylberman, Susan Douglas Rubes, Fairuza Balk

COUNTRY OF ORIGIN: Canada

LANGUAGE: English

RUNNING TIME: 96 minutes

VIDEO: Hemdale/Alliance

DESCRIPTION:

Wonderfully charming story of a young Jewish boy (Zylberman) living in a small town on the Canadian prairie. He is preparing for his bar mitzvah, when the local rabbi is killed in a traffic accident. A new rabbi (Rubinek) arrives but is not quite what everyone expected; he is young and filled with energy and life.

Zylberman and his traditional parents don't see eye to eye about the future. The new rabbi had the same problem with his own parents. He really wanted to be a stand-up comic. By the end of the film, both have fulfilled at least part of their dreams. The performances are outstanding, and the film is filled with a wonderful zest and joy for life. One scene in particular stands out: When Zylberman and his girlfriend run off to see a concert in Winnipeg, Rubinek drives over to bring them home. While there, he meets a musician friend who has a klezmer band, and Rubinek and the two youngsters spend a magical afternoon enjoying the music of this traditional Jewish troupe. The klezmer band is one of Canada's leading Jewish musical groups, Finjan.

TITLE: **OVER THE BROOKLYN BRIDGE**

YEAR PRODUCED: 1984

DIRECTOR: Menahem Golan

CAST: Elliott Gould, Margaux Hemingway, Sid Caesar, Burt Young, Shelley Winters, Carol Kane

COUNTRY OF ORIGIN: United States

LANGUAGE: English

RUNNING TIME: 100 minutes

VIDEO: MGM

DESCRIPTION:

Jewish man needs to borrow money from his family in order to open a restaurant in Manhattan. They refuse to help unless he gets rid of his non-Jewish girlfriend. Poorly done film. Television series called *Brooklyn Bridge* was much better.

TITLE: **OVER THE OCEAN (ME'EVER LAYAM)**

YEAR PRODUCED: 1992

DIRECTOR: Jacob Goldwasser

CAST: Uri Alter, Mili Avital, Motti Giladi, Era Lupid, Aryeh Moskona, Sinai Peter, Daphna Rechter

COUNTRY OF ORIGIN: Israel

LANGUAGE: Hebrew with English subtitles

RUNNING TIME: 89 minutes

VIDEO: Sisu Home Entertainment/CHV Communications

DESCRIPTION:

Comedy about a struggling Israeli family set in the 1960s. The parents are Holocaust survivors and the father believes that the business opportunities overseas are much better than in Israel. With a friend's encouragement, he decides to emigrate to Canada, despite the children's opposition. This is a cute comedy that makes for entertaining viewing.

TITLE: **OVERTURE TO GLORY (DER VILNER SHTOT KHAZN)**

YEAR PRODUCED: 1940

DIRECTOR: Max Nosseck

CAST: Moishe Oysher, Helen Beverly, Florence Weiss

COUNTRY OF ORIGIN: United States

LANGUAGE: Yiddish with English subtitles

RUNNING TIME: 77 minutes

VIDEO: National Center for Jewish Films, Ergo

DESCRIPTION:

Cantor leaves his post in a Vilna synagogue to join the opera in Warsaw. But once there, he misses his wife and child and the friendly surroundings in Vilna.

Oysher was one of the great cantorial voices of the twentieth century, and this film gives him the opportunity to show off his vocal talents.

TITLE: **THE PARTISANS OF VILNA**

YEAR PRODUCED: 1986

DIRECTOR: Josh Waletzky

COUNTRY OF ORIGIN: United States

LANGUAGE: English

RUNNING TIME: 133 Minutes

VIDEO: Facets

DESCRIPTION:

Documentary about the development of a Jewish resistance movement in the Vilna area during World War II.

Before the War, Vilna, the capital city of Lithuania, was called the "Jerusalem" of the west and was a center of Jewish culture and study. Film is a reminder that hundreds of Jews did fight back–in the ghettos and in the forests.

TITLE: **PASSOVER FEVER**

YEAR PRODUCED: 1995

DIRECTOR: Shemi Zarhin

CAST: Gila Almagor, Yossef Shiloah

COUNTRY OF ORIGIN: Israel

LANGUAGE: Hebrew with English subtitles

RUNNING TIME: 100 minutes

VIDEO: Mongrel

DESCRIPTION:

Comedy about three generations of an extended family in today's Israeli society.

When the family gets together for Passover we learn about the problems and happiness the family has experienced. One son was recently killed during army drills, and another son is trying to win back his wife who recently divorced him. A daughter is allergic to everything and a grandson is predicting snow–in April, in Israel.

In addition, the grandmother, Yona, played with great sensitivity by one of Israel's greatest actors, Gila Almagor, is certain her husband has been unfaithful.

A wonderful melange of emotions and characters.

TITLE: **THE PASSOVER PLOT**

YEAR PRODUCED: 1975

DIRECTOR: Michael Campus

CAST: Harry Andrews, Hugh Griffith, Zalman King, Donald Pleasence, Scott Wilson

COUNTRY OF ORIGIN: United States

LANGUAGE: English

RUNNING TIME: 105 minutes

VIDEO: Cannon, Warner

DESCRIPTION:

Based on a controversial book by Hugh J. Schonfield that claims that Jesus planned the scenario leading to the crucifixion and then faked the resurrection.

TITLE: **THE PAWNBROKER**

YEAR PRODUCED: 1965

DIRECTOR: Sidney Lumet

CAST: Rod Steiger, Brock Peters, Jaime Sanchez, Geraldine Fitzgerald

COUNTRY OF ORIGIN: United States

LANGUAGE: English

RUNNING TIME: 100 minutes

VIDEO: Republic

DESCRIPTION:

Still one of the most intriguing Holocaust films ever made.

Steiger plays a Jewish pawnbroker in New York who has isolated himself from everyone and continually broods about his experiences in a concentration camp. The film mixes past and present in an attempt to show how the character confuses them in his mind. Only when his assistant sacrifices his life for him during a holdup does Steiger begin to come out of his shell.

Steiger was nominated for an Academy Award for Best Actor.

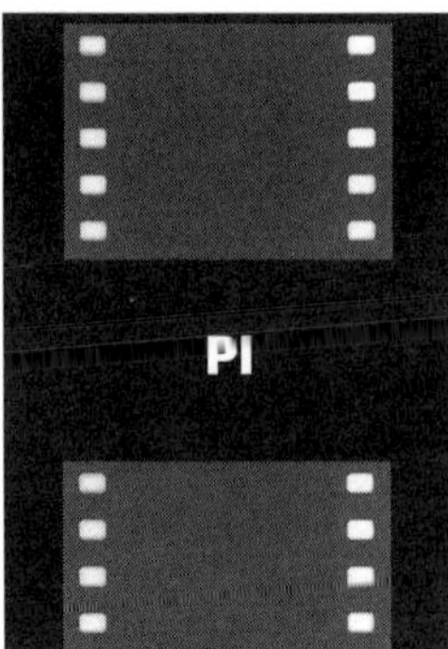

TITLE: **PI**

YEAR PRODUCED: 1998

DIRECTOR: Darren Aronofsky

CAST: Sean Gullette, Mark Margolis, Ben Shenkman

COUNTRY OF ORIGIN: United States

LANGUAGE: English

RUNNING TIME: 85 minutes

VIDEO: Artisan/Alliance

DESCRIPTION:

Max Cohen (Gullette) is a mathematical genius who has difficulty in coping with life and with other people. He built a supercomputer at home in an attempt to understand all existence. At the same time a Hasidic group tries to persuade Max to use his talents to study the Kaballah and a Wall Street firm tries to hire him to work for them.

Interesting but somewhat limited film.

TITLE: **PLAYING FOR TIME**

YEAR PRODUCED: 1980

DIRECTOR: Daniel Mann

CAST: Vanessa Redgrave, Jane Alexander, Maud Adams, Marisa Berenson, Melanie Mayron

COUNTRY OF ORIGIN: United States

LANGUAGE: English

RUNNING TIME: 148 minutes

VIDEO: VCL, Astral

DESCRIPTION:

Powerful television film with a script by Arthur Miller.

Redgrave plays Fania Fenelon, a French cabaret singer who is rounded up by the Nazis and deported to Auschwitz, where she becomes one of the "orchestra girls" who use music to survive the Holocaust.

The casting of Redgrave, an outspoken supporter of Palestinian terrorism, drew a tidal wave of protests from Jewish organizations and from Fania Fenelon herself. But Redgrave's performance was perfect, and the film is one of the best ever produced for television.

TITLE: **THE PLOT AGAINST HARRY**

YEAR PRODUCED: 1989

DIRECTOR: Michael Roemer

CAST: Martin Priest, Ben Lang, Maxine Woods, Helen Nemo

COUNTRY OF ORIGIN: United States

LANGUAGE: English

RUNNING TIME: 80 Minutes

VIDEO: New Yorker

DESCRIPTION:

An aging bookie has just come out of prison and finds the world has changed. Originally shot in 1969 but not released for 20 years.

TITLE: **PORTNOY'S COMPLAINT**

YEAR PRODUCED: 1972

DIRECTOR: Ernest Lehman

CAST: Richard Benjamin, Karen Black, Lee Grant, Jack Somack, Jeannie Berlin, Jill Clayburgh

COUNTRY OF ORIGIN: United States

LANGUAGE: English

RUNNING TIME: 101 minutes

VIDEO: Warner

DESCRIPTION:

One of the worst films I have ever seen. Adaptation of bestselling book by Philip Roth about a Jewish boy's relationship with his mother and the continual guilt trip she has perpetrated on him. Eventually he seeks to escape her by taking up with a non-Jewish woman.

TITLE: **POWER**

YEAR PRODUCED: 1934

DIRECTOR: Lothar Mendes

CAST: Conrad Veidt, Benita Hume, Frank Vosper, Cedric Hardwicke

COUNTRY OF ORIGIN: Britain

LANGUAGE: English

RUNNING TIME: 105 minutes

VIDEO: Discount Video Tapes, Horizon Entertainment

DESCRIPTION:

Jewish ghetto resident in eighteenth century works his way out of the gutter and into a position of power by pleasing the evil duke.

TITLE: **A PRAYER FOR KATARINA HUROVITZOVA**

YEAR PRODUCED: 1969

CAST: Jiri Adamira, Lenka Fiserova, Cestmir Randa

COUNTRY OF ORIGIN: Czechoslovakia

LANGUAGE: Czech with English subtitles

RUNNING TIME: 60 minutes

VIDEO: Facets

DESCRIPTION:

Based on Arnost Lustig's novel, film was kept on shelf for 21 years by Czech government, but was widely acclaimed once released. A beautiful Polish singer tries to trade Nazi war criminals imprisoned in the United States for Jews hoping to emigrate.

TITLE: **A PRICE ABOVE RUBIES**

YEAR PRODUCED: 1998

DIRECTOR: Boaz Yakin

CAST: Renee Zellweger, Christopher Eccleston, Glenn Fitzgerald, Allen Payne, Julianna Margulies

COUNTRY OF ORIGIN: United States

LANGUAGE: English

RUNNING TIME: 117 minutes

VIDEO: Miramax/Alliance

DESCRIPTION:

This story is set in Brooklyn's hasidic community. The film follows Sonia (Zellweger) and her husband Mendel (Fitzgerald) as they carry out the duties and responsibilities of their religious community. Some of the story is a bit unbelievable, but Zellweger and Margulies give outstanding performances that make the film worth watching.

TITLE: **PRINCE OF EGYPT**

YEAR PRODUCED: 1998

DIRECTOR: Brenda Chapman, Steve Hickner, Simon Wells

CAST: Voices of Mel Brooks, Natalie Portman, Sandra Bullock, Ralph Fiennes, Jeff Goldblum, Val Kilmer

COUNTRY OF ORIGIN: United States

LANGUAGE: English

RUNNING TIME: 99 minutes

VIDEO: Dreamworks, Universal Pictures Home Video

DESCRIPTION:

Story of Moses and the Exodus of the Jews from Egypt, as told in a feature length animated film. High quality animation and effects.

TITLE: **PRISONER IN THE MIDDLE**

YEAR PRODUCED: 1974

DIRECTOR: John O'Conner

CAST: David Janssen, Karin Dor, Christopher Stone, Turia Tan, David Semadar, Art Metrano

COUNTRY OF ORIGIN: United States

LANGUAGE: English

RUNNING TIME: 87 minutes

VIDEO: Academy

DESCRIPTION:

Nuclear expert Janssen is the only man who can stop a nuclear warhead from falling into the hands of Middle East fanatics.

TITLE: **PRISONER OF HONOR**

YEAR PRODUCED: 1991

DIRECTOR: Ken Russell

CAST: Richard Dreyfuss, Oliver Reed, Peter Firth, Jeremy Kemp

COUNTRY OF ORIGIN: Britain

LANGUAGE: English

RUNNING TIME: 88 minutes

VIDEO: H.B.O.

DESCRIPTION:

Made-for-cable-television film about the Dreyfus Case. Alfred Dreyfus, a Jewish officer in the French army, is accused and convicted of treason. Georges Picquart (Dreyfuss), the anti-Semitic head of counterintelligence, slowly realizes that Dreyfus has been framed and tries to uncover the truth. He is so adamant in supporting Dreyfus that he too is court-martialed.

The Dreyfus Case outraged the world in the late nineteenth century. Among the spectators in the courtroom was Theodor Herzl, correspondent for a Viennese newspaper. Deeply affected by the trial, he became convinced of the need for a Jewish homeland and went on to found the world Zionist movement.

TITLE: **PRIVATE BENJAMIN**

YEAR PRODUCED: 1980

DIRECTOR: Howard Zieff

CAST: Goldie Hawn, Eileen Brennan, Armand Assante, Sam Wanamaker, Barbara Barrie, Harry Dean Stanton, Albert Brooks

COUNTRY OF ORIGIN: United States

LANGUAGE: English

RUNNING TIME: 110 minutes

VIDEO: Warner

DESCRIPTION:

A coddled, protected Jewish princess gets married. On the wedding night her husband dies. She is left alone, and in an attempt to prove herself, she enlists in the Army.

Despite her complaints, she learns to take care of herself and makes it through basic training. She meets a handsome doctor from France. When she finds out that he is Jewish, she goes to bed with him and they later meet again in Europe. The princess leaves the Army to marry the doctor, only to find out that he is cheating on her. She leaves him and carries on with her life as a capable and worthy woman.

This is a film in which the central character is Jewish and does not try to hide it. At the same time, she and all the other Jewish characters are so flawed that the value and worth of being Jewish are called into question. The father is callow and unfeeling, the husband who dies is an animal when it comes to sex and doesn't seem to care much for his wife's feelings. And athe princess herself starts out as a cupie doll who always relies on someone else to provide her with the things she needs. She eventually grows up, but at what price?

Although the film is very funny on the surface, it raises a number of questions upon reflection.

TITLE: **THE PRODUCERS**

YEAR PRODUCED: 1968

DIRECTOR: Mel Brooks

CAST: Zero Mostel, Gene Wilder, Dick Shawn

COUNTRY OF ORIGIN: United States

LANGUAGE: English

RUNNING TIME: 90 minutes

VIDEO: Columbia

DESCRIPTION:

Classic comedic satire involving unscrupulous Broadway producer (Mostel) and his meek accountant (Wilder).

Producer raises money for a new show, but the only way he can make a profit is if it is a flop. In an attempt to offend audiences and critics, he puts on an outrageous show called Springtime for Hitler. Unfortunately, it's a hit, and our two con artists have to extricate themselves from a difficult situation.

Brooks won an Academy Award for his screenplay.

TITLE: **THE PROPRIETOR**

YEAR PRODUCED: 1996

DIRECTOR: Ismail Merchant

CAST: Jeanne Moreau, Sean Young, Sam Waterston, Christopher Cazenove, Nell Carter, Jean-Pierre Aumont, Austin Pendleton, Charlotte De Turckheim, Pierre Vaneck, Marc Tissot.

COUNTRY OF ORIGIN: United States

LANGUAGE: English, some French with English subtitles

RUNNING TIME: 105 minutes

VIDEO: Warner

DESCRIPTION:

Interesting, although somewhat esoteric film that centers around Adrienne Mark (Jeanne Moreau), a world-famous novelist in her sixties who is haunted by her past.

During World War II her mother, a renowned Parisian couturier, was arrested and was never seen again. Because she was Jewish, the mother transferred ownership of her apartment to a trusted friend. When the war ended, the friend retained the apartment and Adrienne left France to live in the United States. In an attempt to resolve the many unanswered questions in her life, Adrienne returns to Paris to repurchase her mother's apartment. Thrown into the mix is an American motion picture executive who wants to produce a remake of a classic French film based on Adrienne's most famous novel.

The film becomes a bit confusing at times but those sticking with it to the end will be rewarded.

TITLE: **DER PURIMSHPILER (THE JESTER)**

YEAR PRODUCED: 1937

DIRECTOR: Joseph Green

CAST: Miriam Kressyn, Zygmund Turkow, Hymie Jacobson

COUNTRY OF ORIGIN: Poland

LANGUAGE: Yiddish with English subtitles

RUNNING TIME: 90 minutes

VIDEO: Ergo

DESCRIPTION:

Comedy about a wandering Jew who falls in love with a shoemaker's daughter.

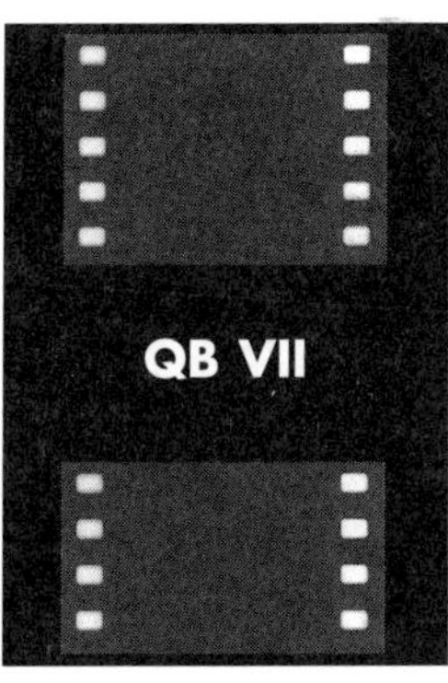

TITLE: **QB VII**

YEAR PRODUCED: 1974

DIRECTOR: Tom Gries

CAST: Anthony Hopkins, Ben Gazzara, Leslie Caron, Lee Remick, Juliet Mills, John Gielgud, Anthony Quayle, Edith Evans, Jack Hawkins, Sam Jaffe

COUNTRY OF ORIGIN: United States

LANGUAGE: English

RUNNING TIME: 313 minutes

VIDEO: Columbia

DESCRIPTION:

TV mini-series based on Leon Uris's bestselling novel.

American Jewish pilot Abraham Cady (Gazzara) is shot down during World War II, recovers in a British hospital, marries his non-Jewish nurse, returns to the United States, and becomes a successful Hollywood screenwriter. His elderly father and his son both settle in Israel.

After his father's death, Cady visits the Jewish homeland and his life is forever changed. He researches the Holocaust and writes a bestselling novel. In the novel, Cady mentions a Dr. Kelno who conducted medical experiments on prisoners in a Nazi concentration camp. Kelno (Hopkins) is now a well-respected and knighted physician in London, and when he reads the novel, he launches a lawsuit against Cady. The final segment of the mini-series deals with the court case, and the results are stunning.

Excellent program that tackles several important issues, including assimilation and the prosecution of war criminals. Shows how easy it is for Jews to lose their identity, and how sometimes it follows them through life, whether they want it to or not. This was one of the first television mini-series to have a strongly Jewish storyline. The lawsuit was based on an actual case brought against Uris by a doctor mentioned in his novel *Exodus*. Its outcome was similar to that in the film.

TITLE: **THE QUARREL**
YEAR PRODUCED: 1992
DIRECTOR: Eli Cohen
CAST: R. H. Thompson, Saul Rubinek
COUNTRY OF ORIGIN: Canada
LANGUAGE: English
RUNNING TIME: 85 minutes
VIDEO: BMG Video

DESCRIPTION:

Two men talking. That is the core of this film. And it is surprisingly engrossing. Chaim Kovler (Thompson) and Hersh Rasseyner (Rubinek) were friends in Europe before the war. Each thought the other had perished in the Holocaust until they meet by chance at Mount Royal Park in Montreal a few years after the war. Each has reacted differently to the Holocaust. Chaim, now a Yiddish writer, is haunted by the past and has rejected his faith. Hersh has become an Orthodox rabbi and is determined to ensure the continuity of Judaism. The two men carry on a debate regarding religion, morality, and many other topics.

Excellent film and outstanding performances by two of Canada's leading actors. Based on a famous Yiddish story by Chaim Grade.

TITLE: **RADIO DAYS**

YEAR PRODUCED: 1987

DIRECTOR: Woody Allen

CAST: Mia Farrow, Seth Green, Michael Tucker, Josh Mostel, Tito Fuente, Danny Aiello, Diane Keaton, Wallace Shawn, Dianne Wiest

COUNTRY OF ORIGIN: United States

LANGUAGE: English

RUNNING TIME: 96 minutes

VIDEO: HBO

DESCRIPTION:

One of Allen's best. Although he does not appear in this film, it is obviously an ode to his childhood, when radio was the main medium of entertainment. Seth Green plays a Jewish teenager who is intended to be the young Allen. And Allen provides the voiceover that ties the various segments of the film together. Before television took over the home entertainment field, people would sit around the radio and listen to variety shows, game shows, and action/adventure programs. Whereas television relies on visual images, often utilizing special effects, to make the viewer see whatever is intended, the imagination was king when radio provided the entertainment.

Allen has assembled a number of scenes in a very loose framework that shows us some of the legendary stories that grew up around the radio business, such as the time burglars ransacking a house answered the telephone and won the grand prize on a game show. The next day the residents found themselves inundated with goods that were completely unexpected. This is a wonderfully nostalgic film that all audiences can appreciate and enjoy.

TITLE: **RAID ON ENTEBBE**

YEAR PRODUCED: 1977

DIRECTOR: Irvin Kershner

CAST: Peter Finch, Charles Bronson, Horst Buchholz, Martin Balsam, John Saxon, Jack Warden, Sylvia Sidney, Yaphet Kotto, Robert Loggia, James Woods

COUNTRY OF ORIGIN: United States

LANGUAGE: English

RUNNING TIME: 113 minutes

VIDEO: HBO

DESCRIPTION:

TV movie about the Israeli commando raid on Entebbe to rescue 104 passengers held hostage by Arab terrorists. Good action film, although not quite as good as *Operation Thunderbolt*. Peter Finch won an Emmy nomination for this role.

TITLE: **REMEMBRANCE OF LOVE (HOLOCAUST SURVIVORS: REMEMBRANCE OF LOVE)**

YEAR PRODUCED: 1982

DIRECTOR: Jack Smight

CAST: Kirk Douglas, Pam Dawber, Chana Eden, Robert Clary, Yoram Gall, Eric Douglas

COUNTRY OF ORIGIN: United States

LANGUAGE: English

RUNNING TIME: 96 minutes

VIDEO: Simon Weisenthal Center

DESCRIPTION:

Holocaust survivor, Joseph Rabin, attends conference in Jerusalem with his daughter, Marci, and tracks down the woman he loved as a young man in the Warsaw Ghetto. Flashbacks feature Kirk Douglas's son, Eric, as the young Rabin.

Film was made for television.

TITLE: **RESCUERS: STORIES OF COURAGE: TWO COUPLES**

YEAR PRODUCED: 1998

DIRECTOR: Tim Hunter, Lynne Littman

CAST: Dana Delany, Martin Donovan, Linda Hamilton, Alfred Molina

COUNTRY OF ORIGIN: United States

LANGUAGE: English

RUNNING TIME: 109 minutes

VIDEO: Paramount Home Video

DESCRIPTION:

The second in the series of dramas about people who risked their lives to save Jewish victims of the Nazi Holocaust.

This cassette contains two episodes. "Aart & Johtje Vos" tells about a newly wed couple in Holland who turn their country house into a hiding place for Jewish refugees.

"Marie Taquet" tells the story of Marie and her husband who hide Jewish boys at their Catholic school for children of Belgian prisoners of war.

TITLE: **RESCUERS: STORIES OF COURAGE: TWO FAMILIES**

YEAR PRODUCED: 1998

DIRECTOR: Tim Hunter, Tony Bill

CAST: Michael Rapaport, Robin Tunney, Daryl Hannah, Tim Matheson

COUNTRY OF ORIGIN: United States

LANGUAGE: English

RUNNING TIME: 105 minutes

VIDEO: Paramount Home Video

DESCRIPTION:

The third in this series of dramas about people who risked their lives in order to save and protect Jewish victims of the Holocaust.

In "Malka Csizmadia," a teenager (Robin Tunney) persuades her mother and two sisters to help a group of Jews escape from a camp behind their home.

In "We Are Circus," the husband and wife (Tim Matheson, Daryl Hannah) owners of a German circus hide a Jewish family.

TITLE: **RESCUERS: STORIES OF COURAGE: TWO WOMEN**

YEAR PRODUCED: 1997

DIRECTOR: Peter Bogdanovich

CAST: Elizabeth Perkins, Al Waxman, Sela Ward, Fritz Weaver, Anne Jackson

COUNTRY OF ORIGIN: United States

LANGUAGE: English

RUNNING TIME: 107 minutes

VIDEO: Paramount Home Video

DESCRIPTION:

True life Holocaust dramas consisting of two stories on each cassette. In each we see the courageous stories of people who risked their lives in order to save Jewish victims from Nazi atrocities.

Executively produced by Barbra Streisand and Cis Corman, these dramas were originally telecast on the Showtime cable system in the United States.

In "Mamusha," Gertruda Babilinska (Perkins) is a Polish nanny for a rich Jewish family in Warsaw. The father disappears at the beginning of the war and the mother takes her son and Gertruda to another city. When the mother dies, Gertruda vows to keep the boy safe.

In "Woman On A Bicycle," Marie-Rose Gineste(Ward) works with her local bishop to hide Jewish refugees in a small town in southern France.

TITLE: **REUNION**

YEAR PRODUCED: 1988

DIRECTOR: Jerry Schatzberg

CAST: Jason Robards, Christian Anholt, Samuel West

COUNTRY OF ORIGIN: France/Germany/Britain

LANGUAGE: English

RUNNING TIME: 120 minutes

VIDEO: Fries

DESCRIPTION:

Elderly American (Robards) returns to Germany to seek out childhood friend he hasn't seen since he emigrated in the 1930s. Flashbacks tell the story of his youth and the rising tide of anti-Semitism that forced his parents to send him to America.

Powerful story told slowly and deliberately.

TITLE: **THE REVOLT OF JOB**

YEAR PRODUCED: 1983

DIRECTOR: Imre Gyongyossy

CAST: Barna Kabay, Ferenc Zenthe, Hedi Temessy, Gabor Feher, Peter Rudolf, Leticia Caro

COUNTRY OF ORIGIN: Hungary/Germany

LANGUAGE: Hungarian with English subtitles

RUNNING TIME: 98 minutes

VIDEO: MGM

DESCRIPTION:

Touching story of a childless Hungarian Jewish couple who adopt a gentile boy and their relationship as the Holocaust overtakes them.

TITLE: **RHAPSODY IN BLUE**

YEAR PRODUCED: 1945

DIRECTOR: Irving Rapper

CAST: Robert Alda, Joan Leslie, Alexis Smith, Oscar Levant, Charles Coburn, Rosemary DeCamp

COUNTRY OF ORIGIN: United States

LANGUAGE: English

RUNNING TIME: 139 minutes

VIDEO: Fox

DESCRIPTION:

Hollywood biography of George Gershwin that places little importance on accuracy but conveys his love of music and his enthusiasm for his work.

The terrific music, especially the performance of the Rhapsody in Blue, is a highlight. Gershwin's Jewishness is not emphasized, but if you listen carefully to the background music when his father is lying on his deathbed, you'll hear an instrumental version of "Ofn Pripichik," which certainly is quite suggestive about the family's ethnicity. The same song was used with powerful effect almost 50 years later in *Schindler's List* and in 1976 in the final scene of *Last Stop, Greenwich Village.*

TITLE: **ROMANCE OF A HORSETHIEF**

YEAR PRODUCED: 1971

DIRECTOR: Abraham Polonsky

CAST: Yul Brynner, Eli Wallach, Jane Birkin, Oliver Tobias, Lainie Kazan, David Opatoshu

COUNTRY OF ORIGIN: United States, Yugoslavia

LANGUAGE: English

RUNNING TIME: 100 minutes

VIDEO: Ace Video

DESCRIPTION:

Wild comedy about Jewish horse traders in eastern Europe in 1904 trying to outsmart Cossack captain Brynner. Has some good moments and Lainie Kazan plays one of her sexier roles.

TITLE: **ROMANTIC STORIES (TEL AVIV STORIES)**

YEAR PRODUCED: 1992

DIRECTOR: Ayelet Menahemi, Yitzhak Ginsberg

CAST: Yael Abecassis, Ruthi Goldberg, Anat Waxman

COUNTRY OF ORIGIN: Israel

LANGUAGE: Dubbed into English

RUNNING TIME: 96 minutes

VIDEO: Astral

DESCRIPTION:

Three short films about independent modern women in Tel Aviv.

One is a model who goes from man to man; another, a writer whose husband has left her and whose life is centered around a cat she saves from a sewer; and the third is a policewoman who takes hostages to prevent her husband from leaving the country before granting her a divorce.

Quality of these films is not of the highest order.

TITLE: **ROSA LUXEMBURG**

YEAR PRODUCED: 1986

DIRECTOR: Margarethe von Trotta

CAST: Barbara Sukowa, Daniel Olbrychski, Otto Sander, Adelheid Arndt

COUNTRY OF ORIGIN: Germany

LANGUAGE: German with English subtitles

RUNNING TIME: 122 minutes

VIDEO: New Yorker

DESCRIPTION:

Biography of the Jewish revolutionary, prominent in German politics in the early years of the twentieth century.

TITLE: **THE ROSE GARDEN**

YEAR PRODUCED: 1989

DIRECTOR: Fons Rademaker

CAST: Liv Ullmann, Maximilian Schell, Peter Fonda

COUNTRY OF ORIGIN: United States

LANGUAGE: English

RUNNING TIME: 112 minutes

VIDEO: Cannon

DESCRIPTION:

Lawyer Gabriele (Ullmann) defends a Holocaust survivor (Schell) charged with assault in modern-day Germany. Only after she takes the case does she realize that the victim was a war criminal.

The film is below average despite fine performances by Ullmann and Schell, and a cameo appearance by Israeli actress Gila Almagor.

TITLE: **ROSEBUD**

YEAR PRODUCED: 1974

DIRECTOR: Otto Preminger

CAST: Peter O'Toole, Richard Attenborough, Cliff Gorman, Claude Dauphin, John V. Lindsay, Peter Lawford, Yosef Shiloa, Isabelle Huppert, Kim Cattrall

COUNTRY OF ORIGIN: United States

LANGUAGE: English

RUNNING TIME: 126 minutes

VIDEO: MGM

DESCRIPTION:

Story of Middle East terrorism. When Arabs kidnap five wealthy teenage girls, American and Israeli agents prepare a plan to effect their rescue.

Probably one of the worse films done by Preminger. O'Toole is not much better.

TITLE: **ROUTES OF EXILE: MOROCCAN JEWISH ODYSSEY**

YEAR PRODUCED: 1982

DIRECTOR: Eugen Rosow

COUNTRY OF ORIGIN: United States

LANGUAGE: English

RUNNING TIME: 79 minutes

VIDEO: Ergo

DESCRIPTION:

Documentary about the remnants of the Jewish community left in Morocco after the mass emigration to Israel of the late 1940's and early 1950's.

TITLE: **SAFE MEN**

YYEAR PRODUCED: 1998

DIRECTOR: John Hamburg

CAST: Sam Rockwell, Steve Zahn, Mark Ruffalo, Harvey Fierstein,
Michael Lerner, John Pais, Christina Kirk

COUNTRY OF ORIGIN: United States

LANGUAGE: English

RUNNING TIME: 89 minutes

VIDEO: Universal Pictures Home Video

DESCRIPTION:

A comedy about two singers with no talent who are mistaken for the best safe crackers in Providence, Rhode Island. The city's Jewish mafia forces them to carry out several "jobs" and the two victims wind up running interference for the actual safecrackers.

Silly story that is completely implausible.

TITLE: **SAINT CLARA**

YEAR PRODUCED: 1996

DIRECTOR: Ari Folman, Ori Sivan

CAST: Lucy Dubinchik, Halil Elohev, Johnny Peterson, Maya Mayron, Israel Damidov

COUNTRY OF ORIGIN: Israel

LANGUAGE: Hebrew and Russian with English subtitles

RUNNING TIME: 85 minutes

VIDEO: New Yorker Video

DESCRIPTION:

Fantasy story that takes place in the future and centers around a group of rebellious teenagers. Clara Chanov is a young Russian immigrant living in a remote industrial town in Israel who discovers she can predict the future. She helps her classmates excel in a school test and the teacher and principal try to track down the reason all the students had identical answers. At the same time, Clara believes that her powers will disappear as soon as she falls in love and she must decide whether to allow herself to do that.

Surrealistic, quixotic film with a number of unusual characters.

TITLE: **SALLAH**

YEAR PRODUCED: 1965

DIRECTOR: Ephraim Kishon

CAST: Topol, Guela Noni, Gila Almagor, Arik Einstein, Shraga Friedman, Esther Greenberg.

COUNTRY OF ORIGIN: Israel

LANGUAGE: Hebrew with English subtitles

RUNNING TIME: 105 minutes

VIDEO: Ergo

DESCRIPTION:

Hilarious comedy that spoofs many facets of Israeli life in the 1950s.

Story about an Oriental Jew who immigrates to Israel with his wife and seven children. Whenever he runs into trouble with the Israeli bureaucracy, Sallah always finds a way around it.

A delightful comedy.

TITLE: **SAM & ME**

YEAR PRODUCED: 1991

DIRECTOR: Deepa Mehta

CAST: Ranjit Chowdhry, Peter Boretski

COUNTRY OF ORIGIN: Canada

LANGUAGE: English

RUNNING TIME: 95 minutes

VIDEO: Astral

DESCRIPTION:

Nikhil, a newly arrived immigrant from India, is hired to work as a companion and care-giver to Sam, an elderly Jew. Sam was also an immigrant to Canada at one time, and now his only desire is to go to Israel to die. Sam and Nikhil soon discover they have many things in common, and a bond of friendship develops between them.

Interestingly, Indian actor Ranjit Chowdhry is Jewish in real life.

Like most Canadian films, this one had a short theatrical life and then was released on video.

TITLE: **SAMSON AND DELILAH**

YEAR PRODUCED: 1949

DIRECTOR: Cecil B. Demille

CAST: Victor Mature, Hedy Lamarr, George Sanders, Angela Lansbury

COUNTRY OF ORIGIN: United States

LANGUAGE: English

RUNNING TIME: 128 minutes

VIDEO: Paramount

DESCRIPTION:

Epic biblical tale of a Jewish boy falling in love with a "shiksa" and the troubles it creates for him, eventually leading to his death.

Entertaining film that won Academy Awards for Art Direction/Set Decoration and Costume Design.

TITLE: **SAMSON AND DELILAH**

YEAR PRODUCED: 1996

DIRECTOR: Nicolas Roeg

CAST: Elizabeth Hurley, Dennis Hopper, Eric Thal

COUNTRY OF ORIGIN: United States

LANGUAGE: English

RUNNING TIME: 200 minutes

VIDEO: Turner Home Video

DESCRIPTION:

The fifth entry in Turner's made-for-cable-television Bible mini-series, and one of the poorest efforts, with numerous subplots and characters that do not show up in the Bible.

TITLE: **SAVE THE TIGER**

YEAR PRODUCED: 1973

DIRECTOR: John D. Avildsen

CAST: Jack Lemmon, Jack Gilford, Laurie Heineman

COUNTRY OF ORIGIN: United States

LANGUAGE: English

RUNNING TIME: 100 minutes

VIDEO: Paramount

DESCRIPTION:

Middle-aged Jewish dress manufacturer sees no way out of financial dilemma except to burn down his business and collect the insurance money.

Lemmon won Academy Award for Best Actor. Film was nominated for Best Story and Screenplay, and Best Supporting Actor (Gilford).

TITLE: **SCANDAL IN A SMALL TOWN**

YEAR PRODUCED: 1988

DIRECTOR: Anthony Page

CAST: Raquel Welch, Christa Denton, Frances Lee McCain, Peter Van Norden, Robin Gammel, Ronny Cox

COUNTRY OF ORIGIN: United States

LANGUAGE: English

RUNNING TIME: 90 minutes

VIDEO: Vidmark

DESCRIPTION:

Waitress in a small-town bar decides to fight the local board of education when she learns that her daughter's high school teacher is spouting anti-Semitic views. When the board refuses to act, she hires a lawyer and takes the matter to court. There have been several real cases similar to the one in this made-for-television film. In Canada's western province of Alberta, one such case wound its way through the courts for many years, and finally ended with the offender removed from teaching and convicted of spreading hatred. Another television film produced at about the same time, *Evil In Clear Water*, is not available on video, but provides a better and more realistic view of the same problem.

SCHINDLER'S LIST

TITLE: **SCHINDLER'S LIST**

YEAR PRODUCED: 1993

DIRECTOR: Steven Spielberg

CAST: Liam Neeson, Ben Kingsley, Ralph Fiennes, Caroline Goodall, Jonathan Sagalle, Embeth Davidtz

COUNTRY OF ORIGIN: United States

LANGUAGE: English

RUNNING TIME: 197 minutes

VIDEO: MCA

DESCRIPTION:

Every once in a while a special film comes along that seems to have been put together with a magic wand, with all the diverse elements fitting together perfectly. With *Schindler's List,* Steven Spielberg seems to have captured that elusive magic, producing a monumental film about the Holocaust and the greatest film of his career. Spielberg's direction is superb; the camera work is inventive and artful without being intrusive; and the acting is outstanding, performed by an ensemble of actors, most of whom were unknown to the public before the film was released. The storyline of *Schindler's List* is fairly straightforward. Oskar Schindler (Neeson), a German raised in Czechoslovakia, attempted to start up several businesses before the war and failed miserably. But Schindler has one talent. He knows how to sell himself and how to manipulate people into helping him.

After the German conquest of Poland, Schindler arrives in Cracow and finds a Jewish accountant (Kingsley) to help him set up an enamel factory. The accountant raises the start-up cash, hires the work force, and runs the business. Schindler makes the contacts and procures the military contracts to make the factory a successful venture. Schindler's relationship with his Jewish workers is symbiotic. He makes a vast amount of money, and the Jews survive a little longer. As the war draws to an end, Schindler decides he will not allow his workers to be shipped off to extermination camps. He uses the fortune he has accumulated to buy back their lives and thus succeeds in saving more than 1,000 Jews. Although this is probably the best Holocaust film ever made, and the most successful, taking in over $300 million worldwide, it is not perfect. I thought Spielberg was really pouring on the schmaltz in the scene where Schindler leaves his workers in an effort to escape capture by the Russians. That scene always makes me squirm a bit. At the same time the final scene of real survivors walking past the grave accompanied by the actors who play them in the film is brilliant and underlines the continuity of the Jewish people. While no film can recreate the horrors of the Holocaust, *Schindler's List* probably comes the closest.

TITLE: **SCHOOL TIES**

YEAR PRODUCED: 1992

DIRECTOR: Robert Mandel

CAST: Brendan Fraser, Chris O'Donnell, Matt Damon, Andrew Lowery, Randall Batinkoff, Amy Locane, Peter Donat, Kevin Tighe

COUNTRY OF ORIGIN: United States

LANGUAGE: English

RUNNING TIME: 110 minutes

VIDEO: Paramount

DESCRIPTION:

An effective and often moving film about anti-Semitism. It would be interesting to view *Gentleman's Agreement* and this film back to back and see how they compare.

In *School Ties,* set in 1955, David Greene (Fraser), a standout quarterback from a working-class background in Scranton, Pennsylvania, is recruited by a WASP prep school in New England determined to have a winning football season. Greene sees this as his only way to an Ivy League college, so he doesn't reveal that he is Jewish. Everything goes well. He makes friends with his society classmates and falls in love with Sally, who also comes from an upper-class family. Under his leadership the football team finally begins to win.

Then an alumnus blurts out the fact the Greene is Jewish and everything changes. Greene is taunted and harassed, and the students are forced to decide whether friendship and class loyalty are more important than truth and honesty. And Greene must decide whether a chance to improve his lot in life is worth abandoning his tradition. Cast is excellent and the film is absorbing.

TITLE: **THE SECRET OF YOLANDA**

YEAR PRODUCED: 1982

DIRECTOR: Yoel Silberg

CAST: Aviva Ger, Asher Zarfati, Shraga Harpaz

COUNTRY OF ORIGIN: Israel

LANGUAGE: English, dubbed

RUNNING TIME: 90 minutes

VIDEO: MGM

DESCRIPTION:

Israeli film dubbed into English. Steamy story about a young woman and the riding instructor who falls for her. Softcore porn.

TITLE: **A SECRET SPACE**

YEAR PRODUCED: 1988

DIRECTOR: Roberta Hodes

CAST: Robert Klein, Phyllis Newman, John Matthews, Sam Schacht, Virginia Graham

COUNTRY OF ORIGIN: United States

LANGUAGE: English

RUNNING TIME: 80 minutes

VIDEO: Ergo

DESCRIPTION:

Young man from a secular family searches for meaning of his Jewish roots as he nears his bar mitzvah.

TITLE: **SECRET WEAPON**

YEAR PRODUCED: 1990

DIRECTOR: Ian Sharp

CAST: Griffin Dunne, Karen Allen, Jeroen Krabbe

COUNTRY OF ORIGIN: United States/Britain

LANGUAGE: English

RUNNING TIME: 95 minutes

VIDEO: Turner

DESCRIPTION:

Television film that doesn't tell us anything new, but details a high-profile espionage case.

Mordecai Vanuunu is a technician in Israel's top-secret nuclear weapons facility. Deciding that the world should know about Israel's nuclear capability, he flees the country and arranges for a British newspaper to break the story, based on information and photographs he supplies.

In Israel, this is considered high treason, and Israeli intelligence arranges for a sexy female agent to lure him into a Mossad trap. Vanuunu is overpowered, shipped home for trial, and sentenced to a long prison term.

Recently a small movement has sprung up to obtain Vanuunu's release. Its members argue that the world knew of Israel's nuclear capability before Vanuunu's revelations and that he may have done Israel a favor. By going public, he warned Israel's enemies to think twice before launching another attack on Israel. During the Gulf War, Israel's nuclear deterrent may have saved it from chemical or biological attack by Iraq.

TITLE: **THE SERPENT'S EGG**

YEAR PRODUCED: 1978

DIRECTOR: Ingmar Bergman

CAST: David Carradine, Liv Ullmann, Gert Frobe, James Whitmore

COUNTRY OF ORIGIN: Germany

LANGUAGE: English

RUNNING TIME: 119 minutes

VIDEO: Live

DESCRIPTION:

English-language film about two Jewish trapeze artists surviving in Berlin during Hitler's rise to power. Not one of Bergman's better efforts, although this was his second English-language film.

TITLE: **THE 17TH BRIDE**

YEAR PRODUCED: 1984

DIRECTOR: Nadav Levitan

CAST: Lisa Hartman, Barry Angel, Rosemary Leach, John Gillo, Stanley Labor

COUNTRY OF ORIGIN: United States

LANGUAGE: English

RUNNING TIME: 92 minutes

VIDEO: Sony

DESCRIPTION:

Set in a small town in Czechoslovakia during the Nazi occupation of that country.

Liza Elias is a beautiful 30-year-old Jewish woman who dreams of marrying the perfect man. When rumors spread through the community that the Nazis will send all unmarried women over the age of 16 to labor camps, the town moves to marry off all of its single women. Liza agrees to marry the son of her father's friend.

When Liza enters the town hall for the wedding ceremony, she sees 16 other couples preparing to do the same in order to avoid deportation. The Nazis, however, put a stop to the ruse. They strip and humiliate the women and prepare to ship them off to the death camps, and Liza faces some important decisions.

TITLE: **THE SEVENTH COIN**

YEAR PRODUCED: 1992

DIRECTOR: Dror Soref

CAST: Peter O'Toole, Alexandra Powers, Navin Chowdry, John Rhys-Davies, Ally Wulker

COUNTRY OF ORIGIN: United States/Israel

LANGUAGE: English

RUNNING TIME: 92 minutes

VIDEO: Hemdale

DESCRIPTION:

Thriller set in modern-day Jerusalem. An Arab youth and an American tourist come into possession of an ancient coin from King Herod's time. Peter O'Toole plays the villain who attempts to take the coin away. The two young people escape O'Toole's grasp and run for their lives.

Most of the film consists of the chase through the Old City of Jerusalem.

TITLE: **SHINE**

YEAR PRODUCED: 1996

DIRECTOR: Scott Hicks

CAST: Geoffrey Rush, Noah Taylor, Alex Rafalowicz, Armin Mueller-Stahl, Lynn Redgrave, John Gielgud

COUNTRY OF ORIGIN: Australia

LANGUAGE: English

RUNNING TIME: 105 minutes

VIDEO: New Line/Alliance

DESCRIPTION:

A man (Mueller-Stahl) whose father never allowed him to pursue his musical talents, and whose entire family was lost in the Holocaust, pushes his own talented son to excel as a pianist.

Set in Australia, this film looks at the confusing and troubled childhood of piano prodigy David Helfgott (Rush). David's father emphasizes several principles in rearing him. One is the primal importance of family and that no one will ever love David as much as his father does. Another, the indestructible beauty of music and how important it is for David to fulfill his musical talents. These principles come into conflict when David is offered an opportunity to study in America and his father refuses to allow him to go because it would break up the family. Later David gets another opportunity, this time in London, and insists on taking it. His father tells David that if he leaves home he can never come back.

The overbearing father and David's insecurity lead to a complete collapse, and David is institutionalized for some 10 years. When finally released, he struggles to live his own life while learning to control and exploit his musical talent. In the end the love of a good woman finally gives David the confidence and ability to carry on with a career in music as well as to live his own life. A fascinating study of a troubled soul that is part fiction and part fact.

Rush is mesmerizing as the adult David Helfgott, and Mueller-Stahl turns in another brilliant performance. Rush received the Academy Award for Best Actor for his performance.

TITLE: **SHIP OF FOOLS**

YEAR PRODUCED: 1965

DIRECTOR: Stanley Kramer

CAST: Vivien Leigh, Simone Signoret, José Ferrer, Lee Marvin, Oskar Werner, Michael Dunn, Elizabeth Ashley, George Segal, José Greco

COUNTRY OF ORIGIN: United States

LANGUAGE: English

RUNNING TIME: 149 minutes

VIDEO: Columbia

DESCRIPTION:

Passengers on vessel bound for Germany in the 1930s, among them several Jews who encounter early signs of Nazi anti-Semitism. Although it would have been easy to change the background of the Jewish passengers, Kramer did not do so and therefore made the film much more interesting.

Won Academy Awards for Best Art Direction/Set Decoration in Black and White and for Best Black and White Cinematography. Nominated for Best Actor (Werner), Best Actress (Signoret), Best Adapted Screenplay, Best Black and White Costume Design, Best Picture, and Best Supporting Actor (Dunn).

TITLE: **SHOAH**

YEAR PRODUCED: 1985

DIRECTOR: Claude Lanzmann

COUNTRY OF ORIGIN: France

LANGUAGE: English, and other languages with English subtitles

RUNNING TIME: 570 minutes

VIDEO: Paramount

DESCRIPTION:

One of the most effective films ever produced about the Holocaust. Described as a documentary, but really much more. It is an opportunity to obtain a modicum of understanding of what the Holocaust was all about.

Although nearly 10 hours long, the film just zips by as one person after another is asked about what he saw and did during the Holocaust. That is exactly what this film is—a series of interviews with people who were there, people who saw what happened, people who can offer personal testimony to the events of the Holocaust. Lanzmann interviews witnesses of three types—-survivors, perpetrators, and people who watched. All give testimony. All bear witness. No one questions whether the Holocaust took place. They were all there. They all saw the events take place with their own eyes. And they describe everything.

The cumulative effect can be devastating, even today. Fifty years after the Holocaust, it is still difficult to understand that such evil could exist and that such horrible things could have happened. Perhaps the lesson of Shoah is that these crimes can be committed and were committed by ordinary people. And if it happened then, it can happen again. In fact history has proven that it can happen again. Maybe not against the Jews, but against any people who are powerless and downtrodden.

TITLE: **THE SHOP ON MAIN STREET**

YEAR PRODUCED: 1965

DIRECTOR: Jan Kadar and Elmar Klos

CAST: Ida Kaminska, Josef Kroner, Hana Slivkova

COUNTRY OF ORIGIN: Czechoslovakia

LANGUAGE: Czech with English subtitles

RUNNING TIME: 126 minutes

VIDEO: Columbia

DESCRIPTION:

Old Jewish woman in occupied Czechoslovakia loses her button shop when Nazis install an Aryan to run it. When the Jews are ordered deported, the Aryan decides to shield the woman. Poignant, passionate drama with one of the great Yiddish actresses of all time in the lead role.

Won Academy Award as Best Foreign Film, and Ida Kaminska was nominated for Best Actress.

TITLE: **SHTETL**

YEAR PRODUCED: 1996

DIRECTOR: Marian Marzynski

COUNTRY OF ORIGIN: United States

LANGUAGE: English

RUNNING TIME: 180 minutes

VIDEO: Ergo

DESCRIPTION:

Very personal documentary produced by Marian Marzynski, a Polish-born Holocaust survivor who returned to Poland to make this film and to obtain answers to many of his own questions.

Marzynski travels to the town of Bransk, which was home to 2,500 Jews before World War II. Accompanying him is a 70-year-old friend, Nathan Kaplan, whose family lived in the town before the war. In Bransk they meet a gentile, Zbyszek Romaniuk, who has become an amateur historian of the town's extinct Jewish community. He serves as their guide. Later Marzynski brings Romaniuk to the United States and introduces him to American Jews whose families came from Bransk. Then Marzynski takes Romaniuk to Israel.

Romaniuk's interest in the Jewish community of Bransk, his obvious discomfort and difficulty in dealing with charges that the Poles collaborated with the Nazis in exterminating the Jews, and the fears of his fellow townspeople that he will help the Jews reclaim their lost property in Bransk all provide a fascinating picture of a man caught between two worlds. *Shtetl* is an emotional and intriguing film that was first broadcast by PBS on April 17, 1996.

TITLE: **SIEGE**
YEAR PRODUCED: 1970
DIRECTOR: Gilberto Tofano
CAST: Gila Almagor, Yehoram Gaon, Dahn Ben Amotz
COUNTRY OF ORIGIN: Israel
LANGUAGE: Hebrew with English subtitles
RUNNING TIME: 95 minutes
VIDEO: Ergo

DESCRIPTION:
Tamar is widowed during the Six-Day War. Her husband's friends pressure her to keep his memory alive, but she wants to move on with her life.

TITLE: **SINAI COMMANDOS**
YEAR PRODUCED: 1968
DIRECTOR: Raphael Nussbaum
CAST: Robert Fuller
COUNTRY OF ORIGIN: United States
LANGUAGE: English
RUNNING TIME: 99 minutes
VIDEO: Atlas, Facets

DESCRIPTION:
Story of Israeli commandos attacking radar sites behind enemy lines in the Sinai during the Six-Day War. Includes actual combat footage.

Fuller is one of the few Americans in this film. He was hired to headline it because he was appearing as a regular on a popular American television series, Ironside, at the time it was made.

TITLE: **THE SINGING BLACKSMITH (YANKL DER SCHMID)**

YEAR PRODUCED: 1938

DIRECTOR: Edgar G. Ulmer

CAST: Moishe Oysher, Miriam Riselle, Florence Weiss

COUNTRY OF ORIGIN: United States

LANGUAGE: Yiddish with English subtitles

RUNNING TIME: 95 minutes

VIDEO: Ergo

DESCRIPTION:

This film is worth seeing because of the magnificent vocal talents of Moishe Oysher and the direction of one of Hollywood's masters of low-budget films, Edgar G. Ulmer.

Oysher plays a philandering married blacksmith who loves women and liquor. Set in the Polish countryside, the film was shot entirely in the United States.

TITLE: **SKOKIE**

YEAR PRODUCED: 1981

DIRECTOR: Herbert Wise

CAST: Danny Kaye, Brian Dennehy, Eli Wallach, Carl Reiner, John Rubinstein, Kim Hunter

COUNTRY OF ORIGIN: United States

LANGUAGE: English

RUNNING TIME: 121 minutes

VIDEO: Academy

DESCRIPTION:

Powerful story of attempt by Jewish residents to stop a Nazi demonstration from marching through the streets of Skokie, Illinois. Danny Kaye gives an outstanding performance as a death camp survivor leading the anti-Nazi forces.

One of the best television films on this topic. Brings into focus the American belief in unfettered free speech versus the right of a minority to prevent the dissemination of hatred.

TITLE: **THE SLINGSHOT**

YEAR PRODUCED: 1993

DIRECTOR: Ake Sandgren

CAST: Jesper Salen, Stellan Skaragard, Basia Frydman, Niclas Olund, Ernst-Hugo Jaregard

COUNTRY OF ORIGIN: Sweden

LANGUAGE: Swedish with English subtitles

RUNNING TIME: 102 minutes

VIDEO: CFP Video

DESCRIPTION:

Story is set in 1920s Sweden. Roland is 12 years old. His mother is a Russian Jew; his father, a Swedish socialist. Roland is a victim of bullying and prejudice. Even his own brother picks on him. But Roland is very inventive. He uses his mother's stock of illegal condoms to make a slingshot, although he eventually gets into trouble over it.

Quirky comedy about how people adapt and sometimes get a measure of revenge against those who persecute them.

TITLE: **SLUMS OF BEVERLY HILLS**

YYEAR PRODUCED: 1998

DIRECTOR: Tamara Jenkins

CAST: Natasha Lyonne, Alan Arkin, Marisa Tomei, Jessica Walter, Carl Reiner, David Krumholtz

COUNTRY OF ORIGIN: United States

LANGUAGE: English

RUNNING TIME: 91 minutes

VIDEO: Fox Home Video

DESCRIPTION:

Coming of age comedy set in 1976. Vivian Abramowitz (Lyonne) is a teenager trying to grow up without a mother and a fly by night father (Arkin) who is looking for a better life for his children.

The father wants his kids to get the advantages of the excellent educational system in Beverly Hills but can't afford a decent home there, so he's constantly moving from one run down apartment to another.

The story, based on the writer/director's own memories, is very funny but filled with over the top incidents and a great deal of sexual content. The performance of Natasha Lyonne is outstanding.

TITLE: **SOFIE**

YEAR PRODUCED: 1992

DIRECTOR: Liv Ullmann

CAST: Karen-Lise Mynster, Ghita Nørby, Erland Josephson

COUNTRY OF ORIGIN: Denmark/Norway/Sweden

LANGUAGE: Danish with English subtitles

RUNNING TIME: 146 minutes

VIDEO: Alliance

DESCRIPTION:

Set in Denmark in the late 1800s. Sofie is a Jewish woman whose family is anxious to see her married. When she falls in love with a non-Jewish painter, they arrange a marriage with a Jewish man in a rural community in northern Denmark.

Sofie has a son, but the marriage is not happy. As her husband's mental condition deteriorates, she takes up with his brother. The story traces 20 years in the life of a woman with a mind of her own.

TITLE: **SOLDIER OF THE NIGHT**

YEAR PRODUCED: 1984

DIRECTOR: Dan Wolman

CAST: Iris Kaner, Ze'ev Shimshoni

COUNTRY OF ORIGIN: Israel

LANGUAGE: Dubbed into English

RUNNING TIME: 89 minutes

VIDEO: MGM

DESCRIPTION:

Israeli-produced thriller about someone murdering soldiers. Into this drama comes a couple who fall passionately in love, except that the young woman begins to have suspicions about her boyfriend.

Poorly dubbed and a bit of a mishmash.

TITLE: **SOLOMON AND SHEBA**

YEAR PRODUCED: 1959

DIRECTOR: King Vidor

CAST: Yul Brynner, Gina Lollobrigida, George Sanders

COUNTRY OF ORIGIN: United States

LANGUAGE: English

RUNNING TIME: 139 minutes

VIDEO: Fox

DESCRIPTION:

Spectacular biblical epic about King David's son and the Queen of Sheba. King Vidor's last film. Originally shot with Tyrone Power in the lead, but he died during filming and Brynner was brought in to replace him.

TITLE: **SONG OF THE SIREN**

YEAR PRODUCED: 1998

DIRECTOR: Eytan Fox

CAST: Dalit Kahan, Boaz Gour-Lavie, Yair Lapid, Orli Zilbershatz

COUNTRY OF ORIGIN: Israel

LANGUAGE: Hebrew with English subtitles

RUNNING TIME: 91 minutes

VIDEO: Ergo

DESCRIPTION:

Story of Talia Katz (Kahan), a yuppie Israeli woman in the advertising business, who lives a self-centered life and is concerned only about her latest love affair. When the missiles start falling on Israel during the Gulf War, she suddenly is forced to face reality and re-evaluate her life.

TITLE: **SOPHIE'S CHOICE**

YEAR PRODUCED: 1987

DIRECTOR: Alan J. Pakula

CAST: Meryl Streep, Kevin Kline, Peter MacNicol, Josh Mostel

COUNTRY OF ORIGIN: United States

LANGUAGE: English

RUNNING TIME: 157 minutes

VIDEO: Fox

DESCRIPTION:

Haunting story of a gentile Polish survivor of Auschwitz and her relationships with a schizophrenic Jewish genius and an aspiring southern writer. Flashbacks to her days in the concentration camp point out her questioning of her survival. The ending is harrowing but totally absorbing.

Flashbacks also point out problems of Polish-Jewish relations when Sophie admits how surprised she was when her father advocated the extermination of the Jews.

Won an Academy Award for Best Actress (Streep) and nominated for Best Adapted Screenplay, Best Cinematography, Best Costume Design, and Best Original Score.

TITLE: **THE SORROW AND THE PITY**

YEAR PRODUCED: 1970

DIRECTOR: Marcel Ophuis

COUNTRY OF ORIGIN: Switzerland

LANGUAGE: French with English subtitles

RUNNING TIME: 265 minutes

VIDEO: Columbia

DESCRIPTION:

Great documentary about the Nazi occupation of France and the French resistance. Lengthy but absorbing. Destroys a lot of myths about the French resistance.

TITLE: **THE STATE OF ISRAEL**
YEAR PRODUCED: 1998
DIRECTOR: Laurence Vulliamy
COUNTRY OF ORIGIN: Israel
LANGUAGE: English
RUNNING TIME: 79 minutes
VIDEO: Ergo

DESCRIPTION:
Documentary about the condition of the State of Israel, features an overview of the origins of the State by Abba Eban and Ehud Olmert, and a debate between writer David Grossman and former Soviet dissident Natan Sharansky. Prominent individuals support the different sides of the debate, including Amos Oz, Elie Wiesel and Shulamit Aloni.

TITLE: **STEAL THE SKY**
YEAR PRODUCED: 1988
DIRECTOR: John Hancock
CAST: Mariel Hemingway, Ben Cross
COUNTRY OF ORIGIN: United States
LANGUAGE: English
RUNNING TIME: 108 minutes
VIDEO: HBO

DESCRIPTION:
Mariel Hemingway plays an Israeli agent who seduces an Iraqi pilot and convinces him to defect and bring a MIG jet fighter with him.

Stranger than fiction? Maybe. But many things are unbelievable until they happen. And this did happen.

A good made for cable television film with some terrific aerial photography.

TITLE: **THE STORY OF RUTH**

YEAR PRODUCED: 1960

DIRECTOR: Henry Koster

CAST: Elana Eden, Stuart Whitman, Tom Tryon, Peggy Wood, Viveca Lindfors, Jeff Morrow

COUNTRY OF ORIGIN: United States

LANGUAGE: English

RUNNING TIME: 132 minutes

VIDEO: Fox

DESCRIPTION:

Biblical story of Ruth and her renunciation of her gods when she finds true faith.

TITLE: **THE STRANGER**

YEAR PRODUCED: 1946

DIRECTOR: Orson Welles

CAST: Edward G. Robinson, Loretta Young, Orson Welles

COUNTRY OF ORIGIN: United States

LANGUAGE: English

RUNNING TIME: 95 Minutes

VIDEO: Aikmon Archive (JEF Films International) / Morningstar

DESCRIPTION:

One of the first films centering on the pursuit of Nazi war criminals.

Edward G. Robinson plays a Nazi hunter who tracks down a prominent Nazi who has escaped to Hartford, Connecticut. The Nazi, played by Orson Welles, succeeds in marrying the daughter (Young) of one of the town's most prominent citizens and hides his true identity behind the facade of a college teacher.

Many of the ground breaking techniques used by Welles in previous films, including the use of shadows and shooting from low and high positions, help to sustain the suspense and tension.

TITLE: **A STRANGER AMONG US**

YEAR PRODUCED: 1992

DIRECTOR: Sidney Lumet

CAST: Melanie Griffith, Eric Thal, John Pankow, Tracey Pollan, Mia Sara

COUNTRY OF ORIGIN: United States

LANGUAGE: English

RUNNING TIME: 109 minutes

VIDEO: Hollywood Films Home Video

DESCRIPTION:

A flawed film, but one that took a certain amount of courage to produce.

Melanie Griffith plays a WASP police detective investigating the murder of a Hasidic Jew in the diamond business. The film provides a close look at New York's Hasidic community. And in that respect it succeeds very well. As a thriller, though, it doesn't always hit the mark. But outside of *The Chosen*, it is one of the most positive views of Judaism ever put on film.

TITLE: **STREETS OF GOLD**

YEAR PRODUCED: 1986

DIRECTOR: Joe Roth

CAST: Klaus Maria Brandauer, Adrian Pasdar, Wesley Snipes, Angela Molina

COUNTRY OF ORIGIN: United States

LANGUAGE: English

RUNNING TIME: 94 minutes

VIDEO: Vestron

DESCRIPTION:

Brandauer plays a boxer from the Soviet Union who is considered one of the greatest fighters of his time, but is not allowed to compete internationally because he is Jewish.

Ten years later, a washed-up, alcoholic fighter stumbling through life in Brooklyn, he spots a couple of kids with a lot of potential sparring in a gym. He begins to train them, and his life begins to turn around.

At the end of the film, one of Brandauer's proteges winds up fighting a Soviet boxer coached by the man who would not let Brandauer represent the U.S.S.R.

TITLE: **THE SUBSTANCE OF FIRE**

YEAR PRODUCED: 1996

DIRECTOR: Daniel Sullivan

CAST: Ron Rifkin, Lee Grant, Tony Goldwin, Eric Bogosian, Timoy Hutton, Sarah Jessica Parker

COUNTRY OF ORIGIN: United States

LANGUAGE: English

RUNNING TIME: 103 minutes

VIDEO: Miramax/Alliance

DESCRIPTION:

Story of New York publisher Isaac Geldhart, a Holocaust survivor who as a child was forced to watch his family being taken away to their deaths in a Nazi extermination camp.

Isaac has committed himself to publishing books on the Holocaust. When this brings his company to the brink of financial disaster, his three children step in and take over.

The focus in this film is on the clashes between family members and the struggle each of them must undergo in deciding between family love and obligation and the cold facts of business logic.

TITLE: **THE SUMMER OF AVIYA**

YEAR PRODUCED: 1988

DIRECTOR: Eli Cohen

CAST: Gila Almagor, Kaipo Cohen, Marina Rosetti, Eli Cohen, Avital Dicker

COUNTRY OF ORIGIN: Israel

LANGUAGE: Hebrew with English subtitles

RUNNING TIME: 96 minutes

VIDEO: Ergo/Mongrel

DESCRIPTION:

One of the best films to come out of Israel in many years—the true story of Gila Almagor's life as a child and her struggle to protect her mother.

Almagor, one of Israel's greatest actors and the author of the autobiography upon which the film is based, plays her mother, and Kaipo Cohen plays Almagor as a child. The film is set in the period shortly after Israel's independence and tells about one summer in the life of 10-year-old Aviya. Aviya's strong and independent mother, a partisan fighter during World War II, lost both her husband and her sanity in the Holocaust. Aviya now has to adjust to life on an Israeli kibbutz, but must also care for her mother and endure periods when she is away at a mental institution. Neither Aviya nor her mother loses hope, even thought they sometimes have to restructure the realities of life to suit their own needs.

A moving and powerful film.

TITLE: **SUMMER OF LA GOULETTE**

YEAR PRODUCED: 1996

DIRECTOR: Ferid Boughedir

CAST: Gamil Ratib, Mustapha Adouani, Buy Nataf

COUNTRY OF ORIGIN: Tunisia, France, Belgium

LANGUAGE: Arabic, French and Italian with English subtitles

RUNNING TIME: 90 minutes

VIDEO: Mongrel Media

DESCRIPTION:

Set in La Goulette, a small harbor town in the suburbs of Tunis, in 1967, the story focuses on three families living in the same building, each one raising a 16-year-old daughter. One family is Arab, one family is Jewish and one is Christian.

The girls vow to lose their virginity and each has her eyes on a boy of a different religion. As a result, a number of taboos are being challenged in this film about the importance of customs and traditions. And all this takes place just before the Six Day War, which changed the history of the area and the relationships between the different ethnic groups forever.

TITLE: **SUMMER OF MY GERMAN SOLDIER**

YEAR PRODUCED: 1978

DIRECTOR: Michael Tuchner

CAST: Kristy McNichol, Bruce Davison, Esther Rolle, Michael Constantine, Barbara Barrie

COUNTRY OF ORIGIN: United States

LANGUAGE: English

RUNNING TIME: 98 minutes

VIDEO: Simon & Schuster, Coronet

DESCRIPTION:

During the summer of 1944, a prisoner-of-war camp is set up in Jenkensville, Georgia. The Bergens are the only Jewish family in town, and their 14-year-old daughter, Patty (McNichol), is having a hard time. She has no friends, her father is overbearing, and her mother ignores her.

She meets one of the German POWs and the two become friends. When he escapes, Patty helps him hide, and their relationship becomes more serious. Well-made television film. Esther Rolle won an Emmy for her portrayal of the Bergens' housekeeper.

TITLE: **SWEET LIGHT IN A DARK ROOM**

YEAR PRODUCED: 1960

DIRECTOR: Jiri Weiss

CAST: Ivan Mistrik, Dana Smutna

COUNTRY OF ORIGIN: Czechoslovakia

LANGUAGE: Czech with English subtitles

RUNNING TIME: 93 minutes

VIDEO: Discount Video Tapes, Horizon Entertainment, Facets

DESCRIPTION:

A student in Prague, during the German occupation, hides a Jewish girl, thereby risking his own life.

TITLE: **SWEET LORRAINE**

YEAR PRODUCED: 1987

DIRECTOR: Steve Gomer

CAST: Maureen Stapleton, Lee Richardson, Trini Alvarado

COUNTRY OF ORIGIN: United States

LANGUAGE: English

RUNNING TIME: 91 minutes

VIDEO: Paramount

DESCRIPTION:

This film has many similarities to *Dirty Dancing*, which was also released in 1987.

It too is set in the Catskills and involves a girl's coming of age at one of the resorts, but without the hot excitement and sexual overtones of *Dirty Dancing*. The story centers around an old, dilapidated Catskill landmark, the Hotel Lorraine. Molly, a college student, comes to work at her grandmother's hotel and falls in love with the place. The hotel is set to be sold to some developers, and Molly tries to save it from being torn down. At the same time, she develops a growing relationship with the local handyman.

A sweet and lovingly produced film with some truly fine performances. In many ways much superior to *Dirty Dancing*.

TITLE: **SWOON**

YEAR PRODUCED: 1991

DIRECTOR: Tom Kalin

CAST: Daniel Schlachet, Craig Chester, Ron Vawter

COUNTRY OF ORIGIN: United States

LANGUAGE: English

RUNNING TIME: 95 minutes

VIDEO: New Line/Alliance (MCA)

DESCRIPTION:

Low-budget film about the infamous 1924 Leopold-Loeb murder case. Nathan Leopold and Richard Loeb were both 18, both Jewish, both brilliant, and both from good families. As a thrill, they kidnapped and killed a 10-year-old boy, believing they could commit the perfect crime and not get caught.

This version of the story (previously portrayed in *Compulsion*) deals explicitly with Leopold and Loeb's homosexuality, and their belief that they were intellectually superior. Shot in 14 days, the film mixes various styles and techniques and may not be to everyone's taste.

TITLE: **SWORD OF GIDEON**

YEAR PRODUCED: 1986

DIRECTOR: Michael Anderson

CAST: Steven Bauer, Michael York, Rod Steiger, Laurent Malet, Colleen Dewhurst, Robert Joy, Leslie Hope

COUNTRY OF ORIGIN: Canada

LANGUAGE: English

RUNNING TIME: 150 minutes

VIDEO: HBO/Alliance

DESCRIPTION:

Based on the bestselling book *Vengeance*, by George Jonas, *Sword of Gideon* is a television mini-series about Israel's attempt to track down and eliminate the perpetrators of the 1972 Munich Olympic massacre.

Opens with Avner (Bauer) being approached by intelligence officials to head up a team of agents to carry out the difficult and dangerous task of finding, identifying, and killing the Arab terrorists responsible for the deaths of the Israeli athletes. At first, Avner's team is very successful. But the longer they remain in Europe, the more difficult the assignment becomes. The terrorists realize they are being stalked and eventually begin to pick off the Israeli agents.

How close to the truth is this film? We can never know. All these Israeli efforts are shrouded in an impenetrable net of secrecy. We do know that every single Arab terrorist connected with the Munich massacre was eliminated, although it took several years, a great deal of effort, and more than one hit team.

Sword of Gideon gives the viewer a small peek into the underground war between Israel and the Arabs. It is one of the best action films about Israel available on home video.

TITLE: **TABLE SETTINGS**

YEAR PRODUCED: 1984

CAST: Robert Klein, Stockard Channing, Dinah Manoff, Eileen Heckart

COUNTRY OF ORIGIN: United States

LANGUAGE: English

RUNNING TIME: 90 minutes

VIDEO: RKO

DESCRIPTION:

Taped performance of James Lapine's comedy about three generations of a Jewish family.

TITLE: **TAKE TWO**

YEAR PRODUCED: 1985

DIRECTOR: Baruch Dienar

COUNTRY OF ORIGIN: Israel

LANGUAGE: English

RUNNING TIME: 100 minutes

VIDEO: Ergo

DESCRIPTION:

Israeli comedy about a cinematographer who has a series of affairs with models and actresses. He hires an American woman as his assistant and falls in love.

TITLE: **THE TANGO LESSON**

YEAR PRODUCED: 1997

DIRECTOR: Sally Potter

CAST: Sally Potter, Pablo Veron

COUNTRY OF ORIGIN: Great Britain

LANGUAGE: English

RUNNING TIME: 101 minutes

VIDEO: Columbia Tristar Home Video/Behaviour

DESCRIPTION:

Story about a Jewish filmmaker who is having trouble with her latest screenplay. When she runs across an Argentinian tango dancer, she is fascinated by both the dancing and the dancer. In return for a role in her next film, the dancer gives her tango lessons and the two fall in love.

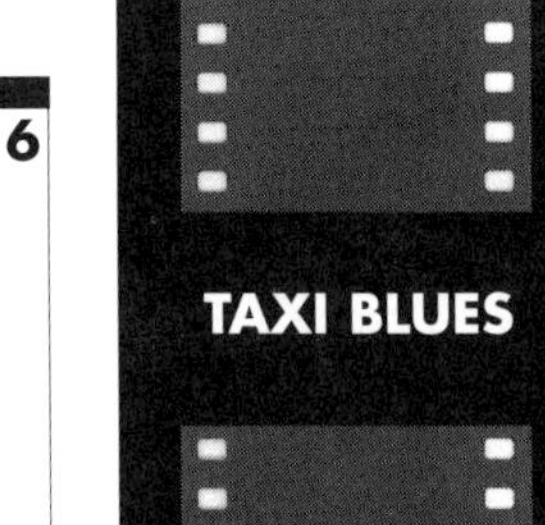

TITLE: **TAXI BLUES**

YEAR PRODUCED: 1990

DIRECTOR: Pavel Lounguine

CAST: Piotr Mamonov, Piotr Zaitchenko

COUNTRY OF ORIGIN: Russia

LANGUAGE: Russian with English subtitles

RUNNING TIME: 110 minutes

VIDEO: New Yorker

DESCRIPTION:

A Moscow taxi driver picks up some musicians. When the last of them, a Jewish saxophone player called Liocha, leaves the cab, he has no money and can't pay. The driver hunts Liocha down and holds him hostage for the fare—even though it means the musician has to do manual labor.

The cabbie is a lower-class black marketeer, while the Jew is a westernized member of the intelligentsia. Each looks down on the other, but both represent segments of post–Cold War Russian society. By the end of the film, the anti-Semitic cabbie and the Jewish musician reach an accommodation that borders on friendship.

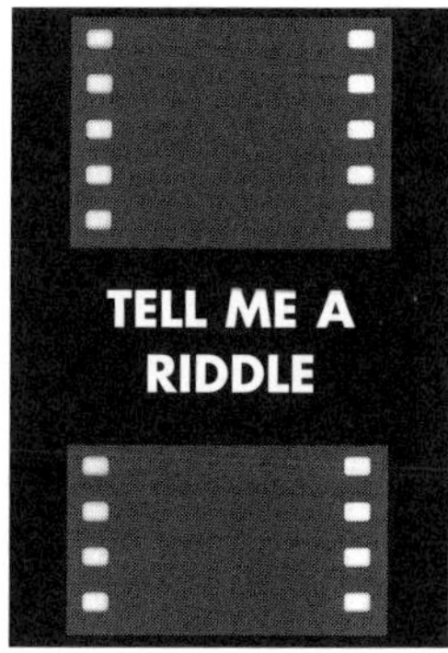

TITLE: **TELL ME A RIDDLE**

YEAR PRODUCED: 1980

DIRECTOR: Lee Grant

CAST: Melvyn Douglas, Lila Kedrova, Peter Coyote

COUNTRY OF ORIGIN: United States

LANGUAGE: English

RUNNING TIME: 90 minutes

VIDEO: Media

DESCRIPTION:

Tender story of an elderly Jewish couple rediscovering their mutual love even though the wife is ill with a terminal disease.

TITLE: **TELL ME THAT YOU LOVE ME**

YEAR PRODUCED: 1984

DIRECTOR: Tzipi Trope

CAST: Nick Mancuso, Barbara Williams, Belinda J. Montgomery

COUNTRY OF ORIGIN: Canada/Israel

LANGUAGE: English

RUNNING TIME: 88 minutes

VIDEO: Live, Vestron/Astral

DESCRIPTION:

A joint Canadian-Israeli production, the story revolves around the relationship between a journalist and her husband. Both have flourishing careers that sometimes conflict. The woman is working on a story on wife abuse and expects to be promoted to editor of the magazine she works for. The husband is a successful lawyer hoping for a one-year posting to New York. All of this causes a rift in the marriage and eventually leads to a divorce.

Although filmed in Israel, the setting is inconsequential and could have been anywhere.

TITLE: **THE TEN COMMANDMENTS**

YEAR PRODUCED: 1956

DIRECTOR: Cecil B. DeMille

CAST: Charlton Heston, Yul Brynner, Anne Baxter, Edward G. Robinson, Yvonne De Carlo, Debra Paget, John Derek, Sir Cedric Hardwicke, Nina Foch, Martha Scott, Judith Anderson, Vincent Price, John Carradine

COUNTRY OF ORIGIN: United States

LANGUAGE: English

RUNNING TIME: 219 minutes

VIDEO: Paramount

DESCRIPTION:

Moses never looked as good as he does in this blockbuster epic, one of the biggest films ever made, with sumptuous sets and costumes.

The film follows the story of Moses from his birth, through adulthood, when he receives the call to return to Egypt to free his people, and the 40 years of wandering in the desert, until his death.

Received seven Academy Award nominations. Won award for Best Special Effects.

TITLE: **TEVYE**

YEAR PRODUCED: 1939

DIRECTOR: Maurice Schwartz

CAST: Maurice Schwartz, Miriam Riselle, Leon Liebgold

COUNTRY OF ORIGIN: United States

LANGUAGE: Yiddish with English subtitles

RUNNING TIME: 96 minutes

VIDEO: National Center for Jewish Films, Ergo

DESCRIPTION:

Based on the Sholem Aleichem story about Tevye the milkman and his daughter Chava, who marries a gentile. A black-and-white *Fiddler on the Roof.*

Tevya was the first non-English film to be included in the National Film Registry set up by the Library of Congress.

TITLE: **THEY WERE TEN**

YEAR PRODUCED: 1961

DIRECTOR: Baruch Dienar

CAST: Ninette, Oded Teomi, Leo Filer

COUNTRY OF ORIGIN: Israel

LANGUAGE: Hebrew with English subtitles

RUNNING TIME: 105 minutes

VIDEO: Ergo

DESCRIPTION:

Story of the founding of a settlement in Palestine in the late nineteenth century.

Ten idealistic Russian Jews arrive in Palestine, where they learn to farm and have to deal with Arab opposition and Turkish harassment. One of the first Israeli films to look at the pioneering period realistically and without ideological coloring.

TITLE: **'38: VIENNA BEFORE THE FALL**

YEAR PRODUCED: 1988

DIRECTOR: Wolfgang Gluck

CAST: Tobias Engel, Sunnyi Melles

COUNTRY OF ORIGIN: Germany

LANGUAGE: German with English subtitles

RUNNING TIME: 97 minutes

VIDEO: Lumivision Corporation

DESCRIPTION:

Wartime Vienna explodes with love and politics. Nominated for an Academy Award for Best Foreign Language Film.

TITLE: **THOROUGHLY MODERN MILLIE**

YEAR PRODUCED: 1967

DIRECTOR: George Roy Hill

CAST: Julie Andrews, Mary Tyler Moore, Carol Channing, James Fox, John Gavin, Beatrice Lillie

COUNTRY OF ORIGIN: United States

LANGUAGE: English

RUNNING TIME: 138 minutes

VIDEO: MCA

DESCRIPTION:

Delightfully zany spoof of the Roaring Twenties. Julie Andrews plays Millie, an innocent country girl who becomes a secretary in order to find a husband. She becomes friends with Mary Tyler Moore and Carol Channing who winds up straightening everything out and setting up the usual happy ending. Nothing much Jewish about all that. The only reason the film is included in this Guide is one scene. Millie does some singing to earn a few extra dollars and has been hired to sing at a wedding. She invites Mary Tyler Moore along and does a terrific Yiddish number. The film is worth seeing just for that.

Won Academy Award for Best Original Score. Nominations included Best Art Direction/Set Decoration, Best Costume Design, Best Song, and Best Supporting Actress (Channing).

TITLE: **THREE DAYS AND A CHILD (NOT MINE TO LOVE)**

YEAR PRODUCED: 1967

DIRECTOR: Uri Zohar

CAST: Oded Kotler, Illy Gorlitzky, Shuy Oshcrov, Judith Soleh

COUNTRY OF ORIGIN: Israel

LANGUAGE: Hebrew with English subtitles

RUNNING TIME: 105 minutes

VIDEO: Ergo

DESCRIPTION:

Story of relationships. A young man (Kotler) returns to his kibbutz from army duty to discover the woman (Soleh) with whom he is in love has married someone else. Later, the woman asks him to babysit her son for three days. Thinking the boy may be his, the man agrees.

TITLE: **THREE DAYS IN APRIL**

YEAR PRODUCED: 1995

DIRECTOR: Oliver Storz

CAST: Karoline Eichhorn, April Hailer, Eva Michel, Birke Bruck

COUNTRY OF ORIGIN: Germany

LANGUAGE: German with English subtitles

RUNNING TIME: 100 Minutes

VIDEO: National Center for Jewish Film

DESCRIPTION:

A train arrives in the small German town of Nesselbuhl, Germany, in April of 1945. The American forces were rapidly approaching and German troops are moving concentration camp inmates farther away from the Allied forces but three cars from the train remain in the town. For three days the train remains while inside Jewish prisoners are dying. No one makes a move to assist them. Instead the cars are pushed onto the main track and down the hill, away from the town.

Only Anna (Eichhorn) the innkeeper's daughter appears to take any interest in the people imprisoned in the train cars.

TITLE: **TICKET TO HEAVEN**

YEAR PRODUCED: 1981

DIRECTOR: Ralph L. Thomas

CAST: Nick Mancuso, Saul Rubinek, Meg Foster, Kim Cattrall, R. H. Thompson, Jennifer Dale

COUNTRY OF ORIGIN: Canada

LANGUAGE: English

RUNNING TIME: 107 minutes

VIDEO: MGM

DESCRIPTION:

A Jewish young man, on the rebound from a failed relationship, joins a cult. His parents and friends kidnap him and hand him over to a deprogrammer.

TITLE: **A TICKLE IN THE HEART**

YEAR PRODUCED: 1996

DIRECTOR: Stefan Schwietert

CAST: Documentary

COUNTRY OF ORIGIN: Germany, Switzerland

LANGUAGE: English

RUNNING TIME: 84 minutes

VIDEO: New Yorker/Mongrel Media

DESCRIPTION:

This charming documentary takes a look at the Epstein Brothers, who are among the last of the great American Klezmorim.

Now in their eighties, the Epsteins look back at their long careers as musicians and exponents of Jewish music. And now in their old age, they are in demand again.

The camera follows the Epsteins to Florida, where they now live, to Berlin where they give a Klezmer concert, to the east European town where their parents come from and to Brooklyn where they had their greatest success in the 1950s and 1960s.

TITLE: **TO BE OR NOT TO BE**

YEAR PRODUCED: 1942

DIRECTOR: Ernst Lubitsch

CAST: Jack Benny, Carole Lombard, Robert Stack, Lionel Atwill, Felix Bressart, Sig Ruman, Helmut Dantine, Stanley Ridges

COUNTRY OF ORIGIN: United States

LANGUAGE: English

RUNNING TIME: 102 minutes

VIDEO: Vestron

DESCRIPTION:

Classic comedy about an acting troupe in Poland when the Nazis invade in 1939. The actors use their skills to work against the Nazi occupation.

Benny's best screen appearance, and Lombard's last film. One of the highlights is the recitation of Shakespeare's "Hath not a Jew eyes?" speech by bit-actor Greenberg (Bressart) at three different points in the film, each recitation having different and increasingly more profound dramatic significance.

This is an excellent anti-Nazi vehicle.

TITLE: **TO BE OR NOT TO BE**

YEAR PRODUCED: 1983

DIRECTOR: Alan Johnson

CAST: Mel Brooks, Anne Bancroft, Tim Matheson, Charles Durning, Jose Ferrer, George Gaynes, Christopher Lloyd, George Wyner, Lewis J. Stadlen, Jack Riley

COUNTRY OF ORIGIN: United States

LANGUAGE: English

RUNNING TIME: 107 minutes

VIDEO: Fox

DESCRIPTION:

Remake of the 1942 classic comedy with Brooks and Bancroft playing a married couple who perform in the Polish theater and get caught up in the resistance to the Nazis.

The film pays frequent tribute to the original and to Jack Benny, who starred in the earlier version.

TITLE: **TO SEE PARIS AND DIE**

YEAR PRODUCED: 1993

DIRECTOR: Alexander Proshkin

CAST: Tatyana Vasiliyeva, Dimitry Malikov, Ekaterina Semenova

COUNTRY OF ORIGIN: Russia

LANGUAGE: Russian with English Subtitles

RUNNING TIME: 110 Minutes

VIDEO: New Yorker/CHV

DESCRIPTION:

Story about an ambitious single mother pushing her only son, Yuri, towards piano greatness. She wants permission from the Soviet Bureaucracy for her son to study in Paris. The time is the 1960's, when such permission was not easy to obtain.

Things become complicated, when one official states that the boy's Jewishness might be a hindrance. This is somewhat strange because there has been no indication that the boy is Jewish. In fact, when Yuri prepares to marry a Jewish girl, the mother complains that she doesn't want Jewish grandchildren.

The true facts don't emerge until the end of the film in this compelling look at Soviet society during the height of the cold war era.

TITLE: **TO SPEAK THE UNSPEAKABLE: THE MESSAGE OF ELIE WIESEL**

YEAR PRODUCED: 1996

DIRECTOR: Judit Elek

COUNTRY OF ORIGIN: Hungary, France

LANGUAGE: Narration in English with some Hungarian and Rumanian with English subtitles

RUNNING TIME: 105 minutes

VIDEO: Mongrel Media

DESCRIPTION:

Documentary recording Elie Wiesel's return to his home town of Sziget, Hungary, where he was born and from which he and his family were deported to Auschwitz.

Wiesel retraces his steps to the Nazi death camps and recalls the last moments he spent with his mother and father. A moving memorial to the victims of the Holocaust.

TITLE: **TOBRUK**

YEAR PRODUCED: 1967

DIRECTOR: Arthur Hiller

CAST: Rock Hudson, George Peppard, Nigel Green, Guy Stockwell, Jack Watson

COUNTRY OF ORIGIN: United States

LANGUAGE: English

RUNNING TIME: 110 minutes

VIDEO: MCA

DESCRIPTION:

World War II action film. Allies, including a group of Palestinian Jewish commandos, are trying to destroy Rommel's fortress in North Africa, so that the Nazi fuel supplies can be blown up. Based on a true story.

TITLE: **TORCH SONG TRILOGY**

YEAR PRODUCED: 1988

DIRECTOR: Paul Bogart

CAST: Harvey Fierstein, Anne Bancroft, Matthew Broderick, Brian Kerwin

COUNTRY OF ORIGIN: United States

LANGUAGE: English

RUNNING TIME: 128 minutes

VIDEO: Columbia

DESCRIPTION:

A gay Jewish man looking for love is the central theme of this adaptation of the Broadway comedy. Fierstein and the rest of the cast give strong performances.

TITLE: **TORN APART**

YEAR PRODUCED: 1989

DIRECTOR: Jack Fisher

CAST: Adrian Pasdar, Cecilla Peck, Amon Zadok

COUNTRY OF ORIGIN: United States

LANGUAGE: English

RUNNING TIME: 95 minutes

VIDEO: Warner

DESCRIPTION:

A Romeo and Juliet love story from the Middle East.

As children, they lived in the same neighborhood and were friends. As adults, their love is forbidden.

Love burns brightly when their paths cross in the Israeli-occupied Gaza Strip. He is now an Israeli soldier, and she is a Palestinian schoolteacher. But their passion is uncontrollable, and they spend as much time together as they can.

As in most stories of this kind, you know that love will not run smooth, and troubles do intervene. But Pasdar and Peck give winning performances and make this an entertaining film.

TITLE: **TRANSPORT FROM PARADISE**

YEAR PRODUCED: 1965

DIRECTOR: Zbynek Brynych

COUNTRY OF ORIGIN: Czechoslovakia

LANGUAGE: Czech with English subtitles

RUNNING TIME: 93 minutes

VIDEO: Facets

DESCRIPTION:

Based on novel by Arnost Lustig about life in the Terezin ghetto before the Jews were shipped off to the death camps.

TITLE: **THE TRIAL OF ADOLPH EICHMANN**

YEAR PRODUCED: 1997

COUNTRY OF ORIGIN: United States

LANGUAGE: English

RUNNING TIME: 120 minutes

VIDEO: PBS

DESCRIPTION:

Excellent documentary broadcast by PBS in the United States with remarkable film clips from the Eichmann trial. Includes interviews with prosecutors and witnesses, and shows the painstaking work undertaken by the Israelis in order to ensure that Eichmann received a fair and open trial.

TITLE: **THE TRIANGLE FACTORY FIRE SCANDAL**

YEAR PRODUCED: 1979

DIRECTOR: Mel Stuart

CAST: Tom Bosley, David Dukes, Tovah Feldshuh, Janet Margolin, Stephanie Zimbalist

COUNTRY OF ORIGIN: United States

LANGUAGE: English

RUNNING TIME: 100 minutes

VIDEO: Live

DESCRIPTION:

Made-for-television film about the Triangle shirtwaist factory fire at the turn of the century, which killed 145 garment workers, most of them Jewish. The scandal that followed led to changes in labor and fire regulations.

TITLE: **TRIUMPH OF THE SPIRIT**

YEAR PRODUCED: 1989

DIRECTOR: Robert M. Young

CAST: Willem Dafoe, Edward James Olmos, Robert Loggia

COUNTRY OF ORIGIN: United States

LANGUAGE: English

RUNNING TIME: 119 minutes

VIDEO: Columbia

DESCRIPTION:

Willem Dafoe portrays Salamo Arouch, a Greek Jewish boxer.

Arouch and his father are deported to Auschwitz. When the Nazis realize that Arouch is a championship boxer, they force him to put on exhibition matches for their entertainment. Whoever loses is sent to the gas chambers.

Arouch faces the moral dilemma that every time he enters the ring, one of the fighters is certain to die. When he learns that his father is on the list to be exterminated, the only way to save him is to find someone to take his place or to volunteer to do so himself. Survival in Auschwitz meant a series of untenable choices, choices to be lived with for the rest of one's life, however long that might be.

Arouch happened to survive and made his way to Israel, where he wrote the book upon which this film is based.

TITLE: **THE TRUCE**

YEAR PRODUCED: 1997

DIRECTOR: Francesco Rosi

CAST: John Turturro, Massimo Ghini Rade Servedzija, Stefano Dionisi, Teco Celio

COUNTRY OF ORIGIN: Italy, France, Germany, Switzerland

LANGUAGE: English

RUNNING TIME: 126 minutes

VIDEO: Miramax / Alliance

DESCRIPTION:

Powerful film based on the book of Primo Levi.

Levi joined the partisans in Italy when the Germans took control of the country. He was quickly tracked down, arrested and imprisoned in Auschwitz. When the Red Army liberated Auschwitz, Levi found the way back to Italy to be cut off by the war and was forced to embark on a year long sojourn that led deep into the Soviet Union and then back through Germany, before he could return to his homeland.

This film tells the story of this difficult trek and Turturro gives a terrific performance as the brillant writer and chemist.

TITLE: **TRUE CONFECTIONS**

YEAR PRODUCED: 1991

DIRECTOR: Gail Singer

CAST: Leslie Hope, Kyle McCulloch, Jill Riley, Judah Katz, Chandra West

COUNTRY OF ORIGIN: Canada

LANGUAGE: English

RUNNING TIME: 95 minutes

VIDEO: Astral

DESCRIPTION:

Autobiographical film based on a book by Sondra Gotleib.

Verna is searching for herself and for the right mate. Should he be the handsome guy, the nerd, or the academic? This romantic comedy takes place in the Jewish community of Winnipeg, Manitoba, and tells the story of a young woman passing into adulthood.

TITLE: **21 HOURS AT MUNICH**

YEAR PRODUCED: 1976

DIRECTOR: William A. Graham

CAST: William Holden, Shirley Knight, Franco Nero, Anthony Quayle, Noel Willman, Paul Smith, Richard Basehart, Martin Gilat, Georg Marischka

COUNTRY OF ORIGIN: United States

LANGUAGE: English

RUNNING TIME: 101 minutes

VIDEO: Orion

DESCRIPTION:

Well-done television film recreating the events surrounding the massacre of the Israeli athletes at the 1972 Munich Olympics. Very accurate as far as the factual events are concerned.

TITLE: **TWILIGHT OF THE GOLDS**

YEAR PRODUCED: 1996

DIRECTOR: Ross Marks

CAST: Jennifer Beals, Faye Dunaway, Brendan Fraser, Garry Marshall, Jon Tenney, Rosie O'Donnell

COUNTRY OF ORIGIN: United States

LANGUAGE: English

RUNNING TIME: 93 minutes

VIDEO: Facets / CFP

DESCRIPTION:

Produced by the Showtime cable network, this film was also shown theatrically in selected markets. Suzanne and Rob (Beals and Tenney) are a Jewish couple who learn they are expecting a child. Rob is involved in genetic research and after testing his wife discovers that the child has a chromosome associated with determining homosexuality. Then the arguements begin. Suzanne's brother (Fraser) is gay and the question is whether the parents want to give birth to such a child.

TITLE: **THE TWO OF US**

YEAR PRODUCED: 1968

DIRECTOR: Claude Berri

CAST: Michel Simon, Alain Cohen, Luce Fabiole, Roger Carel, Paul Preboist

COUNTRY OF ORIGIN: France

LANGUAGE: French with English subtitles

RUNNING TIME: 86 minutes

VIDEO: Distributor unknown but it has been available on video for many years.

DESCRIPTION:

Beautiful film about a Jewish boy sent away from the city during World War II to live with an anti-Semitic farmer. Funny and charming, one of the best Holocaust films.

TITLE: **TWO SISTERS**

YEAR PRODUCED: 1938

DIRECTOR: Ben K. Blake

CAST: Jennie Goldstein

COUNTRY OF ORIGIN: United States

LANGUAGE: Yiddish with English subtitles

RUNNING TIME: 82 minutes

VIDEO: National Center for Jewish Films, Jewish Book Center

DESCRIPTION:

Story of an older sister who sacrifices for her younger sister. Goldstein was one of the leading actresses of the Yiddish theater, but this was her only venture into the world of film.

The NCJF version features new English subtitles.

TITLE: **2000 YEARS OF FREEDOM AND HONOR: THE COCHIN JEWS OF INDIA**

YEAR PRODUCED: 1992

DIRECTOR: Dr. Johanna Spector

COUNTRY OF ORIGIN: United States

LANGUAGE: English

RUNNING TIME: 80 minutes

VIDEO: Ergo

DESCRIPTION:

Documentary tracing the history of the Cochin Jews of India. After almost 2000 years of living in India, the younger generation has largely emigrated to Israel, while the elders have remained in their native land.

TITLE: **TZANAFI FAMILY**

YEAR PRODUCED: 1976

DIRECTOR: Boaz Davidzon

CAST: Gabi Amrani, Levanah Finkelstein, Chaim Banai

COUNTRY OF ORIGIN: Israel

LANGUAGE: Hebrew with English subtitles

RUNNING TIME: 90 minutes

VIDEO: Kol Ami

DESCRIPTION:

Israeli film about a Sephardic family and their trials and tribulations.

TITLE: **UNCLE MOSES**

YEAR PRODUCED: 1932

DIRECTOR: Sidney Goldin, Aubray Scotto

CAST: Maurice Schwartz, Rubin Goldberg

COUNTRY OF ORIGIN: United States

LANGUAGE: Yiddish with English subtitles

RUNNING TIME: 87 minutes

VIDEO: National Center for Jewish Film, Ergo

DESCRIPTION:

East European Jewish immigrants at the turn of the century settle in New York's Lower East Side. Uncle Moses tries to retain traditional family values and falls in love with the tailor's daughter.

Maurice Schwartz was a legendary Yiddish stage actor. Based on book by Sholem Asch.

TITLE: **UNDER THE DOMIM TREE**

YEAR PRODUCED: 1995

DIRECTOR: Eli Cohen

CAST: Kaipo Cohen, Gila Almagor, Juliano Mer, Riki Blich, Orli Perl, Ohad Knoller, Jeniya Catzan

COUNTRY OF ORIGIN: Israel

LANGUAGE: Hebrew with English subtitles

RUNNING TIME: 102 minutes

VIDEO: Fox Loriber/Mongrel

DESCRIPTION:

Sequel to the highly successful *Summer of Aviya.* It is now five years later. Aviya is 15 years old and is living in an Israeli communal settlement for orphaned concentration camp survivors and other troubled youngsters.

On the surface everything seems quite normal, but at night the demons suffered by these children are released. Many of them cannot forget the horrors they lived through, and their dreams are filled with terrifying memories. When things get too unbearable, the teenagers seek refuge under the branches of the domim tree.

Aviya is less central to the storyline than she was in the *Summer of Aviya,* although we find out that her mother, again played by Gila Almagor, has been institutionalized.

An important and powerful film.

TITLE: **UNDER THE WORLD (DEBAJO DEL MUNDO)**

YEAR PRODUCED: 1987

DIRECTOR: Juan Bautista Stagnaro and Beda Docampo Feijoo

CAST: Sergio Renan, Barbara Mugica, Victor Laplace

COUNTRY OF ORIGIN: Argentina

LANGUAGE: Spanish with English subtitles

RUNNING TIME: 106 minutes

VIDEO: New World

DESCRIPTION:

Moving drama about one family's survival in Poland during the Holocaust.

The Nachmans go into hiding in a trench dug under a barn. Later they join a group of Jews hiding in the forests.

Incredible story that makes the viewer doubt that this could have actually happened, but all the incidents depicted actually took place. Some of the survivors of the Nachman family now live in Argentina.

TITLE: **UNDERDOGS: A SPORTS (WAR) MOVIE**

YEAR PRODUCED: 1996

DIRECTOR: Doron Tsabari, Rino Tzror

COUNTRY OF ORIGIN: Israel

LANGUAGE: Hebrew with English subtitles

RUNNING TIME: 85 minutes

VIDEO: Ergo

DESCRIPTION:

Documentary about the fortunes of the Hapoel Beit She'an soccer team and how its success or failure was reflected by the townspeople who lived and died by the team. Story of the haves and have nots in Israeli society.

TITLE: **UNDZERE KINDER (OUR CHILDREN)**

YEAR PRODUCED: 1948

DIRECTOR: Natan Gross, Shaul Goskind

CAST: Nusia Gold, Shimon Dzigan, Yisroel Schumacher

COUNTRY OF ORIGIN: Poland

LANGUAGE: Yiddish with English subtitles

VIDEO: Jewish Book Center

DESCRIPTION:

Filmed at an orphanage near Lodz, this film was suppressed by the Polish government for many years because its content was too Jewish. Includes some classic turns by the famous comedy team of Dzigan and Schumacher.

TITLE: **UNSETTLED LAND**

YEAR PRODUCED: 1988

DIRECTOR: Uri Barbash

CAST: Kelly McGillis, John Shea, Amon Zadok

COUNTRY OF ORIGIN: Israel

LANGUAGE: English

RUNNING TIME: 109 minutes

VIDEO: Nelson, New Line

DESCRIPTION:

Anda, a beautiful Viennese doctor, and her lover, Marcus, arrive in Palestine in 1910 intending to build a new society where Jews will be able to live in equality and peace. Instead they find themselves fighting for survival as they attempt to claw a meager living from the soil and defend themselves from attacks by Bedouin tribesmen who claim the land.

The couple typifies the idealistic youngsters who, with nothing more than their bare hands, laid the foundations for the modern State of Israel.

One of the few films to question what the Jewish pioneers did and the motives behind their actions.

TITLE: **UNSTRUNG HEROES**

YEAR PRODUCED: 1995

DIRECTOR: Diane Keaton

CAST: John Turturro, Andie MacDowell, Michael Richards, Nathan Watt, Maury Chaykin

COUNTRY OF ORIGIN: United States

LANGUAGE: English

RUNNING TIME: 93 minutes

VIDEO: Hollywood Films Home Video

DESCRIPTION:

Steven Lidz (Watt), 12 years old, tries to cope in a world that is collapsing around him.

His mother (MacDowell) has become seriously ill, and his nutty father (Turturro) is absorbed in creating offbeat inventions and caring for Steven's mother. Steven turns to his two eccentric uncles (Chaykin and Richards), who collect garbage and exhibit unusual behavior. This rather special film mixes comedy and tragedy, setting the stage for Steven to grow up and enter the adult world with both feet on the ground—which isn't easy in this family.

The film makes no bones about the fact that the family is Jewish, but some of the Jewish elements have been diluted in an attempt to make the story more universal.

TITLE: **UP YOUR ANCHOR**

YEAR PRODUCED: 1985

DIRECTOR: Dan Wolman

CAST: Yftach Katzur, Zachi Noy

COUNTRY OF ORIGIN: Israel

LANGUAGE: English

RUNNING TIME: 89 minutes

VIDEO: MGM

DESCRIPTION:

Two nerds enlist in the Israeli Navy and attempt to fulfill their sexual fantasies. Very poor soft-porn film.

TITLE: **USED PEOPLE**

YEAR PRODUCED: 1992

DIRECTOR: Beeban Kidron

CAST: Shirley MacLaine, Jessica Tandy, Kathy Bates, Macello Mastroianni, Marcia Gay Harden, Sylvia Sidney

COUNTRY OF ORIGIN: United States

LANGUAGE: English

RUNNING TIME: 116 minutes

VIDEO: Fox

DESCRIPTION:

A Jewish grandmother (MacLaine) is propositioned on the day of her husband's funeral by an Italian-American admirer (Mastroianni).

Sounds a little ludicrous? Much of the film is, but at the same time it is a good drama with some very funny moments. The cast is excellent, with Jessica Tandy as MacLaine's mother, and Bates and Harden as MacLaine's adult, but disturbed daughters.

While the central love story keeps the film moving, the subplots provide most of the comedy. Unfortunately there is no effort to look at the main characters' Jewishness, or at the conflict a relationship between a Jewish woman and an Italian man might create. Moreover, there are few Jewish reference points, and even the shiva scene might be mistaken for a wake.

TITLE: **VICTORY AT ENTEBBE**

YEAR PRODUCED: 1976

DIRECTOR: Marvin J. Chomsky

CAST: Helmut Berger, Kirk Douglas, Linda Blair, Richard Dreyfuss, Helen Hayes, Anthony Hopkins, Burt Lancaster, Elizabeth Taylor

COUNTRY OF ORIGIN: United States

LANGUAGE: English

RUNNING TIME: 119 minutes

VIDEO: Warner

DESCRIPTION:

First of the Entebbe films to be produced for television.

Tells the story of the hijacking of an Air France plane by terrorists who force it to land in Entebbe, Uganda. A few days later, after it becomes clear that the Jewish hostages will not be released, an Israeli commando force lands at the airport and rescues them.

This film is not as good as either *Operation Thunderbolt* or *Raid on Entebbe.*

TITLE: **THE VISAS THAT SAVED LIVES**

YEAR PRODUCED: 1992

DIRECTOR: Katsumi Ohyama

COUNTRY OF ORIGIN: Japan

LANGUAGE: Japanese with English subtitles

RUNNING TIME: 115 minutes

VIDEO: Ergo

DESCRIPTION:

Story of Chiune Sugiharo, the Japanese consul-general in Lithuania in 1940 who issued visas to Jews that would allow them out of Europe. He saved 2,000 to 6,000 Jewish lives.

TITLE: **THE VOW**

YEAR PRODUCED: 1937

DIRECTOR: Henryk Szaro

CAST: Zigmund Turkow, Dina Helpern, Max Bozyk

COUNTRY OF ORIGIN: Poland

LANGUAGE: Yiddish with English subtitles

RUNNING TIME: 90 minutes

VIDEO: Jewish Book Center, Ergo

DESCRIPTION:

Two friends pledge their unborn children to marry. Story line is very similar to *The Dybbuk.*

TITLE: **VOYAGE OF TERROR: THE ACHILLE LAURO AFFAIR**

YEAR PRODUCED: 1990

DIRECTOR: Alberto Negrin

CAST: Burt Lancaster, Eva Marie Saint, Rebecca Schaeffer, Brian Bloom, Robert Culp

COUNTRY OF ORIGIN: United States/Germany/France/Italy

LANGUAGE: English

RUNNING TIME: 120 minutes

VIDEO: Prism

DESCRIPTION:

One of the most audacious acts of Palestinian terrorism was the 1985 hijacking of the luxury cruise-ship *Achille Lauro*. The incident ended very quickly, with the hijackers having little to show for their effort. But the Palestinian cause received a black eye when it was revealed that the terrorists had thrown Leon Klinghoffer, an elderly disabled Jewish man, overboard and allowed him to drown. This video is an edited version of the longer television mini-series. Lancaster and Saint give powerful performances.

TITLE: **VOYAGE OF THE DAMNED**

YEAR PRODUCED: 1976

DIRECTOR: Stuart Rosenberg

CAST: Faye Dunaway, Oskar Werner, Max von Sydow, Orson Welles, Malcolm McDowell, James Mason, Lee Grant, José Ferrer, Luther Adler, Katharine Ross, Sam Wanamaker, Denholm Elliott, Nehemiah Persoff, Julie Harris,
Maria Schell, Ben Gazzara

COUNTRY OF ORIGIN: Britain

LANGUAGE: English

RUNNING TIME: 134 minutes

VIDEO: Fox

DESCRIPTION:

Star-studded film about incident that occurred in 1939. Hitler wanted to prove that no one cared what happened to Jews, so he allowed the passenger vessel *St. Louis* to sail with a full complement of Jewish refugees. They supposedly had visas to enter Cuba, but the visas were revoked before they arrived there. No other country, including the United States and Canada, would allow them in.

The film is episodic, with a number of characters in turn telling their stories. So we have the distinguished doctor removed from his post at a university, the prominent lawyer who has suffered mental problems after being banned from practicing his profession, the middle-class couple who have converted all their assets into cash in order to purchase passage on the ship, and so on. At times the film dissolves into soap opera, but it is still an important entry in the Holocaust genre.

Received several Academy Award nominations, including Best Adapted Screenplay, Best Supporting Actress (Grant), and Best Original Score.

TITLE: **THE WALL**
YEAR PRODUCED: 1982
DIRECTOR: Robert Markowitz
CAST: Tom Conti, Lisa Eichhorn, Gerald Hiken, Rachel Roberts, Philip Sterling, Eli Wallach, Rosanna Arquette, Griffin Dunne, Dianne Wiest
COUNTRY OF ORIGIN: United States
LANGUAGE: English
RUNNING TIME: 150 minutes
VIDEO: HBO

DESCRIPTION:
TV movie based on John Hersey's book of the same name centers on the Nazi occupation of Warsaw and the persecution of the Jews resettled in the Ghetto. As conditions deteriorate, the resistance movement gains strength, until in April of 1943 all-out warfare erupts when the Germans decide to liquidate the Ghetto.

Shot on location in Poland.

TITLE: **A WALL IN JERUSALEM**

YEAR PRODUCED: 1970

DIRECTOR: Michelle Wiart

CAST: Documentary

COUNTRY OF ORIGIN:

LANGUAGE: English

RUNNING TIME: 91 minutes

VIDEO: Ergo

DESCRIPTION:

Moving black-and-white documentary tracing the history of the Zionist movement and the establishment of the Jewish community in Palestine, from early pioneering days to the Six-Day War. Narrated by Richard Burton.

TITLE: **THE WANDERING JEW**

YEAR PRODUCED: 1920

DIRECTOR:

CAST: Rudolf Schildkraut, Joseph Schildkraut

COUNTRY OF ORIGIN: Austria

LANGUAGE: Silent film

RUNNING TIME: 65 minutes

VIDEO: Glenn Video Vistas

DESCRIPTION:

Rare Austrian film version of the "wandering Jew" legend.

TITLE: **THE WANNSEE CONFERENCE**

YEAR PRODUCED: 1984

DIRECTOR: Heinz Schirk

CAST: Dietrich Mattsusch, Gerd Bockmann, Friedrich Beckhaus, Gunter Spoerrie, Martin Luttge

COUNTRY OF ORIGIN: Germany/Austria

LANGUAGE: German with English subtitles

RUNNING TIME: 87 minutes

VIDEO: Ergo

DESCRIPTION:

On January 20, 1942, the Nazi Empire was at its peak, and Hitler decided it was time to set up the ways and means of effecting the Final Solution to the Jewish Problem. On that day 14 leaders of the Nazi hierarchy met in the posh Berlin suburb of Wannsee to formulate a plan. The meeting lasted only 85 minutes and was a total success. There was no resistance to Reinhard Heydrich's proposal for the Final Solution.

Producer Manfred Korytowski drew upon the original secretarial notes to reconstruct the meeting in virtually real time. The actors were chosen because they physically resembled the characters they played.

An outstanding and mesmerizing film.

TITLE: **WAR AND LOVE**

YEAR PRODUCED: 1984

DIRECTOR: Moshe Mizrahi

CAST: Kyra Sedgwick, Sebastian Keneas, Alan Feinstein, Cheryl Gianni, David Spielberg, Lee Wallace

COUNTRY OF ORIGIN: United States

LANGUAGE: English

RUNNING TIME: 112 minutes

VIDEO: MGM

DESCRIPTION:

True story based on Jack Eisner's autobiography, *The Survivor.*

Tells the story of a Jewish boy from Warsaw, Jacek, who is in his early teens when Poland is invaded by Germany in 1939. Jacek's heart is broken when Halina, the neighbor he has fallen in love with, is taken by her parents to the countryside to escape the Nazis. Jacek escapes from the Warsaw Ghetto and finds Halina. The young couple voluntarily returns to Warsaw to fight against the Nazis. After the Ghetto is destroyed, the two lovers are sent to concentration camps, where they are separated and struggle to survive. In 1945, Jacek returns to Poland and searches for Halina.

Aside from documentaries, this was the first film with scenes actually shot at Auschwitz. In addition, the Ghetto Uprising scenes are stirring and effective.

TITLE: **WAR AND REMEMBRANCE**
YEAR PRODUCED: 1988
DIRECTOR: Dan Curtis
CAST: Robert Mitchum, Jane Seymour, Hart Bochner, Victoria Tennant, Barry Bostwick, Polly Bergen, David Dukes, Michael Woods, Sharon Stone, Robert Morley, Sami Frey, Topol, John Rhys-Davies, Ralph Bellamy, John Gielgud
COUNTRY OF ORIGIN: United States
LANGUAGE: English
RUNNING TIME: 1440 minutes
VIDEO: MPI

DESCRIPTION:
A mini-series sequel—twelve videocassettes, and approximately 24 hours in length–to The *Winds of War*, completing the story, but with some major cast changes. Jane Seymour replaces Ali MacGraw as Natalie, and Hart Bochner takes over the role of Byron from Jan-Michael Vincent. Another change was necessitated by the death of John Houseman. John Gielgud came in to play the brilliant but politically naive Aaron Jastrow.

The unprecedented length of this mini-series made it extremely difficult for people to sit down and view the entire saga, even though it was broadcast in two parts. At the same time, any history buff will probably revel in all the detail and the many events described. It's almost like reliving World War II, day by day.

Some of the episodes are very effective. I've never seen such explicit and realistic scenes as those depicting Jews being forced into the gas chambers at Auschwitz. The images are heartrending.

TITLE: **WARSZAWA (WARSAW—YEAR 5703)**

YEAR PRODUCED: 1993

DIRECTOR: Janusz Kijowski

CAST: Lambert Wilson, Julie Delpy, Hanna Schygulla

COUNTRY OF ORIGIN: France/Germany

LANGUAGE: French with English subtitles

RUNNING TIME: 116 minutes

VIDEO: Cineplex-Odeon

DESCRIPTION:

In the winter of 1943 a young Jewish couple escapes from the Warsaw Ghetto. The man (Wilson) makes his way to a safe house in the Aryan section of the city, only to find it occupied by Germans. Another tenant (Schygulla) offers to take him in, and they spend the night together. The next day, she goes out to find the man's "sister," Fryda (Delpy), and brings her back to the apartment. The tensions between the three rise until Fryda seems to go over the edge, yelling out the window that there are Jews hiding in the apartment.

TITLE: **THE WAY WE WERE**

YEAR PRODUCED: 1973

DIRECTOR: Sydney Pollack

CAST: Barbra Streisand, Robert Redford, Bradford Dillman, Viveca Lindfors, Herb Edelman

COUNTRY OF ORIGIN: United States

LANGUAGE: English

RUNNING TIME: 118 minutes

VIDEO: Columbia

DESCRIPTION:

Terrific love story with a lot of meaning behind the glitzy facade of a Hollywood film. Jewish radical Streisand meets WASP hunk Redford. Streisand comes from a working-class background and is committed to social causes. She is an outsider trying to make a difference. Redford is of upper-class origin, has no commitment to anything other than himself, but is mesmerized by Streisand's devotion to her causes. He is the consummate insider with nothing to prove. They meet in college and then again during World War II. They fall in love and get married, despite the differences between them. Redford becomes a successful Hollywood screenwriter. Streisand is forced to suppress her convictions and tries to live the Hollywood life.

The House Un-American Activities Committee's pursuit of some of the most creative people in Hollywood brings matters to a head. Streisand, unable to sit back when people she knows are attacked and vilified, speaks out. Realizing that there are too many differences between them, Streisand and Redford split up. Years later we see Streisand in New York handing out leaflets. She has returned to her roots. She is dressed like a New Yorker and has taken up causes that she believes in. She has also remarried. This time her husband is Jewish.

The Way We Were deals with the differences between the Jewish Streisand and the gentile Redford. They try to paper them over but ultimately return to their roots. This is one time that assimilation does not work, despite the efforts Streisand makes. She must be true to herself.

One of the best and most honest treatments of this subject ever done on film. Won Academy Awards for Best Song and Best Score. Nominations included Best Actress (Streisand), Best Art Direction/Set Decoration, and Best Cinematography.

TITLE: **WEAPONS OF THE SPIRIT**

YEAR PRODUCED: 1990

DIRECTOR: Pierre Sauvage

COUNTRY OF ORIGIN: France

LANGUAGE: French with English subtitles

RUNNING TIME: 90 minutes

VIDEO: Ergo, National Center for Jewish Film

DESCRIPTION:

Le Chambon-sur-Lignon was a village in occupied France whose 5,000 Christian inhabitants took in and sheltered 5,000 Jewish refugees. The director, Pierre Sauvage, returns to his birth place to determine why these brave villagers risked their lives and all they owned to save these Jews.

TITLE: **WELCOME TO THE DOLLHOUSE**

YEAR PRODUCED: 1996

DIRECTOR: Todd Solonde

CAST: Heather Matarazzo, Daria Kalinina, Matthew Faber

COUNTRY OF ORIGIN: United States

LANGUAGE: English

RUNNING TIME: 87 minutes

VIDEO: Columbia/Malofilm

DESCRIPTION:

An independent film done with a cast of unknowns that really hits home.

The film centers around Dawn Wiener (Matarazzo) an 11-year old grown up in a suburban Jewish family.

Dawn is constantly tormented and harassed at school and constantly put down at home because of her geeky appearance.

This is a film that will mean something to all the geeks in the world.

TITLE: **WHEN EVERY DAY IS THE FOURTH OF JULY**

YEAR PRODUCED: 1978

DIRECTOR: Dan Curtis

CAST: Katy Kurtzman, Dean Jones, Louise Sorel

COUNTRY OF ORIGIN: United States

LANGUAGE: English

RUNNING TIME: 100 minutes

VIDEO: Live

DESCRIPTION:

A 9-year-old Jewish girl asks her lawyer father to defend a mute handyman accused of murder. When he agrees to take on the case, the town turns on him.

Followed by a sequel, *Long Days of Summer.*

TITLE: **WHERE IS MY CHILD?**

YEAR PRODUCED: 1937

DIRECTOR: Abraham Leff, Harry Lynn

CAST: Celia Adler, Anna Lillian, Morris Strassberg

COUNTRY OF ORIGIN: United States

LANGUAGE: Yiddish with English subtitles

RUNNING TIME: 92 minutes

VIDEO: National Center for Jewish Film, Facets

DESCRIPTION:

Jewish immigrants during the 1911–1937 period experience tragedy in adapting to their new homeland. Film's heroine gives her newborn son up for adoption and quickly regrets her decision. New English subtitles.

TITLE: **THE WHITE ROSE**

YEAR PRODUCED: 1983

DIRECTOR: Michael Verhoeven

CAST: Lena Stolze, Wulf Kessler, Oliver Siebert, Ulrich Tuker

COUNTRY OF ORIGIN: Germany

LANGUAGE: German with English subtitles

RUNNING TIME: 108 minutes

VIDEO: MGM

DESCRIPTION:

True story of a group of German students who opposed the Hitler regime in the 1940s. They distributed leaflets in Munich and ran a clandestine anti-Nazi propaganda operation. Most of them were arrested and executed.

A very well done film about a story from World War II that very few people know about.

TITLE: **WILLIE & PHIL**

YEAR PRODUCED: 1980

DIRECTOR: Paul Mazursky

CAST: Michael Ontkean, Margot Kidder, Ray Sharkey

COUNTRY OF ORIGIN: United States

LANGUAGE: English

RUNNING TIME: 116 minutes

VIDEO: Fox

DESCRIPTION:

Willie, a Jewish high school teacher, meets Phil, an Italian fashion photographer, at a Truffaut film festival. Both young men are searching for the meaning of life when they meet Jeannette and their lives become interlocked. But this relationship is unsatisfying. Willie continues searching for meaning. He loves his friends and the daughter he has with Jeannette, but there is still something missing. He searches everywhere but within himself and his own background. He is somewhat ambivalent about his Jewishness, and marrying out of his faith does not appear to concern him very much.

At the end of the film, as in life, many questions are left unanswered.

TITLE: **THE WINDS OF WAR**

YEAR PRODUCED: 1983

DIRECTOR: Dan Curtis

CAST: Robert Mitchum, Ali MacGraw, Ralph Bellamy, Polly Bergen, Jan-Michael Vincent, David Dukes, John Houseman, Peter Graves, Topol

COUNTRY OF ORIGIN: United States

LANGUAGE: English

RUNNING TIME: 883 minutes

VIDEO: Paramount

DESCRIPTION:

Television mini-series available on seven video cassettes, based on Herman Wouk's bestselling novel.

The Second World War from the viewpoint of an American naval family. Robert Mitchum and his sons always seem to be where the action is. The youngest son is in Poland when the Germans invade. He falls in love with an American Jewish girl who is visiting her family. A large part of the film deals with her attempts to escape from Poland. The other son is a naval pilot stationed at Pearl Harbor when the Japanese launch their surprise attack on December 7, 1941.

Some of the battle scenes, especially the attack on Pearl Harbor, are very well done and worth seeing. The rest is too long, but the mini-series did well enough to result in an even longer, but better, sequel, *War and Remembrance.*

TITLE: **A WOMAN AT WAR**
YEAR PRODUCED: 1994
DIRECTOR: Edward Bennett
CAST: Martha Plimpton, Eric Stoltz
COUNTRY OF ORIGIN: United States
LANGUAGE: English
RUNNING TIME: 115 minutes
VIDEO: Republic

DESCRIPTION:
A Jewish young woman, Helene Moskiewicz (Plimpton), joins the Belgian resistance and infiltrates Gestapo headquarters. True story with excellent performance by Plimpton as headstrong and determined Moskiewicz, who refuses to accept occupation without a fight.

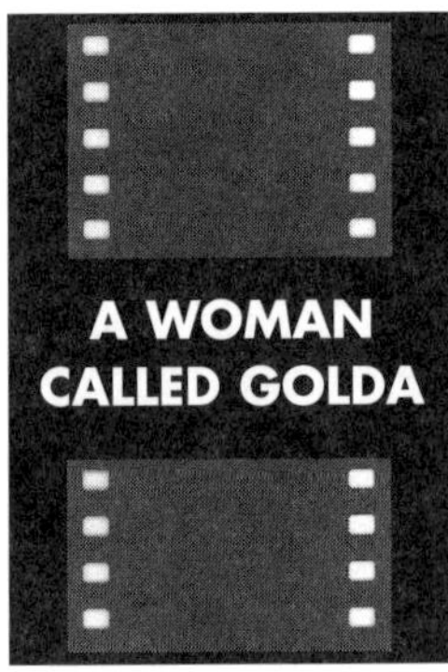

TITLE: **A WOMAN CALLED GOLDA**
YEAR PRODUCED: 1982
DIRECTOR: Alan Gibson
CAST: Ingrid Bergman, Ned Beatty, Judy Davis, Anne Jackson, Robert Loggia, Leonard Nimoy
COUNTRY OF ORIGIN: United States
LANGUAGE: English
RUNNING TIME: 192 minutes
VIDEO: Paramount

DESCRIPTION:
Ingrid Bergman in her final screen appearance plays Golda Meir in the biography of Israel's first woman Prime Minister. Produced as a television mini-series and has some powerful moments.

Story is told in a series of flashbacks as Golda returns to the school she attended in Milwaukee as a child. We see Golda's earliest memories of pogroms suffered by the Jews of her hometown in Eastern Europe and her determination to emigrate to Palestine.

Some of the most moving scenes deal with the situation during and after the Yom Kippur War and Golda's sense of accomplishment when she meets President Anwar Sadat of Egypt during his historic visit to Israel. One of the best and most complimentary films about Israel. Bergman won an Emmy for her performance, and the film was awarded an Emmy as Outstanding Drama Special.

TITLE: **THE WOODEN GUN**

YEAR PRODUCED: 1979

DIRECTOR: Ilan Moshenson

CAST: Eric Rosen, Judith Sole, Leo Yung, Ophelia Strahl

COUNTRY OF ORIGIN: Israel

LANGUAGE: Hebrew with English subtitles

RUNNING TIME: 91 minutes

VIDEO: Ergo

DESCRIPTION:

Two rival groups of Israeli youngsters struggle during the difficult years of the early 1950s. The film studies the young people being raised in freedom in a Jewish state, and their alienation from their parents' generation, especially the Holocaust survivors who arrived in Israel after the war.

TITLE: **THE WORDMAKER**

YEAR PRODUCED: 1991

DIRECTOR: Eli Cohen

CAST: Sinai Peter, Irena Selezniova, Anat Waxman, Nessim Zohar, Gal Zaid

COUNTRY OF ORIGIN: Israel

LANGUAGE: Hebrew with English subtitles, English

RUNNING TIME: 90 minutes

VIDEO: National Center for Jewish Films

DESCRIPTION:

Story of Eliezer Ben-Yehuda (Peter), the zealous champion of the Hebrew language who took a language that had not been in daily use for almost 2000 years and revived it and reinvented it for modern day use.

TITLE: **THE WORLD OF SHOLOM ALEICHEM**

YEAR PRODUCED: 1959

DIRECTOR: Don Richardson

CAST: Zero Mostel, Nancy Walker, Jack Gilford, Gertrude Berg

COUNTRY OF ORIGIN: United States

LANGUAGE: English

RUNNING TIME: 90 minutes

VIDEO: Ergo

DESCRIPTION:

Three classic Sholom Aleichem stories presented for a television production with an all-star cast of Jewish performers.

"A Tale of Chelm" tells about a bookseller sent by his wife to buy a goat; "Bontche Schweig" is an inspirational tale of a poor man who dies and goes to heaven; and "The High School" shows a couple's efforts to get their son into the school of their choice.

TITLE: **YENTL**

YEAR PRODUCED: 1983

DIRECTOR: Barbra Streisand

CAST: Barbra Streisand, Mandy Patinkin, Amy Irving, Nehemiah Persoff, Steven Hill

COUNTRY OF ORIGIN: United States

LANGUAGE: English

RUNNING TIME: 134 minutes

VIDEO: Fox

DESCRIPTION:

A young girl (Streisand) in an Eastern European shtetl seeks to study the Talmud, and masquerades as a man in order to enter a yeshiva. The masquerade leads to a series of problems for her.

Streisand treats Jewish traditions and customs with loving care and has produced an excellent film. The only drawback is the rather undistinguished music; furthermore, Streisand has plenty of songs, but if she was going to cast Mandy Patinkin in a musical, she should have given him a few. But Streisand fans will love this film.

Based on a short story by Isaac Bashevis Singer.

Film won an Academy Award for Best Original Score and was nominated for Best Song, Best Art Direction/Set Decoration, and Best Supporting Actress (Irving).

TITLE: **YIDDISHE MAMA**

YEAR PRODUCED: 1939

CAST: Esther Field, Simon Wolf, Cantor Max Rosenblatt

COUNTRY OF ORIGIN: United States

LANGUAGE: Yiddish with English subtitles

RUNNING TIME: 80 minutes

VIDEO: Kol Ami, Jewish Book Center

DESCRIPTION:

A Jewish widow guides her offspring through the problems of being Jewish immigrants in America.

TITLE: **YIDL MITN FIDL (A JEW WITH HIS FIDDLE)**

YEAR PRODUCED: 1936

DIRECTOR: Joseph Green

CAST: Molly Picon, Simche Fostel, Max Bozyk, Leon Liebgold

COUNTRY OF ORIGIN: United States

LANGUAGE: Yiddish with English subtitles

RUNNING TIME: 92 minutes

VIDEO: National Center for Jewish Films, Ergo

DESCRIPTION:

Classic Yiddish musical comedy. Molly Picon poses as a man in order to join a group of vagabond musicians roaming the countryside in 1930s Poland and falls in love with one of them.

Joseph Green was one of the most prominent Yiddish directors in America, although many of his films, including this one, were actually made in Poland. This film was the most successful Yiddish musical of all time. It includes several songs that were to become Yiddish standards. Molly Picon dominated the Yiddish stage for decades and witnessed its steady decline as Jews moved away from the big cities and integrated into American society, losing their facility with the Yiddish language. In her later years, Picon made a comeback of sorts, appearing in a number of English-language films. Her most prominent role came as Yente the Matchmaker in *Fiddler on the Roof.*

TITLE: **THE YOUNG LIONS**

YEAR PRODUCED: 1958

DIRECTOR: Edward Dmytryk

CAST: Marlon Brando, Montgomery Clift, Dean Martin, Hope Lange, Barbara Rush, Maximilian Schell, Mai Britt, Lee Van Cleef

COUNTRY OF ORIGIN: United States

LANGUAGE: English

RUNNING TIME: 167 minutes

VIDEO: Fox

DESCRIPTION:

Realistic antiwar film with Brando playing a disillusioned Nazi army officer, and Martin and Clift playing American soldiers. Clift's character is Jewish, and he falls in love with a non-Jewish woman from New England. Anti-Semitism raises its head when the woman's father pointedly emphasizes his family's long roots in America, and the crosses in the family plot succeed in making the point that the father is not pleased with his daughter's choice of a boyfriend.

TITLE: **ZALMAN; OR, THE MADNESS OF GOD**

YEAR PRODUCED: 1975

CAST: Joseph Wiseman

COUNTRY OF ORIGIN: United States

LANGUAGE: English

RUNNING TIME: 120 minutes

VIDEO: WNET/Thirteen Non-Broadcast

DESCRIPTION:

Based on Elie Wiesel's mystical story about a rabbi's struggle against religious persecution in Russia after the Stalinist era.

TITLE: **ZEBRAHEAD**

YEAR PRODUCED: 1992

DIRECTOR: Anthony Drazan

CAST: Michael Rapaport, Ray Starkey, N'Bushe Wright, Paul Butler, De Shonn Castle, Helen Shaver

COUNTRY OF ORIGIN: United States

LANGUAGE: English

RUNNING TIME: 102 minutes

VIDEO: Columbia

DESCRIPTION:

Romeo and Juliet with a black and Jewish element.

A very realistic, contemporary film set in a racially mixed area of Detroit. Zack, a redheaded Jewish boy (Rapaport), is immersed in black culture. He loves the music, the talk, and the attitudes of the black community, and most of his friends are black.

When Zack falls in love with a black girl, Nikki (Wright), a backlash is set off. His black friends don't like it, and neither does his father. Nikki also suffers a backlash from friends and relatives, and eventually tragedy strikes.

Unfortunately, much of the action is contrived, and there is no discussion of Zack's Jewish background and how this might affect the relationship.

Interesting film to watch, but it could have been better.

FILMS

Alphabetical Listing of Films

A

A la Mode (1994) (F)
Aaron's Magic Village (1997)
Abraham (1994)
About The Jews of Yemen: A Vanishing Culture (1986)
Actor: The Paul Muni Story (1978)
Adam's Rib (1991) (R)
Alan & Naomi (1992)
Almonds and Raisins (1984)
The Ambassador (1984)
American Matchmaker (1940) (Y)
American Pop (1981)
An American Tail (1986)
Amongst Friends (1993)
Angel of Death (1986)
Angry Harvest (1985) (G)
Anne Frank Remembered (1995)
Annie Hall (1977)
Antonia and Jane (1991)
The Apprenticeship of Duddy Kravitz (1974)
The Architecture of Doom (1989) (SWE)
The Assignment (1997)
The Assisi Underground (1984)
Atalia (1984) (H)
The Attic: The Hiding of Anne Frank (1988)
Au Revoir Les Enfants (1987) (F)
Auditions (1995) (H)
Austeria (1988) (P)
Avalon (1990)

B

Bachelor Girl (1987)
Beaches (1988)
Because of that War (1988) (H)
Ben Gurion: An Appointment With Destiny (1968)

sA = Arabic
CR = Croatian
CZ = Czech
DAN = Danish
F = French
G = German
Y = Yiddish
H = Hebrew
HU = Hungarian
I = Italian
JAP = Japanese
NOR =Norwegian
P = Polish
POR = Portuguese
R = Russian
RU = Rumanian
SP = Spanish
SWE = Swedish
Silent

The Benny Goodman Story (1955)
Best Boy (1979)
Beyond the Walls (1985)
Biloxi Blues (1988)
The Birdcage (1996)
Black Sunday (1977)
Blazing Saddles (1974)
Blazing Sand (1960)
Blind Man's Bluff (1993) (H)
Blood Money: Nazi Gold (1987)
The Blum Affair (1948) (G)
The Boat Is Full (1981) (G)
Border Street (1948) (P)
Born in Berlin (1991) (H) (G) (SWE)
The Boxer and Death (1963) (CZ)
Boy Takes Girl (1983) (H)
The Boys from Brazil (1978)
Brighton Beach Memoirs (1986)
A Brivele der Mamen (1938) (Y)
Broadway Bound (1992)
Broken Glass (1996)
Brotherhood of the Rose (1989)
Brussels Transit (1980) (Y)
But Where Is Daniel Wax? (1974) (H)

C

Cabaret (1972)
Cafe au Lait (1993) (F)
A Call To Remember (1997)
The Cantor's Son (1937) (Y)
Carpati (1996) (R) (Y)
Cast a Giant Shadow (1966)
Catskill Honeymoon (1949) (Y)
Cemetery Club (1993)
Chariots of Fire (1981)
Charlie Grant's War (1980)
Children of Rage (1975)

The Chosen (1981)
Chronicle of the Uprising In The Warsow Ghetto According to Marek Edelman (1994) (p)
Cold Days (1966) (HU)
Commissar (1968) (R)
Compulsion (1959)
Conflict (Judith) (1966)
Conspiracy of Hearts (1960)
Crimes and Misdemeanors (1990)
Crossfire (1947)
Crossfire (1989) (H)
Crossing Delancey (1988)
Cup Final (1992) (H)

D

The Damned (1969)
Dangerous Moves (1984)
Dark Lullabies (1985)
David (1979)
David and Bathsheba (1951)
A Day in October (1992)
Day of Atonement (1992)
Dead End Street (1983) (H)
Deadly Currents (1991)
Descending Angel (1990)
Diamonds (1972)
Diamonds of the Night (1964) (CZ)
The Diary of Anne Frank (1959)
Dirty Dancing (1987)
Dita Saxova (1967) (CZ)
The Doomsday Gun (1994)
Double Edge (1991)
Drifting (1982) (H)
Driving Miss Daisy (1989)
The Dunera Boys (1985)
The Dybbuk (1937) (Y)

E

Eagles Attack at Dawn (1974)
East and West (1923) (Silent)
Echoes of Conflict (1989) (H)
The Eddie Cantor Story (1953)
The Eighty-First Blow (1974) (Y) (H)
Eli Eli (1940) (Y)
End of Innocence (1990)
Enemies: A Love Story (1989)
Escape from Sobibor (1987)
Escape to the Sun (1972)
Esther and the King (1960)
Europa, Europa (1991) (G) (R)
Every Time We Say Goodbye (1986)
The Execution (1985)
Exodus (1960)
Eyewitness (1981)

F

Falling Over Backwards (1990)
Family of Cops (1995)
Family of Cops II: Breach of Faith (1997)
Family Prayers (1993)
Fate (1990)
Father (1990)
Festival at the Poolroom (1975) (H)
Fictitious Marriage (1988) (H)
Fiddler on the Roof (1971)
Finals (1983) (H)
The Fixer (1968)
Flames in the Ashes (1986) (Y) (H)
Flames of Revolt: The Irgun (1990) (H)
Forbidden (1984)
Forced March (1990)
Freud Leaving Home (1991) (SWE)
Friendship in Vienna (1988)

The Frisco Kid (1979)
The Front (1976)
Funny Girl (1968)
Funny Lady (1974)

G

Gaby: A True Story (1987)
The Garden of the Finzi-Continis (1971) (I)
A Generation (1954) (P)
Genghis Cohn (1994)
Gentleman's Agreement (1947)
Getting Away with Murder (1996)
The Glory Boys (1984)
God, Man and Devil (1949) (Y)
The Golem (1920) (Silent)
Good Evening, Mr. Wallenberg (1992) (SWE) (G) (HU)
Goodbye, Columbus (1969)
Goodbye, New York (1984)
The Governess (1998)
The Great Dictator (1940)
Green Fields (1937) (Y)
Green Fields (1989) (H)
Greta (1986) (P)

H

Hamsin (1983) (H)
Hannah and Her Sisters (1986)
Hanna K. (1983)
Hannah's War (1988)
Hate (1995) (F)
The Heartbreak Kid (1972)
Heavy Metal (1981)
The Heritage (1993)
The Hero (1969)
Hershaleh (1977) (H)
Hester Street (1974) (Y)
Hide and Seek (1980) (H)

Hill 24 Doesn't Answer (1955)
His People (1925) (Silent)
His Wife's Lover (1931) (Y)
History of the World, Part I (1981)
Hit the Dutchman (1992)
Hollywoodism: Jews, Movies and the American Dream (1997)
Holocaust (1978)
Homicide (1991)
Hotel Terminus (1987) (F)
The House on Chelouche Street (1973) (H)
The House on Garibaldi Street (1979)
Hungry Hearts (1922) (Silent)
Hunted (1979) (G)

I

I Don't Buy Kisses Anymore (1992)
I Don't Give a Damn (1988) (H)
I Love You, Alice B. Toklas (1968)
I Love You...Don't Touch Me (1998)
I Love You, I Love You Not (1997)
I Love You, Rosa (1972) (H)
The Illegals (1947)
I'm Not Rappaport (1997)
The Imported Bridegroom (1990)
The Impossible Spy (1987)
In The Presence of Mine Enemies (1997)
Independence Day (1996)
The Infiltrator (1994)
Infinity (1996)
The Inheritors (1985) (G)
Inside the Third Reich (1982)
Intimate Story (1981) (H)
Iron Eagle 2 (1988)
Israel: A Nation Is Born (1992)
Ivan and Abraham (1993) (Y)
Ivanhoe (1952)
Ivanhoe (1997)

J

Jacob (1994)
Jacob the Liar (1974) (G)
The Jazz Singer (1927)
The Jazz Singer (1952)
The Jazz Singer (1980)
The Jew (1995) (POR)
Jewish Luck (1925) (Silent)
The Jolly Paupers (1937) (Y)
Jolson Sings Again (1949)
The Jolson Story (1946)
Jonah Who Lived in the Whale (1993)
Joseph (1995)
Joshua Then and Now (1985)
Jud Suess (1940) (G)
Judgment at Nuremberg (1961)
Judith (Conflict) (1966)
Julia (1977)
Jumpin' Night in the Garden of Eden (1988)
Justine (1969)

K

Kapo (1959)
Kazablan (1974) (H)
King David (1985)
King for a Day (1982) (H)
King of Comedy (1983)
Korczak (1990) (P)
Kuni Lemel in Cairo (1983) (H)
Kuni Lemel in Tel Aviv (1977) (H)

L

Ladies' Tailor (1990) (R)
The Last Angry Man (1959)
The Last Butterfly (1990)
The Last Klezmer (1995)
The Last Metro (1980) (F)

The Last Sea (1980) (Y) (H)
The Last Seven Months of Anne Frank (1988)
The Last Winter (1984)
Late Summer Blues (1987) (H)
Laughter Through Tears (1928) (Silent)
Laura Adler's Last Love Affair (1990) (Y) (H)
Le Golem: The Legend of Prague (1935) (F)
Leon the Pig Farmer (1992)
Lepke (1974)
Les Misérables (1995) (F)
Les Patriotes (1994) (F)
Les Violons du Bal (1974) (F)
Lies My Father Told Me (1975)
Life is Beautiful (1997) (I)
The Light Ahead (1939) (Y)
The Little Drummer Girl (1984)
Little Odessa (1994)
The Living Orphan (1939) (Y)
Loan Me Your Wife (1988) (H)
Lodz Ghetto (1988)
Long Days of Summer (1980)
Long Is the Road (1948) (Y) (G) (P)
The Long Way Home (1997)
The Longest Hatred (1991)
Lost in Yonkers (1993)
The Lover (1990)
Luna Park (1991) (R)
Lupo (1970) (H)

M

Madame Rosa (1977) (F)
Madman (1979)
The Magician of Lublin (1979)
A Majority of One (1961)
Mamele (1938) (Y)
The Man Who Captured Eichmann (1996)
Marathon Man (1976)

Marjorie Morningstar (1958)
Marry Me, Marry Me (1969) (F)
Masada (1981)
Max and Helen (1990)
Me and the Colonel (1958)
Mendel (1997) (N)
Mina Tenanbaum (1994) (F)
Mindbender (1995)
Miracle at Midnight (1998)
Miracle at Moreaux (1986)
Mirele Efros (1939) (Y)
Miss Rose White (1992)
Mr. Emmanuel (1944)
Mr. Halpern & Mr. Johnson (1983)
Mr. Klein (1977) (F)
Mr. Saturday Night (1992)
Moses (1975)
Moses (1996)

Motel the Operator (1939) (Y)
Mother Night (1996)
Mothers of Today (Hayntike Mames) (1939) (Y)
The Murder of Mary Phagan (1987)
The Murderers Among Us (1989)
Music Box (1989)
My Favorite Year (1982)
My Knees Were Jumping: Remembering The Kinder Transport (1996)
My Michael (1975) (H)
My Mother's Courage (1996) (G)

N

Nadia (1987) (H)
The Nasty Girl (1989) (G)
Neighbors (1938) (Y)
Never Forget (1991)
Newland (1994) (H)
Next Stop, Greenwich Village (1976)

The Nightmare Years (1989)
Noa at Seventeen (1982) (H)
Not Like Sheep to the Slaughter: The Story of the Bialystock Ghetto (1990) (H)
Not in This Town (1997)
Not Quite Paradise (1986)

O

The Odessa File (1974)
Oliver (1968)
On My Way To Father's Land (1995) (H)
Once Upon a Time in America (1984)
One of Us (1989) (H)
The Only Way (1970)
Operation Thunderbolt (1977)
The Oppermanns (1982) (G)
The Outside Chance of Maximilian Glick (1988)
Over the Brooklyn Bridge (1984)
Over the Ocean (1992) (H)
Overture to Glory (1940) (Y)

P

The Partisans of Vilna (1986)
Passover Fever (1995) (H)
The Passover Plot (1975)
The Pawnbroker (1965)
Pi (1998)
Playing for Time (1980)
The Plot Against Harry (1989)
Portnoy's Complaint (1972)
Power (1934)
A Prayer for Katarina Hurovitzova (1969) (CZ)
A Price Above Rubies (1998)
Prince of Egypt (1998)
Prisoner in the Middle (1974)
Prisoner of Honor (1991)
Private Benjamin (1980)

The Producers (1968)
The Proprietor (1996)
Der Purimshpiler (1937) (Y)

Q

QB VII (1974)
The Quarrel (1992)

R

Radio Days (1987)
Raid on Entebbe (1977)
Remembrance of Love (1982)
Rescuers: Stories of Courage: Two Couples (1998)
Rescuers: Stories of Courage: Two Families (1998)
Rescuers: Stories of Courage: Two Women (1997)
Reunion (1988)
The Revolt of Job (1983) (HU)
Rhapsody in Blue (1945)
Romance of a Horsethief (1971)
Romantic Stories (1992)
Rosa Luxemburg (1986) (G)
The Rose Garden (1989)
Rosebud (1974)
Routes of Exile: Moroccan Jewish Odessy (1982)

S

Safe Men (1998)
Saint Clara (1996) (H)
Sallah (1965) (H)
Sam & Me (1991)
Samson and Delilah (1949)
Samson and Delilah (1996)
Save the Tiger (1973)
Scandal in a Small Town (1988)
Schindler's List (1993)
School Ties (1992)
Secret of Yolanda (1982)

A Secret Space (1988)
Secret Weapon (1990)
The Serpent's Egg (1978)
The 17th Bride (1984)
The Seventh Coin (1992)
Shine (1996)
Ship of Fools (1965)
Shoah (1985)
The Shop on Main Street (1965) (CZ)
Shtetl (1996)
Siege (1970) (H)
Sinai Commandos (1968)
The Singing Blacksmith (1938) (Y)
Skokie (1981)
Slingshot (1993) (SWE)
Slums of Beverly Hills (1998)
Sofie (1992) (DAN)
Soldier of the Night (1984)
Solomon and Sheba (1959)
Song of the Siren (1994) (H)
Sophie's Choice (1982)
The Sorrow and the Pity (1970) (F)
The State of Israel (1998)
Steal the Sky (1988)
The Story of Ruth (1960)
The Stranger (1946)
A Stranger Among Us (1992)
Streets of Gold (1986)
The Substance of Fire (1996)
The Summer of Aviya (1988) (H)
The Summer of La Goulette (1996) (F) (I) (A)
Summer of My German Soldier (1978)
Sweet Light in a Dark Room (1960) (CZ)
Sweet Lorraine (1987)
Swoon (1991)
Sword of Gideon (1986)

T

Table Settings (1984)

Take Two (1985)

The Tango Lesson (1998)

Taxi Blues (1990) (R)

Tell Me a Riddle (1980)

Tell Me That You Love Me (1984)

The Ten Commandments (1956)

Tevye (1939) (Y)

They Were Ten (1961) (H)

'38: Vienna Before the Fall (1988) (G)

Thoroughly Modern Millie (1967)

Three Days and a Child (1967) (H)

Three Days in April (1995) (G)

Ticket to Heaven (1981)

A Tickle in the Heart (1996)

To Be or Not to Be (1942)

To Be or Not to Be (1983)

To See Paris and Die (1993) (R)

To Speak The Unspeakable: The Message of Elie Wiesel (1996) (Hu) (Ru)

Tobruk (1967)

Torch Song Trilogy (1988)

Torn Apart (1989)

Transport From Paradise (1965) (CZ)

The Trial of Adolph Eichmann (1997)

The Triangle Factory Fire Scandal (1979)

Triumph of the Spirit (1989)

The Truce (1997)

True Confections (1991)

21 Hours at Munich (1976)

Twilight of the Golds (1996)

The Two of Us (1968) (F)

Two Sisters (1938) (Y)

2000 Years of Freedom and Honor: The Cochin Jews of India (1992)

Tzanafi Family (1976) (H)

U

Uncle Moses (1932) (Y)
Under the Domim Tree (1995) (H)
Under the World (1987) (SP)
Underdogs: A Sports (War) Movie (1996) (H)
Undzere Kinder (1948) (Y)
Unsettled Land (1988)
Unstrung Heroes (1995)
Up Your Anchor (1985) (H)
Used People (1992)

V

Victory at Entebbe (1976)
The Visas That Saved Lives (1992) (JAP)
The Vow (1937) (Y)
Voyage of Terror: The Achille Lauro Affair (1990)
Voyage of the Damned (1976)

W

The Wall (1982)
A Wall in Jerusalem (1970)
The Wandering Jew (1920) (Silent)
The Wannsee Conference (1984) (G)
War and Love (1984)
War and Remembrance (1988)
Warszawa (1993) (P)
The Way We Were (1973)
Weapons of the Spirit (1990) (F)
Welcome to the Dollhouse (1996)
When Every Day Is the Fourth of July (1978)
Where Is My Child? (1937) (Y)
The White Rose (1983) (G)
Willie & Phil (1980)
The Winds of War (1983)
A Woman at War (1994)
A Woman Called Golda (1982)

The Wooden Gun (1979) (H)
The Wordmaker (1991) (H)
The World of Sholom Aleichem (1959)

Y

Yentl (1983)
Yiddishe Mama (1939) (Y)
Yidl Mitn Fidl (1936) (Y)
The Young Lions (1958)

Z

Zalman; or, The Madness of God (1975)
Zebrahead (1992)

FILMS

ACTORS

ALPHABETICAL

CHRONOLOGICAL

DIRECTORS

GENRES

LANGUAGES

DISTRIBUTORS

Chronological Listing of Films

1920
The Golem (Silent)
The Wandering Jew (Silent)

1922
Hungry Hearts (Silent)

1923
East and West (Silent)

1925
His People (Silent)
Jewish Luck (Silent)

1927
The Jazz Singer (1927)

1928
Laughter Through Tears (Silent)

1931
His Wife's Lover (Y)

1932
Uncle Moses (Y)

1934
Power

1935
Le Golem: The Legend of Prague (F)

1936
Yidl Mitn Fidl (1936) (Y)

1937
The Cantor's Son (Y)
The Dybbuk (Y)
Green Fields (Y)
The Jolly Paupers (Y)
Der Purimshpiler (Y)
The Vow (Y)
Where Is My Child? (Y)

1938
A Brivele der Mamen (Y)
Mamele (Y)
Neighbors (Y)
The Singing Blacksmith (Y)
Two Sisters (Y)

1939
The Light Ahead (Y)
The Living Orphan (Y)
Mirele Efros (Y)
Motel the Operator (Y)
Mothers of Today (Hayntike Mames) (Y)
Tevye (Y)
Yiddishe Mama (Y)

1940
American Matchmaker (Y)
Eli Eli (Y)
The Great Dictator
Jud Suess (G)
Overture to Glory (Y)

1942
To Be or Not to Be

1944
Mr. Emmanuel

1945
Rhapsody in Blue

1946
The Jolson Story
The Stranger

1947
Crossfire
Gentleman's Agreement
The Illegals

1948
The Blum Affair (G)
Border Street (P)
Long Is the Road (Y) (G) (P)
Undzere Kinder (Y)

1949
Catskill Honeymoon (Y)
God, Man and Devil (Y)
Jolson Sings Again
Samson and Delilah

1951
David and Bathsheba

1952
Ivanhoe
The Jazz Singer

1953
The Eddie Cantor Story

1954
A Generation (P)

1955
The Benny Goodman Story
Hill 24 Doesn't Answer

1956
The Ten Commandments

1958
Marjorie Morningstar
Me and the Colonel
The Young Lions

1959
Compulsion
The Diary of Anne Frank
Kapo
The Last Angry Man
Solomon and Sheba
The World of Sholom Aleichem

1960
Blazing Sand
Conspiracy of Hearts
Esther and the King
Exodus
Story of Ruth
Sweet Light in a Dark Room (CZ)

1961
Judgment at Nuremberg
A Majority of One
They Were Ten (H)

1963

The Boxer and Death (CZ)

1964

Diamonds of the Night (CZ)

1965

The Pawnbroker
Sallah (H)
Ship of Fools
The Shop on Main Street (CZ)
Transport from Paradise (CZ)

1966

Cast a Giant Shadow
Cold Days (HU)
Judith (Conflict)

1967

Dita Saxova (CZ)
Thoroughly Modern Millie
Three Days and a Child (H)
Tobruk

1968

Ben Gurion: An Appointment With Destiny
Commissar (R)
The Fixer
Funny Girl
I Love You, Alice B. Toklas
Oliver
The Producers
Sinai Commandos
The Two of Us (F)

1969

The Damned
Goodbye, Columbus
The Hero
Justine
Marry Me, Marry Me (F)
Prayer for Katarina Hurovitzova (CZ)

1970

Lupo (H)
The Only Way
Siege (H)
The Sorrow and the Pity (F)
A Wall in Jerusalem

1971

Fiddler on the Roof
The Garden of the Finzi-Continis (I)
Romance of a Horsethief

1972

Cabaret
Diamonds
Escape to the Sun
The Heartbreak Kid
I Love You, Rosa (H)
Portnoy's Complaint

1973

The House on Chelouche Street (H)
Save the Tiger
The Way We Were

1974

The Apprenticeship of Duddy Kravitz
Blazing Saddles
But Where Is Daniel Wax? (H)
Eagles Attack at Dawn
The Eighty-first Blow (Y) (H)

Funny Lady
Hester Street (Y)
Jacob The Liar (G)
Kazablan (H)
Lepke
Les Violons du Bal (F)
The Odessa File
Prisoner in the Middle
QB VII
Rosebud

1975

Children of Rage
Festival at the Poolroom (H)
Lies My Father Told Me
Moses
My Michael (H)
The Passover Plot
Zalman; or, The Madness of God

1976

The Front
Marathon Man
Next Stop, Greenwich Village
21 Hours at Munich
Tzanafi Family (H)
Victory at Entebbe
Voyage of the Damned

1977

Annie Hall
Black Sunday
Hershaleh (H)
Julia
Kuni Lemel in Tel Aviv (H)
Madame Rosa (F)
Mr. Klein (F)
Operation Thunderbolt
Raid on Entebbe

1978

Actor: The Paul Muni Story
The Boys from Brazil
Holocaust
The Serpent's Egg
Summer of My German Soldier
When Every Day Is the Fourth of July

1979

Best Boy
David
The Frisco Kid
The House on Garibaldi Street
Hunted (G)
Madman
The Magician of Lublin
The Triangle Factory Fire Scandal
The Wooden Gun (H)

1980

Brussels Transit (Y)
Charlie Grant's War
Hide and Seek (H)
The Jazz Singer
The Last Metro (F)
The Last Sea (Y) (H)
Long Days of Summer
Playing for Time
Private Benjamin
Tell Me a Riddle
Willie & Phil

1981

American Pop

The Boat Is Full (G)
Chariots of Fire
The Chosen
Eyewitness
Heavy Metal
History of the World, Part I
Intimate Story (H)
Masada
Skokie
Ticket to Heaven

1982
Drifting (H)
Inside the Third Reich
King for a Day (H)
My Favorite Year
Noa at Seventeen (H)
The Oppermanns (G)
Remembrance of Love
Routes of Exile: Moroccan Jewish Odyssey
Secret of Yolanda
The Wall
A Woman Called Golda

1983
Boy Takes Girl (H)
Dead End Street (H)
Finals (H)
Hamsin (H)
Hanna K.
King of Comedy
Kuni Lemel in Cairo (H)
Mr. Halpern & Mr. Johnson
The Revolt of Job (HU)
To Be or Not to Be
The White Rose (G)
The Winds of War
Yentl

1984
Almonds and Raisins
The Ambassador
The Assisi Underground
Atalia (H)
Dangerous Moves
Forbidden
The Glory Boys
Goodbye New York
The Last Winter
The Little Drummer Girl
Once Upon a Time in America
Over the Brooklyn Bridge
The 17th Bride
Soldier of the Night
Table Settings
Tell Me That You Love Me
The Wannsee Conference (G)
War and Love

1985
Angry Harvest (G)
Beyond the Walls
Dark Lullabies
The Dunera Boys
The Execution
The Inheritors (G)
Joshua Then and Now
King David
Shoah
Take Two
Up Your Anchor (H)

1986

About The Jews of Yemen: A Vanishing Culture

An American Tail

Angel of Death

Brighton Beach Memoirs

Every Time We Say Goodbye

Flames in the Ashes (Y) (H)

Greta (P)

Hannah and Her Sisters

Miracle at Moreaux

Not Quite Paradise

The Partisans of Vilna

Rosa Luxemburg (G)

Streets of Gold

Sword of Gideon

1987

Au Revoir les Enfants (F)

Bachelor Girl

Blood Money: Nazi Gold

Dirty Dancing

Escape from Sobibor

Gaby: A True Story

Hotel Terminus (F)

The Impossible Spy

Late Summer Blues (H)

The Murder of Mary Phagan

Nadia (H)

Radio Days

Sophie's Choice

Sweet Lorraine

Under the World (SP)

1988

The Attic

Austeria (P)

Beaches

Because of that War (H)

Biloxi Blues

Crossing Delancey

Fictitious Marriage (H)

Friendship in Vienna

Hannah's War

I Don't Give a Damn (H)

Iron Eagle 2

A Jumpin' Night in the Garden of Eden

The Last Seven Months of Anne Frank

Loan Me Your Wife (H)

The Outside Chance of Maximilian Glick

Reunion

Scandal in a Small Town

A Secret Space

Steal the Sky

The Summer of Aviya (H)

38: Vienna Before the Fall (G)

Torch Song Trilogy

Unsettled Land

War and Remembrance

1989

Architecture of Doom (SWE)

Brotherhood of the Rose

Crossfire (H)

Driving Miss Daisy

Echoes of Conflict (H)

Enemies: A Love Story

Green Fields (H)

Murderers Among Us

Music Box

The Nasty Girl (G)

The Nightmare Years

One of Us (H)

The Plot Against Harry

The Rose Garden
Torn Apart
Triumph of the Spirit

1990

Avalon
Crimes and Misdemeanors
Descending Angel
End of Innocence
Falling Over Backwards
Fate
Father
Flames of Revolt: The Irgun (H)
Forced March
The Imported Bridegroom
Korczak (P)
Ladies' Tailor (R)
The Last Butterfly
Laura Adler's Last Love Affair (Y) (H)
The Lover
Max and Helen
Not Like Sheep To The Slaughter: The Story of The Bialystock Ghetto (H)
Secret Weapon
Taxi Blues (R)
Voyage of Terror: The Achille Lauro Affair
Weapons of the Spirit (F)

1991

Adam's Rib (R)
Antonia and Jane
Born in Berlin (H) (G) (SWE)
Deadly Currents
Double Edge
Europa, Europa (G) (R)
Freud Leaving Home (SWE)
Homicide
The Longest Hatred
Luna Park (R)
Never Forget
Prisoner of Honor
Sam & Me
Swoon
True Confections
The Wordmaker (H)

1992

Alan & Naomi
Broadway Bound
Cup Final (H)
A Day in October
Day of Atonement
Good Evening, Mr. Wallenberg (SWE)(G)(HU)
Hit the Dutchman
I Don't Buy Kisses Anymore
Israel: A Nation is Born
Leon the Pig Farmer
Miss Rose White
Mr. Saturday Night
Over the Ocean (H)
The Quarrel
Romantic Stories
School Ties
The Seventh Coin
Sofie (DAN)
A Stranger Among Us
Two Thousand Years of Freedom and Honor: The Cochin Jews of India
Used People
The Visas that Saved Lives (JAP)
Zebrahead

1993

Amongst Friends

Blind Man's Bluff (H)

Cafe au Lait (F)

Cemetery Club

Family Prayers

The Heritage (H)

Ivan and Abraham (Y)

Jonah Who Lived in the Whale

Lost in Yonkers

Schindler's List

Slingshot (SWE)

To See Paris and Die (R)

Warszawa (P)

1994

A la Mode (F)

Abraham

Chronicle of the Uprising In The Warsaw Ghetto According to Marek Edelman (P)

The Doomsday Gun

Genghis Cohn

The Infiltrator

Jacob

Les Patriotes (F)

Little Odessa

Mina Tenanbaum (F)

Newland (H)

Song of the Siren (H)

A Woman at War

1995

Anne Frank Remembered

Auditions (H)

Family of Cops

Hate (F)

The Jew (POR)

Joseph

The Last Klezmer

Les Misérables (F)

Mindbender

On My Way to Father's Land (H)

Passover Fever (H)

Three Days in April (G)

Under the Domim Tree (H)

Unstrung Heroes

1996

The Birdcage

Broken Glass

Carpati (R) (Y)

Getting Away with Murder

Independence Day

Infinity

The Man Who Captured Eichmann

Moses

Mother Night

My Knees Were Jumping: Remembering the Kindertransports

My Mother's Courage

The Proprietor

Saint Clara (H)

Samson and Delilah

Shine

Shtetl

Substance of Fire

Summer of La Goulette (A) (F) (I)

A Tickle in the Heart

To Speak the Unspeakable: The Message of Elie Wiesel (HU) (RU)

Twilight of the Golds

Underdogs: A Sports (War) Movie (H)

Welcome to the Dollhouse

1997

Aaron's Magic Village

The Assignment
A Call To Remember
Family of Cops II: Breach of Faith
Hollywoodism: Jews, Movies and the American Dream
I Love You, I Love You Not
I'm Not Rappaport
In the Presence of Mine Enemies
Invanhoe
Life Is Beautiful (I)
✓The Long Way Home
Mendel (N)
Not In This Town
Rescuers: Stories of Courage: Two Women
The Tango Lesson
Trial of Adolph Eichmann
The Truce

1998

The Governess
I Love You...Don't Touch Me
✓Miracle at Midnight
Pi
A Price Above Rubies
Prince of Egypt
Rescuers: Stories of Courage: Two Couples
Rescuers: Stories of Courage: Two Families
Safe Men
Slums of Beverly Hills
The State of Israel

ACTORS

ALPHABETICAL

CHRONOLOGICAL

DIRECTORS

GENRES

LANGUAGES

DISTRIBUTORS

JUDITH ABARBANEL:	The Cantor's Son (1937);
	American Matchmaker (1940)
YAEL ABECASSIS:	Romantic Story (1992)
	The Heritage (1993)
F. MURRAY ABRAHAM:	Madman (1979)
ALON ABUTBUL:	One of Us (1989)
	The Heritage (1993)
JIRI ADAMIRA:	A Prayer for Katarina Hurovitzova (1969)
MAUD ADAMS:	Playing for Time (1980)
SHULAMIT ADAR:	Laura Adler's Last Love Affair (1990)
CELIA ADLER:	Where is My Child? (1937)
JULIUS ADLER:	Catskill Honeymoon (1949)
LUTHER ADLER:	The Last Angry Man (1959)
	Cast A Giant Shadow (1966)
	Voyage of the Damned (1976)
MUSTAPHA ADOUANI:	Summer of La Goulette (1996)
DANNY AIELLO:	The Front (1976)
	Once Upon a Time in America (1984)
	Radio Days (1987)
	Cemetery Club (1993)
ANOUK AIMEE:	Justine (1969)
EDDIE ALBERT:	The Heartbreak Kid (1972)
JACK ALBERTSON:	Justine (1969)
CHAVA ALBERSTEIN:	Intimate Story (1981)
ALAN ALDA:	Crimes and Misdemeanors (1990)
ROBERT ALDA:	Rhapsody in Blue (1945)
JANE ALEXANDER:	Playing for Time (1980)
	Friendship in Vienna (1988)
	I Don't Buy Kisses Anymore (1992)
SHARON ALEXANDER:	One of Us (1989)
ROMA ALEXANDROVITCH:	Ivan and Abraham (1993)
KAREN ALLEN:	Secret Weapon (1990)
NANCY ALLEN:	Les Patriotes (1994)
STEVE ALLEN:	The Benny Goodman Story (1955)
WOODY ALLEN:	The Front (1976)
	Annie Hall (1977)
	Hannah and Her Sisters (1986)
	Crimes and Misdemeanors (1990)
GILA ALMAGOR:	Sallah (1965)
	Siege (1970)
	The House on Chelouche Street (1973)

	Hide and Seek (1980)
	Every Time We Say Goodbye (1986)
	The Summer of Aviya (1988)
	The Rose Garden (1989)
	Under the Domim Tree (1995)
	Passover Fever (1995)
URI ALTER:	Over The Ocean (1992)
TRINI ALVARADO:	Sweet Lorraine (1987)
GABI AMRANI:	Tzanafi Family (1976)
	King For a Day (1982)
HERBERT ANDERSON:	The Benny Goodman Story (1955)
JUDITH ANDERSON:	The Ten Commandments (1956)
ANTHONY ANDREWS:	Hanna's War (1988)
HARRY ANDREWS:	The Passover Plot (1975)
JULIE ANDREWS:	Thoroughly Modern Millie (1967)
SUSAN ANDREWS:	Angel of Death (1986)
BARRY ANGEL:	The 17th Bride (1984)
JEAN HUGHES ANGLADE:	Jonah Who Lived in the Whale (1993)
CHRISTIAN ANHOLT:	Reunion (1988)
ETTI ANKRI:	Newland (1994)
AMY AQUINO:	Allan & Naomi (1992)
ALEXANDRE ARBATT:	Dangerous Moves (1984)
ANNE ARCHER:	Family Prayers (1993)
ADAM ARKIN:	Not In This Town (1997)
ALAN ARKIN:	The Magician of Lublin (1979)
	Joshua Then and Now (1985)
	Escape From Sobibor (1987)
	The Doomsday Gun (1994)
	Mother Night (1996)
	Slums of Beverly Hills (1998)
GABI ARMENI:	Lupo (1970)
LUCI ARNAZ:	The Jazz Singer (1980)
ADELHEID ARNDT:	Rosa Luxemburg (1986)
PATRICIA ARQUETTE:	Infinity (1996)
ROSANNA ARQUETTE:	The Wall (1982)
AYALA ASHEROV:	Auditions (1995)
ELIZABETH ASHLEY:	Ship of Fools (1965)
EDWARD ASNER:	Friendship in Vienna (1988)
ARMAND ASSANTE:	Private Benjamin (1980)
YVAN ATTAL:	Les Patriotes (1994)
RICHARD ATTENBOROUGH:	Rosebus (1974)

ANAT ATZMAN:	Dead End Street (1983)
	Every Time We Say Goodbye (1986)
TALI ATZMON:	Auditions (1995)
JULIET AUBREY:	Jonah Who Lived in the Whale (1993)
JEAN-PIERRE AUMONT:	The Proprietor (1996)
MILI AVITAL:	Over The Ocean (1992)
AKI AVNI:	Auditions (1995)
DAN AYCKROYD:	Driving Miss Daisy (1989)
	Getting Away with Murder (1996)
FELIX AYLMER:	Mr. Emmanuel (1944)
HANK AZARIA:	The Birdcage (1996)
HANA AZULAI-HASFARY:	Nadia (1987)
JENNIFER BABTIST:	Goodbye New York (1984)
ED BAGLEY JR:	Not In This Town (1997)
DIANE BAKER:	The Diary of Anne Frank (1959)
KATHY BAKER:	Not In This Town (1997)
LENNY BAKER:	Next Stop Greenwich Village (1976)
MOHAMMED BAKRI:	Hanna K. (1983)
	Beyond the Walls (1985)
	Double Edge (1991)
	Cup Final (1992)
DANIEL BALDWIN:	Family of Cops (1995)
FAIRUZA BALK:	The Outside Chance of Maximilian Glick (1988)
KAYE BALLARD:	Fate (1990)
MARTIN BALSAM:	Marjorie Morningstar (1958)
	Raid on Entebbe (1977)
	The House on Garibaldi Street (1979)
CHAIM BANAI:	Tzanafi Family (1976)
MEIR BANAI:	Nadia (1987)
YOSSI BANAI:	Les Patriotes (1994)
YUVAL BANAI:	Nadia (1987)
ANNE BANCROFT:	To Be or Not To Be (1983)
	Torch Song Trilogy (1988)
	Broadway Bound (1992)
SCHLOMO BAR-ABA:	Fictitious Marriage (1988)
ALEX BARDNINI:	Long Is The Road (1948)
YEHUDA (YUDA) BARKAN:	Lupo (1970)
	Festival at the Pool Room (1975)
	Fate (1990)
BARBARA BARRIE:	Summer of my German Soldier (1978)
	Private Benjamin (1980);

	The Execution (1985)
JAN BART:	Catskill Honeymoon (1949)
RICHARD BASEHART:	21 Hours at Munich (1976)
MICHAL BAT-ADAM:	I Love You Rosa (1972)
	The House on Chelouche Street (1973)
	Atalia (1984)
ALAN BATES:	The Fixer (1968)
KATHY BATES:	Used People (1992)
RANDALL BATINKOFF:	School Ties (1992)
STEVEN BAUER:	Sword of Gideon (1986)
MONIKA BAUMGARTNER:	The Nasty Girl (1989)
ANNE BAXTER:	The Ten Commandments (1956)
JENNIFER BEALS:	Day of Atonement (1992)
	Twilight of the Golds (1996)
NED BEATTY:	A Woman Called Golda (1982)
MICHAEL BECK:	Madman (1979)
HARTMUT BECKER:	Escape From Sobibor (1987)
ISRAEL BECKER:	Long Is The Road (1948)
KLAUS BECKER:	The Blum Affair (1948)
FRIEDRICH BECKHAUS:	The Wannsee Conference (1984)
RALPH BELLAMY:	The Winds of War (1983)
	War and Remembrance (1988)
MONICA BELLUCCI:	Joseph (1995)
JEAN-PAUL BELMONDO:	Les Miserables (1995)
DAHN BEN AMOTZ:	Siege (1970)
ROBERTO BENIGNI:	Life Is Beautiful (1997)
RICHARD BENJAMIN:	Goodbye Columbus (1969)
	Portnoy's Complaint (1972)
HEINZ BENNENT:	The Last Metro (1980)
JACK BENNY:	To Be or Not To Be (1942)
ROBBY BENSON:	The Chosen (1982)
DANIEL BENZALI:	A Day in October (1992)
MARISA BERENSON:	Cabaret (1972)
	Playing for Time (1980)
GERTRUDE BERG:	The World of Sholom Aleichem (1959)
POLLY BERGEN:	The Winds of War (1983)
	War and Remembrance (1988)
GUSTAV BERGER:	The Living Orphan (1939)
	God Man and Devil (1949)
HELMUT BERGER:	The Damned (1969)
	The Garden of the Finzi-Continis (1971)
	Victory at Entebbe (1976)

SENTA BERGER:	Cast A Giant Shadow (1966)
INGRID BERGMAN:	A Woman Called Golda (1982)
MILTON BERLE:	Lepke (1974)
JEANNIE BERLIN:	The Heartbreak Kid (1972)
	Portnoy's Complaint (1972)
WARREN BERLINGER:	Lepke (1974)
HERSCHEL BERNARDI:	Green Fields (1937)
	The Front (1976)
	Actor (1978)
SANDRA BERNHARD:	King of Comedy (1983)
CLAUDE BERRI:	Marry Me Marry Me (1969)
RICHARD BERRY:	Day of Atonement (1992)
HELEN BEVERLY:	Green Fields (1937)
	The Light Ahead (1939)
	Overture To Glory (1940)
RICHARD BEYMER:	The Diary of Anne Frank (1959)
MAYIM BIALIK:	Beaches (1988)
PAUL BILDT:	The Blum Affair (1948)
JANE BIRKIN:	Romance of a Horsethief (1971)
LEN BIRMAN:	Lies My Father Told Me (1975)
ILSE BISHOFOVA:	Diamonds of the Night (1964)
JACQUELINE BISSET:	Forbidden (1984)
KAREN BLACK:	Portnoy's Complaint (1972)
LINDA BLAIR:	Victory at Entebbe (1976)
JULIA BLAKE:	Father (1990)
HANS-CHRISTIAN BLECH:	The Blum Affair (1948)
RIKI BLICH:	Under the Domim Tree (1995)
BRIAN BLOOM:	Voyage of Terror (1990)
CLAIRE BLOOM:	Crimes and Misdemeanors (1990)
HART BOCHNER:	War and Remembrance (1988)
GERD BOCKMANN:	The Wannsee Conference (1984)
EUGENE BODO:	Neighbors (1938)
DIRK BOGARDE:	The Fixer (1968)
	The Damned (1969)
	Justine (1969)
LEENA BOGDANOVA:	Adam's Rib (1991)
ERIC BOGOSIAN:	The Substance of Fire (1996)
ROMANE BOHRINGER:	Mina Tenanbaum (1994)
CURT BOIS:	The Boat is Full (1980)
JOSEPH BOLOGNA:	My Favorite Year (1982)
CONNIE BOOTH:	Leon the Pig Farmer (1992)

PETER BORETSKI:	Sam & Me (1991)
OLEG BORISOV:	Luna Park (1991)
EVA BOROWIK:	Greta (1986)
TOM BOSLEY:	The Triangle Factory Fire Scandal (1979)
BARRY BOSTWICK:	War and Remembrance (1988)
JOSEPH BOTTOMS:	Holocaust (1978)
MICHEL BOUJENAH:	Les Miserables (1995)
EDIE BOWZ:	Hit the Dutchman (1992)
LARA FLYNN BOYLE:	Jacob (1994)
MAX BOZYK:	Yidl Mitn Fidl (1936)
	The Dybbuk (1937)
	The Jolly Paupers (1937)
	The Vow (1937);
	Mamele (1938)
	Catskill Honeymoon (1949)
ROSE BOZYK:	Catskill Honeymoon (1949)
KLAUS MARIA BRANDAUER:	Streets of Gold (1986)
MARLON BRANDO:	The Young Lions (1958)
NICOLETTA BRASCHI:	Life Is Beautiful (1997)
KEEFE BRASSELLE:	The Eddie Cantor Story (1953)
EILEEN BRENNAN:	Private Benjamin (1980)
	I Don't Buy Kisses Anymore (1992)
NICK BRIMBLE:	Ivanhoe (1997)
MAI BRITT:	The Young Lions (1958)
MATTHEW BRODERICK:	Biloxi Blues (1988)
	Torch Song Trilogy (1988)
	Infinity (1996)
VLASTIMIL BRODSKY:	Jacob the Liar (1974)
M. BRONIEWSKI:	Border Street (1948)
CHARLES BRONSON:	Raid on Entebbe (1977)
	Family of Cops (1995)
	Family of Cops II: Breach of Faith (1997)
ALBERT BROOKS:	Private Benjamin (1980)
JOEL BROOKS:	The Man Who Captured Eichmann (1996)
MEL BROOKS:	Blazine Saddles (1974)
	History of the World Part 1 (1981)
	To Be or Not To Be (1983)
	Prince of Egypt (1998)
GEORGIA BROWN:	The Fixer (1968)
	Actor (1978)
PETER BROWN:	Eagles Attack at Dawn (1974)

BIRKE BRUCK: Three Days in April (1995)

YUL BRYNNER: The Ten Commandments (1956)
Solomon and Sheba (1959)
Cast A Giant Shadow (1966)
Romance of a Horsethief (1971)

HORST BUCHHOLZ: Raid on Entebbe (1977)
Life Is Beautiful (1997)

ANIA BUKSTEIN: Newland (1994)

SANDRA BULLOCK: Prince of Egypt (1998)

KIM BURFIELD: The Hero (1969)

ELLEN BURSTYN: The Ambassador (1984)
Hanna's War (1988)
Cemetery Club (1993)

MIKE BURSTYN (BURSTEIN): Hershaleh (1977)
Kuni Lemel in Tel Aviv (1977)
Kuni Lemel in Cairo (1983)

SERGIO BUSTRIC: Life Is Beautiful (1997)

PAUL BUTLER: Zebrahead (1992)

ROLAN BYKOV: Commissar (1968)

GABRIEL BYRNE: Hanna K. (1983)

JAMES CAAN: Funny Lady (1974)

SID CAESAR: Over the Brooklyn Bridge (1984)

MICHAEL CAINE: Hannah and Her Sisters (1986)

MICHAEL CALLAN: Lepke (1974)

GODFREY CAMBRIDGE: The Last Angry Man (1959)

CHERYL CAMPBELL: Chariots of Fire (1981)

DOUGLAS CAMPBELL: Charlie Grant's War (1980)

JOHN CANDY: Heavy Metal (1981)

DYAN CANNON: The End of Innocence (1990)

GIORGIO CANTARINI: Life Is Beautiful (1997)

ROGER CAREL: The Two of Us (1968)

LETICIA CARO: The Revolt of Job (1983)

LESLIE CARON: QB VII (1974)
Dangerous Moves (1984)

DAVID CARRADINE: The Serpent's Egg (1978)

JOHN CARRADINE: The Ten Commandments (1956)

BARBARA CARRERA: Masada (1981)

NELL CARTER: The Proprietor (1996)

ISADORE CASHIER: His Wife's Lover (1931)
The Light Ahead (1939)

VINCENT CASSEL:	Hate (1995)
DE SHONN CASTLE:	Zebrahead (1992)
KIM CATTRALL:	Rosebud (1974)
	Ticket to Heaven (1981)
JENIYA CATZAN:	Under the Domim Tree (1995)
CHRISTOPHER CAZENOVE:	The Proprietor (1996)
TECO CELIO:	The Truce (1997)
CAROL CHANNING:	Thoroughly Modern Millie (1967)
STOCKARD CHANNING:	Table Settings (1984)
CHARLES CHAPLIN:	The Great Dictator (1940)
JOSEPHINE CHAPLIN:	Escape to the Sun (1972)
IAN CHARLESON:	Chariots of Fire (1981)
MAURY CHAYKIN:	Iron Eagle 2 (1988)
	Unstrung Heroes (1995)
CRAIG CHESTER:	Swoon (1991)
RANJIT CHOWDHRY:	Sam & Me (1991)
NAVIN CHOWDRY:	The Seventh Coin (1992)
ROBERT CLARY:	Remembrance of Love (1982)
JILL CLAYBURGH:	Portnoy's Complaint (1972)
	Hanna K. (1983)
	Day of Atonement (1992)
MONTGOMERY CLIFT:	The Young Lions (1958)
	Judgment at Nuremberg (1961)
LEE J. COBB:	Exodus (1960)
CHARLES COBURN:	Rhapsody in Blue (1945)
GEORGE COE:	The End of Innocence (1990)
ALAIN COHEN:	The Two of Us (1968)
ELI COHEN:	The Summer of Aviya (1988)
KAIPO COHEN:	The Summer of Aviya (1988)
	Under the Domim Tree (1995)
DABNEY COLEMAN:	Never Forget (1991)
JOAN COLLINS:	Esther and the King (1960)
PAULINE COLLINS:	My Mother's Courage (1996)
LUISA COLPEYN:	Marry Me Marry Me (1969)
BOBBY COLT:	Catskill Honeymoon (1949)
ANJANETTE COMER:	Lepke (1974)
MICHAEL CONSTANTINE:	Justine (1969)
	Summer of my German Soldier (1978)
TOM CONTI:	The Wall (1982)
TOM COURTENAY:	The Last Butterfly (1990)
GRETA COWAN:	The Imported Bridegroom (1990)

RONNY COX:	Scandal in a Small Town (1988)
PETER COYOTE:	Tell Me a Riddle (1980)
NORMA CRANE:	Fiddler on the Roof (1971)
HUME CRONYN:	Broadway Bound (1992)
BEN CROSS:	Chariots of Fire (1981)
	The Assisi Underground (1984)
	Steal the Sky (1988)
BILLY CRYSTAL:	Mr. Saturday Night (1992)
ROBERT CULP:	Voyage of Terror (1990)
TONY CURTIS:	Lepke (1974)
CYRIL CUSACK:	Children of Rage (1975)
ZBIGNIEW CYBULSKI:	A Generation (1954)
WILLEM DAFOE:	Triumph of the Spirit (1989)
PAUL DAHLKE:	Long Is The Road (1948)
JENNIFER DALE:	Ticket to Heaven (1981)
EWA DALKOWSSKA:	Korczak (1990)
ISRAEL DAMIDOV:	Saint Clara (1996)
MATT DAMON:	School Ties (1992)
CHARLES DANCE:	In the Presence of Mine Enemies (1997)
CLAIRE DANES:	I Love You, I Love You Not (1997)
BLYTHE DANNER:	Inside the Third Reich (1982)
	Brighton Beach Memoirs (1986)
	Never Forget (1991)
	A Call To Remember (1997)
SYBIL DANNING:	Operation Thunderbolt (1977)
RAMI DANON:	Newland (1994)
RAY DANTON:	A Majority of One (1961)
FLORENCE DAREL:	A La Mode (1994)
GERARD DARMON:	Day of Atonement (1992)
CLAUDE DAUPHIN:	Madame Rosa (1977)
NIGEL DAVENPORT:	Chariots of Fire (1981)
EMBETH DAVIDTZ:	Schindler's List (1993)
JUDY DAVIS:	A Woman Called Golda (1982)
OSSIE DAVIS:	I'm Not Rappaport (1997)
BRUCE DAVISON:	Summer of my German Soldier (1978)
PAM DAWBER:	Remembrance of Love (1982)
ASSAF DAYAN:	Operation Thunderbolt (1977)
	Beyond the Walls (1985)
ROSEMARY DECAMP:	Rhapsody in Blue (1945)
YVONNE DE CARLO:	The Ten Commandments (1956)

DANA DELANY:	Rescuers: Stories of Courage: Two Couples (1998)
ALAIN DELON:	Mr. Klein (1977)
JULIE DELPY:	Europa Europa (1991)
	Warszawa (1993)
DOM DELUISE:	Blazing Saddles (1974)
	History of the World Part 1 (1981)
	An American Tail (1986)
WILLIAM DEMAREST:	The Jazz Singer (1927)
	The Jolson Story (1946)
	Jolson Sings Again (1949)
CATHERINE DENEUVE:	The Last Metro (1980)
ROBERT DENIRO:	King of Comedy (1983)
	Once Upon a Time in America (1984)
BRIAN DENNEHY:	Skokie (1981)
SANDY DENNIS:	The Execution (1985)
CHRISTA DENTON:	Scandal in a Small Town (1988)
GERARD DEPARDIEU:	The Last Metro (1980)
JOHN DEREK:	The Ten Commandments (1956)
	Exodus (1960)
BRUCE DERN:	Black Sunday (1977)
MARUSCHKA DETMERS:	Hanna's War (1988)
ERNEST DEUTSCH:	The Golem (1920)
WILLIAM DEVANE:	Marathon Man (1976)
COLLEEN DEWHURST:	Annie Hall (1977)
	Sword of Gideon (1986)
NEIL DIAMOND:	The Jazz Singer (1980)
ANGIE DICKENSON:	Cast A Giant Shadow (1966)
AVITAL DICKER:	The Summer of Aviya (1988)
MARLENE DIETRICH:	Judgment at Nuremberg (1961)
BRADFORD DILLMAN:	Compulsion (1959)
	The Way We Were (1973)
STEFANO DIONISI:	The Truce (1997)
BOB DISHY:	Brighton Beach Memoirs (1986)
OMRI DOLEV:	Late Summer Blues (1987)
EWA DOMANSKA:	Austeria (1988)
JAMES DONALD:	Cast A Giant Shadow (1966)
PETER DONAT:	School Ties (1992)
LUDWIG DONATH:	Jolson Sings Again (1949)
MARTIN DONOVAN:	Rescuers: Stories of Courage: Two Couples (1998)
PAUL DOOLEY:	The Murder of Mary Phagan (1987)
KARIN DOR:	Prisoner in the Middle (1974)

ERIC DOUGLAS:	Remembrance of Love (1982)
KIRK DOUGLAS:	Cast A Giant Shadow (1966)
	Victory at Entebbe (1976)
	Remembrance of Love (1982)
MELVYN DOUGLAS:	Tell Me a Riddle (1980)
RICHARD DREYFUSS:	The Apprenticeship of Duddy Kravitz (1974)
	Victory at Entebbe (1976);
	Prisoner of Honor (1991)
	Lost in Yonkers (1993)
CAROL DRINKWATER:	Father (1990)
MINNIE DRIVER:	The Governess (1998)
LUCY DUBINCHIK:	Saint Clara (1996)
YUDEL DUBINSKY:	American Matchmaker (1940)
HOWARD DUFF:	Actor (1978)
OLYMPIA DUKAKIS:	Cemetery Club (1993)
DAVID DUKES:	The Triangle Factory Fire Scandal (1979)
	The Winds of War (1983);
	War and Remembrance (1988)
FAYE DUNAWAY:	Voyage of the Damned (1976)
	Double Edge (1991)
	Twilight of the Golds (1996)
MICHAEL DUNN:	Ship of Fools (1965)
GRIFFIN DUNNE:	The Wall (1982)
	Secret Weapon (1990)
MILDRED DUNNOCK:	The Jazz Singer (1952)
KIRSTEN DUNST:	Mother Night (1996)
GIUSTINO DURANO:	Life Is Beautiful (1997)
CHARLES DURNING:	To Be or Not To Be (1983)
CHARLES S. DUTTON:	The Murder of Mary Phagan (1987)
ROBERT DUVALL:	The Man Who Captured Eichmann (1996)
SHELLEY DUVALL:	Annie Hall (1977)
SHIMON DZIGAN:	The Jolly Paupers (1937)
	Undzere Kinder (1948)

CHRISTOPHER ECCLESTON:	A Price Above Rubies (1998)
HERB EDELMAN:	The Way We Were (1973)
CHANA EDEN:	Remembrance of Love (1982)
ELANA EDEN:	The Story of Ruth (1960)
RICHARD EGAN:	Esther and the King (1960)
KURT EHRHARDT:	The Blum Affair (1948)
KAROLINE EICHHORN:	Three Days in April (1995)

LISA EICHHORN:	The Wall (1982)
ARIK EINSTEIN:	Sallah (1965)
GABI ELDOR:	Boy Takes Girl (1983)
YONA ELIAN:	The Last Winter (1984)
	Loan Me Your Wife (1988)
ARIAH (ARIE) ELIAS:	Kazablan (1974)
	Hershaleh (1977)
DENHOLM ELLIOTT:	The Apprenticeship of Duddy Kravitz (1974)
	Voyage of the Damned (1976)
	The Boys from Brazil (1978)
HALIL ELOHEV:	Saint Clara (1996)
TINA ENGEL:	The Boat is Full (1980)
TOBIAS ENGEL:	'38: Vienna Before the Fall (1988)
MARILYN ERSKINE:	The Eddie Cantor Story (1953)
EDITH EVANS:	QB VII (1974)
MATTHEW FABER:	Welcome to the Dollhouse (1996)
LUCE FABIOLE:	The Two of Us (1968)
MIA FARROW:	Hannah and Her Sisters (1986)
	Radio Days (1987)
	Crimes and Misdemeanors (1990);
	Miracle At Midnight (1998)
ANGELA FEATHERSTONE:	Family of Cops (1995)
	Family of Cops II: Breach of Faith (1997)
FEDER SISTERS:	Catskill Honeymoon (1949)
GABOR FEHER:	The Revolt of Job (1983)
ALAN FEINSTEIN:	War and Love (1984)
RAPHAEL FEJTO:	Au Revoir Les Enfants (1986)
TOVA FELDSHUH:	Holocaust (1978)
	The Triangle Factory Fire Scandal (1979)
	A Day in October (1992);
	Aaron's Magic Village (1997)
CONCHATA FERRELL:	Family Prayers (1993)
JOSE FERRER:	Ship of Fools (1965)
	Voyage of the Damned (1976)
	To Be or Not To Be (1983)
ESTHER FIELD:	Mothers of Today (1939)
	Yiddishe Mama (1939)
	Eli Eli (1940)
RALPH FIENNES:	Schindler's List (1993)
	Prince of Egypt (1998)

HARVEY FIERSTEIN:	Torch Song Trilogy (1988)
	Safe Men (1998)
LEO FILER:	They Were Ten (1961)
PETER FINCH:	Judith (1966)
	Raid on Entobbe (1977)
FYVUSH FINKEL:	Aaron's Magic Village (1997)
LEVANAH FINKELSTEIN:	Tzanafi Family (1976)
	The Heritage (1993)
PETER FIRTH:	Prisoner of Honor (1991)
MARIO FISCHEL:	David (1979)
JAKOB FISCHER:	Long Is The Road (1948)
LENKA FISEROVA:	A Prayer for Katarina Hurovitzova (1969)
CARRIE FISHER:	Hannah and Her Sisters (1986)
GERALDINE FITZGERALD:	The Pawnbroker (1965)
GLENN FITZGERALD:	A Price Above Rubies (1998)
JOE FLAHERTY:	Heavy Metal (1981)
LOUISE FLETCHER:	The Magician of Lublin (1979)
NINA FOCH:	The Ten Commandments (1956)
JANE FONDA:	Julia (1977)
PETER FONDA:	The Rose Garden (1989)
JOAN FONTAINE:	Ivanhoe (1952)
HARRISON FORD:	The Frisco Kid (1979)
FREDERIC FORREST:	The Music Box (1989)
WILLIAM FORREST:	The Eddie Cantor Story (1953)
BRIGITTE FOSSEY:	The Last Butterfly (1990)
SIMCHE FOSTEL:	Yidl Mitn Fidl (1936)
MEG FOSTER:	Ticket to Heaven (1981)
JAMES FOX:	Thoroughly Modern Millie (1967)
ANNE FRANCIS:	Funny Girl (1968)
DON FRANCKS:	Heavy Metal (1981)
IRIT FRANK:	Finals (1983)
MARK FRANKEL:	Leon the Pig Farmer (1992)
ARTHUR FRANZ:	The Eddie Cantor Story (1953)
EDUARD FRANZ:	The Jazz Singer (1952)
BRENDAN FRASER:	School Ties (1992)
	Twilight of the Golds (1996)
MORGAN FREEMAN:	Eyewitness (1981)
	Driving Miss Daisy (1989)
LEONARD FREY:	Fiddler on the Roof (1971)
SAMI FREY:	War and Remembrance (1988)
LAZAR FRIED:	Eli Eli (1940)
JAN FRIEDL:	Bachelor Girl (1987)

SHRAGA FRIEDMAN:	Sallah (1965)
GERT FROBE:	The Serpent's Egg (1978)
BASIA FRYDMAN:	The Slingshot (1993)
LEO FUCHS:	American Matchmaker (1940)
	The Frisco Kid (1979)
	Avalon (1990)
TITO FUENTE:	Radio Days (1987)
PENNY FULLER:	Miss Rose White (1992)
ROBERT FULLER:	Sinai Commandos (1968)
EDWARD FURLONG:	Little Odessa (1994)
JOSEPH FURST:	The Dunera Boys (1985)
DAN FUTTERMAN:	The Birdcage (1996)
MICHAEL GAHR:	The Nasty Girl (1989)
MAX GAIL:	Not In This Town (1997)
YORAM GALL :	Remembrance of Love (1982)
PETER GALLAGHER:	The Murder of Mary Phagan (1987)
	The Lover (1990)
ROBIN GAMMEL:	Scandal in a Small Town (1988)
YEHORAM GAON:	Siege (1970)
	Eagles Attack at Dawn (1974)
	Kazablan (1974)
	Operation Thunderbolt (1977)
	Dead End Street (1983)
ALLEN GARFIELD:	Family Prayers (1993)
JOHN GARFIELD	Gentleman's Agreement (1947)
GIANNO GARKO:	Kapo (1959)
JUDY GARLAND:	Judgment at Nuremberg (1961)
VITTORIO GASSMAN:	Abraham (1994)
JOHN GAVIN:	Thoroughly Modern Millie (1967)
BEN GAZZARA:	QB VII (1974)
	Voyage of the Damned (1976)
LUCY GEHRMAN:	A Brivele Der Mamen (1939)
MISHA GEHRMAN:	A Brivele Der Mamen (1939)
HEINRICH GEORGE:	Jud Suess (1940)
AVIVA GER:	The Secrets of Yolanda (1982)
	Goodbye New York (1984)
RICHARD GERE:	King David (1985)
ERWIN GERSCHONNECK:	Jacob the Liar (1974)
BERTA GERSTEN:	Mirele Efros (1939)
	The Benny Goodman Story (1955)
MASSIMO GHINA:	The Truce (1997)

STATHIS GIALLEUS:	Cast A Giant Shadow (1966)
CHERYL GIANNI:	War and Love (1984)
GIANCARLO GIANNINI:	Jacob (1994)
JOHN GIELGUD:	QB VII (1974)
	Chariots of Fire (1981)
	Inside the Third Reich (1982);
	War and Remembrance (1988)
	Shine (1996)
MOTTI GILADI:	Over The Ocean (1992)
MARTIN GILAT:	21 Hours at Munich (1976)
BILLIE GILBERT:	The Great Dictator (1940)
JACK GILFORD:	The World of Sholom Aleichem (1959)
	Save the Tiger (1973)
JOHN GILLO:	The 17th Bride (1984)
LILIANA GLABCZYNSKA:	Austeria (1988)
JACKIE GLEASON:	Mr. Halpern & Mr. Johnson (1983)
BRIAN GLOVER:	Leon the Pig Farmer (1992)
MATHIAS GNAEDINGER:	The Boat is Full (1980)
PAULETTE GODDARD:	The Great Dictator (1940)
ISHAI GOLAN:	Mindbender (1995)
NUSIA GOLD:	Undzere Kinder (1948)
DINAH GOLDBERG:	Catskill Honeymoon (1949)
RUBY GOLDBERG:	Uncle Moses (1932)
RUTHI GOLDBERG:	Romantic Stories (1992)
CHANAN GOLDBLATT:	King For a Day (1982)
JEFF GOLDBLUM:	Next Stop Greenwich Village (1976)
	Independence Day (1996)
	Prince of Egypt (1998)
SIDNEY GOLDIN:	East and West (1923)
JENNIE GOLDSTEIN:	Two Sisters (1938)
MICHAEL GOLDSTEIN:	Green Fields (1937)
TONY GOLDWYN:	The Doomsday Gun (1994)
	The Substance of Fire (1996)
MACHA GOLOUBKINA:	Adam's Rib (1991)
CAROLINE GOODALL:	Schindler's List (1993)
HENRY GOODMAN:	Broken Glass (1996)
JOHN GOODMAN:	Mother Night (1996)
BILL GOODWIN:	The Jolson Story (1946)
	Jolson Sings Again (1949)
EVE GORDON:	Avalon (1990)
ILLY GORLITZKY:	Three Days and a Child (1967)

CLIFF GORMAN:	Rosebud (1974)
LOUIS GOSSETT JR:	Iron Eagle 2 (1988)
ELLIOTT GOULD:	Over the Brooklyn Bridge (1984)
HAROLD GOULD:	Actor (1978)
BOAZ GOUR-LAVIE:	Song of the Siren (1994)
ANDREI GOUTINE:	Luna Park (1991)
JOSEPH GRABER:	Kazablan (1974)
JANUSZ GRABOWSKI:	Greta (1986)
VIRGINIA GRAHAM:	A Secret Space (1988)
GLORIA GRAHAME:	Crossfire (1947)
PALLE GRANDITSKY:	Freud Leaving Home (1991)
LEE GRANT:	Portnoy's Complaint (1972)
	Voyage of the Damned (1976)
	The Substance of Fire (1996)
PETER GRAVES:	The Winds of War (1983)
SPALDING GRAY:	Beaches (1988)
NIGEL GREEN:	Tobruk (1967)
SETH GREEN:	Radio Days (1987)
ESTHER GREENBERG:	Sallah (1965)
	Lupo (1970)
ELLEN GREENE:	Next Stop Greenwich Village (1976)
JENNIFER GREY:	Dirty Dancing (1987)
JOEL GREY:	Cabaret (1972)
HELMUT GRIEM:	The Damned (1969)
	Cabaret (1972)
HUGH GRIFFITH:	Exodus (1960)
	The Fixer (1968)
	Oliver (1968)
	The Passover Plot (1975)
MELANIE GRIFFITH:	A Stranger Among Us (1992)
TOMASZ GROCHOCZKI:	Greta (1986)
CHARLES GRODIN:	The Heartbreak Kid (1972)
AYRE GROSS:	Mother Night (1996)
HELEN GROSS:	Neighbors (1938)
MICHAEL GROSS:	Alan & Naomi (1992)
IRVING GROSSMAN:	Catskill Honeymoon (1949)
ALEC GUINESS:	A Majority of One (1961)
SEAN GULLETTE:	Pi (1998)
STEVE GUTTENBERG:	The Boys from Brazil (1978)
KIM GYNGELL:	Bachelor Girl (1986)
GRETA GYNT:	Mr. Emmanuel (1944)

LUKAS HAAS:	The Music Box (1989)
	Alan & Naomi (1992)
SHELLEY HACK:	King of Comedy (1983)
JOAN HACKETT:	Long Days of Summer (1980)
GENE HACKMAN:	The Birdcage (1996)
SHARON HACOHEN:	Crossfire (1989)
YAEL HADAR:	Auditions (1995)
CHAIM HADAYA:	Hide and Seek (1980)
SUHEIL HADDAD:	Cup Final (1992)
UTA HAGEN:	The Boys from Brazil (1978)
JULIE HAGERTY:	Goodbye New York (1984)
APRIL HAILER:	Three Days in April (1995)
BARBARA HALE:	Jolson Sings Again (1949)
DINA HALPERN:	The Dybbuk (1937)
LINDA HAMILTON:	Rescuers: Stories of Courage: Two Couples (1998)
LIONEL HAMPTON:	The Benny Goodman Story (1955)
ROGER HANIN:	Day of Atonement (1992)
TOM HANKS:	Every Time We Say Goodbye (1986)
DARYL HANNAH:	Rescuers: Stories of Courage: Two Families (1998)
HAYA HARAREET:	Hill 24 Doesn't Answer (1955)
MARCIA GAY HARDEN:	Used People (1992)
CEDRIC HARDWICKE:	Power (1934)
	The Ten Commandments (1956)
SHRAGE HARPAZ:	The Secret of Yolanda (1982)
JESSICA HARPER:	My Favorite Year (1982)
KAMIE HARPER:	Friendship in Vienna (1988)
VALERIE HARPER:	The Execution (1985)
JULIE HARRIS:	Voyage of the Damned (1976)
RICHARD HARRIS:	The Hero (1969)
	Abraham (1994)
ELIZABETH HARTMAN:	The Fixer (1968)
LISA HARTMAN:	The 17th Bride (1984)
LAURENCE HARVEY:	Escape to the Sun (1972)
RUTGER HAUER:	Inside the Third Reich (1982)
	Escape From Sobibor (1987)
FRANCOIS HAUTESERRE:	A La Mode (1994)
NIGEL HAVERS:	Chariots of Fire (1980)
JUNE HAVOC:	Gentleman's Agreement (1947)
JACK HAWKINS:	Judith (1966)
	Escape to the Sun (1972)
	QB VII (1974)
GOLDIE HAWN:	Private Benjamin (1980)

JILL HAWORTH:	Exodus (1960)
HELEN HAYES:	Victory at Entebbe (1976)
SUSAN HAYWARD:	David and Bathsheba (1951)
JOHN HEARD:	Beaches (1988)
	The End of Innocence (1990)
EILEEN HECKART:	Table Settings (1984)
LAURIE HEINEMAN:	Save the Tiger (1973)
INGRID HELD:	The Last Butterfly (1990)
GUR HELLER:	Echoes of Conflict (1989)
DINA HELPERN:	The Vow (1937)
MARGAUX HEMINGWAY:	Over the Brooklyn Bridge (1984)
MARIEL HEMINGWAY:	Steal the Sky (1988)
ED HERLIHY:	King of Comedy (1983)
BARBARA HERSHEY:	Diamonds (1972)
	Hannah and Her Sisters (1986)
	Beaches (1988)
	Abraham (1994)
CHARLTON HESTON:	The Ten Commandments (1956)
KEN HIGELIN:	A La Mode (1994)
GERALD HIKEN:	The Wall (1982)
STEVEN HILL:	Yentl (1983)
CIARAN HINDS:	Ivanhoe (1997)
GREGORY HINES:	History of the World Part 1 (1981)
JUDD HIRSCH:	Independence Day (1996)
YOAV HITE:	Auditions (1995)
FLORENCE HOATH:	The Governess (1998)
AVI HOFFMAN:	The Imported Bridegroom (1990)
DUSTIN HOFFMAN:	Marathon Man (1976);
GERT GUNTER HOFFMANN:	Blazing Sand (1960)
MARCO HOFSCHNEIDER:	Europa Europa (1991)
RENE HOFSCHNEIDER:	Europa Europa (1991)
RAMI HOIBERGER:	Auditions (1995)
WILLIAM HOLDEN:	21 Hours at Munich (1976)
JERRY HOLLAND:	American Pop (1981)
HAL HOLLBROOK:	Julia (1977)
CELESTE HOLM:	Gentleman's Agreement (1947)
IAN HOLM:	The Fixer (1968)
	Chariots of Fire (1981)
LESLIE HOPE:	Sword of Gideon (1986)
	True Confections (1991)
ANTHONY HOPKINS:	QB VII (1974)
	Victory at Entebbe (1976)

DENNIS HOPPER:	Samson and Delilah (1996)
BOB HOSKINS:	The Dunera Boys (1985)
JOHN HOUSEMAN:	The Winds of War (1983)
ARLISS HOWARD:	The Infiltrator (1994)
	The Man Who Captured Eichmann (1996)
GUSTI HUBER:	The Diary of Anne Frank (1959)
ROCK HUDSON:	Tobruk (1967)
	The Ambassador (1984)
BENITA HUME:	Power (1934)
MARK HUMPHREY:	Iron Eagle 2 (1988)
BONNIE HUNT:	Getting Away with Murder (1996)
HELEN HUNT:	Mr. Saturday Night (1992)
KIM HUNTER:	Skokie (1981)
ISABELLE HUPPERT:	Rosebud (1974)
ELIZABETH HURLEY:	Samson and Delilah (1996)
WILLIAM HURT:	Eyewitness (1981)
ANJELICA HUSTON:	Enemies: A Love Story (1989)
	Crimes and Misdemeanors (1990)
TIMOTHY HUTTON:	The Substance of Fire (1996)
SACHA IAKOVIEV:	Ivan and Abraham (1993)
JOHN IRELAND:	Escape to the Sun (1972)
AMY IRVING:	Yentl (1983)
	Crossing Delancey (1988)
	I'm Not Rappaport (1997)
JUDITH IVEY:	Brighton Beach Memoirs (1986)
MOSHE IVGI:	Kuni Lemel in Cairo (1983)
	Cup Final (1992)
ANNE JACKSON:	A Woman Called Golda (1982)
	Rescuers: Stories of Courage: Two Women (1997)
DEREK JACOBI:	Inside the Third Reich (1982)
LOU JACOBI:	The Diary of Anne Frank (1959)
	Next Stop Greenwich Village (1976);
	The Magician of Lublin (1979)
	Avalon (1990)
	I Don't Buy Kisses Anymore (1992)
LISA JACOBS:	The Attic (1988)
STEVE JACOBS:	Father (1990)
HENRIETTA JACOBSON:	Catskill Honeymoon (1949)
HYMIE JACOBSON:	Der Purimshpiler (1937)

YVES JACQUES:	The Lover (1990)
SAM JAFFE:	Gentleman's Agreement (1947)
	QB VII (1974)
LADISLAV JANSKY:	Diamonds of the Night (1964)
DAVID JANSSEN:	Prisoner in the Middle (1974)
ERNST-HUGO JAREGARD:	The Slingshot (1993)
RICK JASON:	Eagles Attack at Dawn (1974)
AL JOLSON:	The Jazz Singer (1927)
CAROLYN JONES:	Marjorie Morningstar (1958)
DEAN JONES:	When Every Day is the Fourth of July (1978)
	Long Days of Summer (1980)
FREDDIE JONES:	The Last Butterfly (1990)
RICHARD JORDAN:	The Murder of Mary Phagan (1987)
ERLAND JOSEPHSON:	Sofie (1992)
ROBERT JOY:	Miracle at Moreaux (1986)
	Sword of Gideon (1986)
CURT JURGENS:	Me and the Colonel (1958)
BARNA KABAY:	The Revolt of Job (1983)
DALIT KAHAN:	Song of the Siren (1994)
MADELINE KAHN:	Blazing Saddles (1974)
	History of the World Part 1 (1981)
	An American Tail (1986)
DARIA KALININA:	Welcome to the Dollhouse (1996)
JACOB KALISH:	East and West (1923)
IDA KAMINSKA:	The Shop on Main Street (1965)
CAROL KANE:	Hester Street (1974)
	Annie Hall (1977)
	Over the Brooklyn Bridge (1984)
IRIS KANER:	Soldier of the Night (1984)
VALERIE KAPRISKY:	The Lover (1990)
ALEX KARRAS:	Blazing Saddles (1974)
ANDREI KASIANOV:	Adam's Rib (1991)
MATHIEU KASSOVITZ:	Cafe Au Lait (1993)
JUDAH KATZ:	True Confections (1991)
YEFTACH KATZUR:	Atalia (1984)
	Up Your Anchor (1985)
DANNY KAYE:	Me and the Colonel (1958)
	Skokie (1981)
LAINIE KAZAN:	Romance of a Horsethief (1971)
	My Favorite Year (1982)
	Beaches (1988);

	I Don't Buy Kisses Anymore (1992)
STACY KEACH:	The Lover (1990)
DIANE KEATON:	Annie Hall (1977)
	The Little Drummer Girl (1984)
	Radio Days (1987)
STEVEN KEATS:	Hester Street (1974)
MOSHE KEDEM:	The Dunera Boys (1985)
LILA KEDROVA:	Escape to the Sun (1972)
	Tell Me a Riddle (1980)
MARTHE KELLER:	Marathon Man (1976)
	Black Sunday (1977)
	The Nightmare Years (1989)
GENE KELLY:	Marjorie Morningstar (1958)
MOIRA KELLY:	Little Odessa (1994)
ROZ KELLY:	American Pop (1981)
JOSEF KEMER:	The Last Butterfly (1990)
JEREMY KEMP:	Prisoner of Honor (1991)
SEBASTIAN KENEAS:	War and Love (1984)
BRIAN KERWIN:	Torch Song Trilogy (1988)
WULF KESSLER:	The White Rose (1983)
EVELYN KEYES:	The Jolson Story (1946)
SANDRINE KIBERLAIN:	Les Patriotes (1994)
MICHAEL KIDD:	Actor (1978)
MARGOT KIDDER:	Willie & Phil (1980)
VAL KILMER:	Prince of Egypt (1998)
NEVO KIMCHI:	Auditions (1995)
ALAN KING:	The Infiltrator (1994)
ZALMAN KING:	The Passover Plot (1975)
BEN KINGSLY:	The Murderers Among Us (1989)
	Schindler's List (1993)
	Joseph (1995)
	Moses (1996);
	The Assignment (1997)
KLAUS KINSKI:	Operation Thunderbolt (1977)
	The Little Drummer Girl (1984)
CHRISTINA KIRK:	Safe Men (1998)
SALLY KIRKLAND:	Hit the Dutchman (1992)
ROBERT KLEIN:	Table Settings (1984)
	A Secret Space (1988)
KEVIN KLINE:	Sophie's Choice (1982)
EUGENE KLOPFER:	Jud Suess (1940)
JACK KLUGMAN:	Goodbye Columbus (1969)

MILAN KNAZKO:	The Last Butterfly (1990)
SHIRLEY KNIGHT:	21 Hours at Munich (1976)
OHAD KNOLLER:	Under the Domim Tree (1995)
AMOS KOLLEK:	Goodbye New York (1984)
	Double Edge (1991)
HARVEY KORMAN:	Blazing Saddles (1974)
	History of the World Part 1 (1981)
ROBERT KOSOY:	Miracle at Moreaux (1986)
ODED KOTLER:	Blazing Sand (1960)
	Three Days and a Child (1967)
	My Michael (1975)
YAPHET KOTTO:	Raid on Entebbe (1977)
HUBERT KOUNDE:	Cafe Au Lait (1993)
	Hate (1995)
JEROEN KRABBE:	Crossing Delancey (1988)
	Secret Weapon (1990)
WERNER KRAUSS:	Jud Suess (1940)
MIRIAM KRESSYN:	Der Purimshpiler (1937)
ALICE KRIGE:	Chariots of Fire (1981)
	King David (1985)
	Max and Helen (1990)
	Joseph (1995)
JOSEF KRONER:	The Shop on Main Street (1965)
DAVID KRUMHOLTZ:	Slums of Beverly Hills (1998)
GENE KRUPA:	The Benny Goodman Story (1955)
AGNIESZKA KRUSZEWSKA:	Greta (1986)
ANTONIN KUMBERA:	Diamonds of the Night (1964)
KATY KURTZMAN:	When Every Day is the Fourth of July (1978)
STEFAN KVIETIK:	The Boxer and Death (1963)
STANLEY LABOR:	The 17th Bride (1984)
DIANE LADD:	Cemetery Club (1993)
HEDY LAMARR:	Samson and Delilah (1949)
BURT LANCASTER:	Judgment at Nuremberg (1961)
	Moses (1975)
	Victory at Entebbe (1976);
	Voyage of Terror (1990)
MICHELINE LANCTOT:	The Apprenticeship of Duddy Kravitz (1974)
MARTIN LANDAU:	Crimes and Misdemeanors (1990)
	Max and Helen (1990)
	Joseph (1995)
ANGELA LANDSBURY:	Samson and Delilah (1949)

DIANNE LANE: Descending Angel (1990)
NATHAN LANE: The Birdcage (1996)
BEN LANG: The Plot Against Harry (1989)
HOPE LANG: The Young Lions (1958)
JESSICA LANGE: The Music Box (1989)
FRANK LANGELLA: The Doomsday Gun (1994)
CAAROLYN LANGFORD: King For a Day (1982)
ERA LAPID: Over The Ocean (1992)
YAIR LAPID: Song of the Siren (1994)
VICTOR LAPLACE: Under the World (1987)
DAVID LASCHER: A Call To Remember (1997)
MICHAEL LASKIN: The Man Who Captured Eichmann (1996)
CHANA LASLO: Kuni Lemel in Cairo (1983)
JACK LAUFER: The Man Who Captured Eichmann (1996)
ARIEH LAVI: Hill 24 Doesn't Answer (1955)
DALIAH LAVI: Blazing Sand (1960)
EFRAT LAVIE: Kazablan (1974)
My Michael (1975)
JUDE LAW: I Love You, I Love You Not (1997)
PETER LAWFORD: Exodus (1960)
Rosebud (1974)
GABRIELLE LAZURE: Joshua Then and Now (1985)
ROSEMARY LEACH: The 17th Bride (1984)
CLORIS LEACHMAN: History of the World Part 1 (1981)
OTTO LEDERER: The Jazz Singer (1927)
MICHELE LEE: Broadway Bound (1992)
PEGGY LEE: The Jazz Singer (1952)
SHERYL LEE: Mother Night (1996)
MARGOT LEICESTER: Broken Glass (1996)
VIVIAN LEIGH: Ship of Fools (1965)
JACK LEMMON: Save the Tiger (1973)
The Murder of Mary Phagan (1987);
Getting Away with Murder (1996)
ROBERT SEAN LEONARD: I Love You, I Love You Not (1997)
MICHAEL LERNER: Safe Men (1998)
JOAN LESLIE: Rhapsody in Blue (1945)
MARK LESTER: Oliver (1968)
J. LESZCZYNSKI: Border Street (1948)
OSCAR LEVANT: Rhapsody in Blue (1945)
RACHEL LEVIN: Gaby: A True Story (1987)
BEN LEVINE: Drifting (1982)

LUCY LEVINE:	His Wife's Lover (1931)
EUGENE LEVY:	Heavy Metal (1981)
HEMDA LEVY:	Hamsin (1983)
JOSE LEWGOY:	The Jew (1995)
JENNY LEWIS:	Friendship in Vienna (1988)
JERRY LEWIS:	King of Comedy (1983)
RONALD LEWIS:	Cospiracy of Hearts (1960)
LEON LIEBGOLD:	Yidl Mitn Fidl (1936)
	The Dybbuk (1937)
	Tevye (1939)
MARILYN LIGHTSONE:	Lies My Father Told Me (1975)
LILI LILIANA:	The Dybbuk (1937)
ANNA LILLIAN:	Where is My Child? (1937)
BEATRICE LILLIE:	Thoroughly Modern Millie (1967)
DINA LIMON:	Boy Takes Girl (1983)
VIVECA LINDFORS:	The Story of Ruth (1960)
	The Way We Were (1973)
ROBERT LINDSAY:	Ghenghis Cohn (1994)
JOSEPH LINDSEY:	Amongst Friends (1993)
MARK LINN-BAKER:	My Favorite Year (1982)
MICHAEL LIPKIN:	But Where is Daniel Wax? (1974)
MARIA LIPKINA:	Ivan and Abraham (1993)
CLEAVON LITTLE:	Blazing Saddles (1974)
BERTA LITWINA:	Long Is The Road (1948)
CHRISTOPHER LLOYD:	To Be or Not To Be (1983)
AMY LOCANE:	School Ties (1992)
ROBERT LOGGIA:	Raid on Entebbe (1977)
	A Woman Called Golda (1982)
	Gaby: ATrue Story (1987);
	Triumph of the Spirit (1989)
GINA LOLLOBRIGIDA:	Solomon and Sheba (1959)
CAROLE LOMBARD:	To Be or Not To Be (1942)
TADEUSZ LOMNICKI:	A Generation (1954)
MICHAEL LONSDALE:	Mr. Klein (1977)
SOPHIA LOREN:	Judith (1966)
CHAD LOWE:	In the Presence of Mine Enemies (1997)
ELINA LOWENSOHN:	In the Presence of Mine Enemies (1997)
ANDREW LOWERY:	School Ties (1992)
PATTI LUPONE:	Driving Miss Daisy (1989)
	Family Prayers (1993)
MARTIN LUTTGE:	The Wannsee Conference (1984)

JEFFREY LYNAS:	Lies My Father Told Me (1975)
	Actor (1978)
SUSAN LYNCH:	Ivanhoe (1997)
CHERYL LYNN:	Fate (1990)
MEREDITH SCOTT LYNN:	I Love You...Don't Touch Me (1998)
NATASHA LYONNE:	Slums of Beverly Hills (1998)
ANDIE MACDOWELL:	Unstrung Heroes (1995)
ALI MACGRAW:	Goodbye Columbus (1969)
	The Winds of War (1983)
VLADIMIR MACHKOV:	Ivan and Abraham (1993)
STEPHEN MACHT:	The Last Winter (1984)
	Friendship in Vienna (1988)
SHIRLEY MACLAINE:	Used People (1992)
PETER MACNICOL:	Sophie's Choice (1982)
WILLIAM H. MACY:	Homicide (1991)
GEORGE MAHARIS:	Exodus (1960)
LAURENT MALET:	Sword of Gideon (1986)
DIMITRY MALIKOV:	To See Paris and Die (1993)
PIOTR MAMONOV:	Taxi Blues (1990)
NICK MANCUSO:	The House on Garibaldi Street (1979)
	Ticket to Heaven (1981);
	Tell Me That You Love Me (1984)
	The Lover (1990)
GASPARD MANESSE:	Au Revoir Les Enfants (1986)
PAUL MANN:	Fiddler on the Roof (1971)
DINAH MANOFF:	Table Settings (1984)
JOE MANTEGNA:	Homicide (1991)
	Family Prayers (1993)
	A Call To Remember (1997)
JANET MARGOLIN:	The Triangle Factory Fire Scandal (1979)
STUART MARGOLIN:	Iron Eagle 2 (1988)
MARK MARGOLIS:	Pi (1998)
DAVID MARGULIES:	Family Prayers (1993)
JULIANA MARGULIES:	A Price Above Rubies (1998)
FERDINAND MARIAN:	Jud Suess (1940)
E.G. MARSHALL:	Compulsion (1959)
GARRY MARSHALL:	Twilight of the Golds (1996)
CRISTINA MARSILLACH:	Every Time We Say Goodbye (1986)
DEAN MARTIN:	The Young Lions (1958)
ALESSANDRA MARTINES:	Les Miserables (1995)
LEE MARVIN:	Ship of Fools (1965)

JAMES MASON:	Voyage of the Damned (1976)
	The Boys from Brazil (1978)
	The Assisi Underground (1984)
LOLA MASON:	The End of Innocence (1990)
RAYMOND MASSEY:	David and Bathsheba (1951)
MARCELLO MASTROIANNI:	Used People (1992)
RICHARD MASUR:	Les Patriotes (1994)
HEATHER MATARAZZO:	Welcome to the Dollhouse (1996)
TIM MATHESON:	To Be or Not To Be (1983)
	Rescuers: Stories of Courage: Two Families (1998)
WALTER MATTHAU:	I'm Not Rappaport (1997)
JOHN MATTHEWS:	A Secret Space (1988)
DIETRICH MATTSUSCH:	The Wannsee Conference (1984)
VICTOR MATURE:	Samson and Delilah (1949)
JULIE MAUDUECH:	Cafe Au Lait (1993)
MAYA MAYRON:	Saint Clara (1996)
MAY MCAVOY:	The Jazz Singer (1927)
FRANCES LEE MCCAIN:	Scandal in a Small Town (1988)
KYLE MCCULLOCH:	True Confections (1991)
RODDY MCDOWALL:	Funny Lady (1974)
MALCOLM MCDOWELL:	Voyage of the Damned (1976)
PATRICK MCGAW:	Amongst Friends (1993)
KELLY MCGILLIS:	Unsettled Land (1988)
ELIZABETH MCGOVERN:	Once Upon a Time in America (1984)
DOROTHY MCGUIRE:	Gentleman's Agreement (1947)
DON MCKELLAR:	In the Presence of Mine Enemies (1997)
KRISTY MCNICHOL:	The Summer of my German Soldier (1978)
JAYNE MEADOWS:	David and Bathsheba (1951)
KAY MEDFORD:	Funny Girl (1968)
SUNNYI MELLES:	'38: Vienna Before the Fall (1988)
JULIANO MER:	Under the Domim Tree (1995)
PAUL MERCURIO:	Joseph (1995)
JONATHAN RHYS MEYERS:	The Governess (1998)
SOLOMON MICHAELS:	Jewish Luck (1925)
EVA MICHEL:	Three Days in April (1995)
BETTE MIDLER:	Beaches (1988)
MIKHAL MIKHALESKO:	Catskill Honeymoon (1949)
	God Man and Devil (1949)
SYLVIA MILES:	Crossing Delancey (1988)
BARRY MILLER:	The Chosen (1982)
PENELOPE ANN MILLER:	Biloxi Blues (1988)
REBECCA MILLER:	The Murder of Mary Phagan (1987)

JULIET MILLS:	QB VII (1974)
MARTIN MILNER:	Compulsion (1959)
SAL MINEO:	Exodus (1960)
LIZA MINNELLI:	Cabaret (1972)
IVAN MISTRIK:	Sweet Light in a Dark Room (1960)
WARREN MITCHELL:	The Dunera Boys (1985)
YVONNE MITCHELL:	Conspiracy of Hearts (1960)
CHRIS MITCHUM:	Angel of Death (1986)
ROBERT MITCHUM:	Crossfire (1947)
	The Winds of War (1983)
	The Ambassador (1984);
	War and Remembrance (1988)
	Brotherhood of the Rose (1989)
MATTHEW MODINE:	Jacob (1994)
URSULA MODRZYNSKA:	A Generation (1954)
DONALD MOFFAT:	The Music Box (1989)
BETINNA MOISSI:	Long Is The Road (1948)
ALFRED MOLINA:	Rescuers: Stories of Courage: Two Couples (1998)
ANGELA MOLINA:	Streets of Gold (1986)
BELINDA J. MONTGOMERY:	Tell Me That You Love Me (1984)
ELIZABETH MONTGOMERY:	Broken Glass (1996)
RON MOODY:	Oliver (1968)
KIERON MOORE:	David and Bathsheba (1951)
MARY TYLOR MOORE:	Thoroughly Modern Millie (1967)
NONNA MORDYUKOVA:	Commissar (1968)
AVRAHAM MORE:	Loan Me Your Wife (1988)
JEANNE MOREAU:	Mr. Klein (1977)
	The Proprietor (1996)
	I Love You, I Love You Not (1997)
MARSHA MOREAU:	Miracle at Moreaux (1986)
ABRAHAM MOREVSKY:	The Dybbuk (1937)
MICHAEL MORIARTY:	Holocaust (1978)
ROBERT MORLEY:	War and Remembrance (1988)
LIBBY MORRIS:	Not Quite Paradise (1986)
JEFF MORROW:	The Story of Ruth (1960)
DAVID MORSE:	Brotherhood of the Rose (1989)
NATALIE MORSE:	My Mother's Courage (1996)
ARYEH MOSKONA:	Over The Ocean (1992)
JOSH MOSTEL:	Sophie's Choice (1982)
	Radio Days (1987)
ZERO MOSTEL:	The World of Sholom Aleichem (1959)

	The Producers (1968)
	The Front (1976)
ARMIN MUELLER-STAHL:	Angry Harvest (1985)
	The Music Box (1989)
	Avalon (1990)
	Shine (1996);
	In the Presence of Mine Enemies (1997)
BARBARA MUGICA:	Under the World (1987)
EDWARD MULHARE:	Hill 24 Doesn't Answer (1955)
PAUL MUNI:	The Last Angry Man (1959)
MICHAEL MYERS:	Goodbye Columbus (1969)
KAREN-LISE MYNSTER:	Sofie (1992)
MARIE-JOSE NAT:	Les Violons Du Bal (1974)
BUY NATAF:	Summer of La Goulette (1996)
HILLEL NEEMAN:	Boy Takes Girl (1983)
LIAM NEESON:	Schindler's List (1993)
CRAIG T. NELSON:	The Murderers Among Us (1989)
	I'm Not Rappaport (1997)
HELEN NEMO:	The Plot Against Harry (1989)
FRANCO NERO:	21 Hours at Munich (1976)
PAUL NEWMAN:	Exodus (1960)
PHYLLIS NEWMAN:	A Secret Space (1988)
LEONARD NIMOY:	A Woman Called Golda (1982)
	Never Forget (1991)
NINETTE:	They Were Ten (1961)
PHILIPPE NOIRET:	Justine (1969)
LLOYD NOLAN:	Hannah and Her Sisters (1986)
NICK NOLTE:	Mother Night (1996)
GEULA NONI:	Sallah (1965)
GHITA NORBY:	Freud Leaving Home (1991)
	Sofie (1992)
KLAUS NOVAK:	The Inheritors (1985)
ZACHI NOY:	Up Your Anchor (1985)
BRUCE NOZICK:	Hit the Dutchman (1992)
JACK OAKIE:	The Great Dictator (1940)
CHRIS O'DONNELL:	School Ties (1992)
ROSIE O'DONNELL:	Twilight of the Golds (1996)
SHAI K. OFIR:	The House on Chelouche Street (1973)
	Operation Thunderbolt (1977)
KATSUMI OHYAMA:	The Visas That Saved Lives (1992)

WARNER OLAND:	The Jazz Singer (1927)
DANIEL OLBRYCHSKI:	Rosa Luxemburg (1986)
LENA OLIN:	Enemies: A Love Story (1989)
LAURENCE OLIVIER:	Marathon Man (1976)
	Tho Boys from Brazil (1978)
	The Jazz Singer (1980);
	Mr. Halpern & Mr. Johnson (1983)
EDWARD JAMES OLMOS:	Triumph of the Spirit (1989)
NICLAS OLUND:	The Slingshot (1993)
MICHAEL ONTKEAN:	Willie & Phil (1980)
DAVID OPATOSHU:	The Light Ahead (1939)
	Exodus (1960)
	The Fixer (1968)
	Romance of a Horsethief (1971)
MENASHA OPPENHEIM:	The Jolly Paupers (1937)
JERRY ORBACH:	Dirty Dancing (1987)
	Crimes and Misdemeanors (1990)
	Broadway Bound (1992);
	Mr. Saturday Night (1992)
JOAN ORENSTEIN:	Charlie Grant's War (1980)
SHUY OSHEROV:	Three Days and a Child (1967)
GABI OSTERMAN:	I Love You Rosa (1972)
MAUREEN O'SULLIVAN:	Hannah and Her Sisters (1986)
PETER O'TOOLE:	Rosebud (1974)
	Masada (1981)
	My Favorite Year (1982)
	The Seventh Coin (1992)
MOISHE OYSHER:	The Cantor's Son (1937)
	The Singing Blacksmith (1938)
	Overture To Glory (1940)
JOANNA PACULA:	Not Quite Paradise (1986)
	Escape From Sobibor (1987)
DEBRA PAGET:	The Ten Commandments (1956)
JOHN PAIS:	Safe Men (1998)
BETSY PALMER:	The Last Angry Man (1959)
LILLI PALMER:	Conspiracy of Hearts (1960)
	The Boys from Brazil (1978)
JOHN PANKOW:	A Stranger Among Us (1992)
IRENE PAPAS:	Moses (1975)
	The Assisi Underground (1984)
	Jacob (1994)

MARISA PAREDES:	Life Is Beautiful (1997)
COREY PARKER:	Broadway Bound (1992)
SARAH JESSICA PARKER:	The Substance of Fire (1996)
LARRY PARKS:	The Jolson Story (1946)
	Jolson Sings Again (1949)
STEVE PARLAVECCHIO:	Amongst Friends (1993)
ADRIAN PASDAR:	Streets of Gold (1986)
	Torn Apart (1989)
MANDY PATINKIN:	Yentl (1983)
	Broken Glass (1996)
STUART PAUL:	Fate (1990)
DAVID PAYMER:	Mr. Saturday Night (1992)
ALLEN PAYNE:	A Price Above Rubies (1998)
CECILLA PECK:	Torn Apart (1989)
GREGORY PECK:	Gentleman's Agreement (1947)
	David and Bathsheba (1951)
	The Boys from Brazil (1978)
NIA PEEPLES:	I Don't Buy Kisses Anymore (1992)
ZIPORA PELED:	The Last Winter (1984)
ALEX PELEG:	Intimate Story (1981)
AUSTIN PENDLETON:	The Proprietor (1996)
JOE PENNY:	Family of Cops II: Breach of Faith (1997)
GEORGE PEPPARD:	Tobruk (1967)
ANTHONY PERKINS:	The Glory Boys (1984)
ELIZABETH PERKINS:	Avalon (1990)
	Rescuers: Stories of Courage: Two Women (1997)
MILLIE PERKINS:	The Diary of Anne Frank (1959)
ORLI PERL:	Under the Domim Tree (1995)
VALERIE PERRINE:	The Magician of Lublin (1979)
LISA JANE PERSKY:	American Pop (1981)
NEHEMIAH PERSOFF:	Voyage of the Damned (1976)
	Yentl (1983)
	An American Tail (1986)
JOE PESCI:	Once Upon a Time in America (1984)
SINAI PETER:	The Wordmaker (1991)
	Over The Ocean (1992)
BROCK PETERS:	The Pawnbroker (1965)
JOHNNY PETERSON:	Saint Clara (1996)
PENNY PEYSER:	The Frisco Kid (1979)
MICHAEL PHELMAN:	Newland (1994)
MICHEL PICCOLI:	Dangerous Moves (1984)
SLIM PICKENS:	Blazing Saddles (1974)

MOLLY PICON:	East and West (1923)
	Yidl Mitn Fidl (1936)
	Mamele (1938);
	Fiddler on the Roof (1971)
WALTER PIDGEON:	Funny Girl (1968)
FRANTISEK PIECZKA:	Austeria (1980)
LYN PIERSE:	Bachelor Girl (1986)
FILIPE PINHEIRO:	The Jew (1995)
OLIVER PLATT:	The Infiltrator (1994)
DONALD PLEASENCE:	The Passover Plot (1975)
	Hanna's War (1988)
MARTHA PLIMPTON:	A Woman at War (1994)
	I'm Not Rappaport (1997)
JOAN PLOWRIGHT:	Avalon (1990)
AMANDA PLUMMER:	Miss Rose White (1992)
CHRISTOPHER PLUMMER:	Eyewitness (1981)
	An American Tail (1986)
KEN POGUE:	Miracle at Moreaux (1986)
JEAN POIRET:	The Last Metro (1980)
ROMAN POLANSKI:	A Generation (1954)
YEHUDA POLIKER:	Because of That War (1988)
KEVIN POLLAK:	Avalon (1990)
TRACEY POLLAN:	A Stranger Among Us (1992)
NATALIE PORTMAN:	Prince of Egypt (1998)
MARTIN POTTER:	The Only Way (1970)
SALLY POTTER:	The Tango Lesson (1997)
ALEXANDRA POWERS:	The Seventh Coin (1992)
PAUL PREBOIST:	The Two of Us (1968)
VINCENT PRICE:	The Ten Commandments (1956)
MARTIN PRIEST:	The Plot Against Harry (1989)
JURGEN PROCHNOW:	Forbidden (1984)
ROBERT PROSKY:	The Murder of Mary Phagan (1987)
WOJCIECH PSZONIAK:	Angry Harvest (1985)
	Austeria (1988)
	Korczak (1990)
BILL PULLMAN:	Independence Day (1996)
RANDY QUAID:	The Apprenticeship of Duddy Kravitz (1974)
	Inside the Third Reich (1982)
ANTHONY QUAYLE:	QB VII (1974)
	Moses (1975)

	21 Hours at Munich (1976)
	Masada (1981)
KATHLEEN QUINLAN:	The Last Winter (1984)
AIDAN QUINN:	Avalon (1990)
	The Assignment (1997)
FRANCINE RACETTE:	Au Revoir Les Enfants (1986)
ALEX RAFALOWICZ:	Shine (1996)
HAROLD RAMIS:	Heavy Metal (1981)
CHARLOTTE RAMPLING:	The Damned (1969)
SHULI RAND:	Newland (1994)
CESTMIR RANDA:	A Prayer for Katarina Hurovitzova (1969)
TONY RANDALL:	King of Comedy (1983)
MICHAEL RAPAPORT:	Zebrahead (1992)
	Rescuers: Stories of Courage: Two Families (1998)
GAMIL RATIB:	Summer of La Goulette (1996)
TSVI RATNER-STAUBER:	Family Prayers (1993)
DAPHNA RECHTER:	Over The Ocean (1992)
ROBERT REDFORD:	The Way We Were (1973)
LYNN REDGRAVE:	Shine (1996)
VANESSA REDGRAVE:	Julia (1977)
	Playing for Time (1980)
	Little Odessa (1994)
DONNA REED:	The Benny Goodman Story (1955)
OLIVER REED:	Oliver (1968)
	Prisoner of Honor (1991)
SASKIA REEVES:	Antonia and Jane (1991)
REGINE:	Marry Me Marry Me (1969)
SEYMOUR REICHZEIT:	Motel the Operator (1939)
CARL REINER:	Skokie (1981)
	Slums of Beverly Hills (1998)
PAUL REISER:	Family Prayers (1993)
LEE REMICK:	QB VII (1974)
SERGIO RENAN:	Under the World (1987)
ZEEV REVACH:	Festival at the Pool Room (1975)
	Loan Me Your Wife (1988)
CLIVE REVILL:	Escape to the Sun (1972)
FERNANDO REY:	Angel of Death (1986)
CYNTHIA RHODES:	Dirty Dancing (1987)
JOHN RHYS-DAVIES:	War and Remembrance (1988)
	The Seventh Coin (1992)

SVELTANA RIABOVA:	Adam's Rib (1991)
MANDY RICE-DAVIES:	Kuni Lemel in Tel Aviv (1977)
JEAN-LOUIS RICHARD:	The Last Metro (1980)
MICHAEL RICHARDS:	Unstrung Heroes (1995)
LEE RICHARDSON:	Sweet Lorraine (1987)
RALPH RICHARDSON:	Exodus (1960)
PETER RIEGERT:	Crossing Delancey (1988)
	The Infiltrator (1994)
	Infinity (1996)
RON RIFKIN:	The Chosen (1982)
	The Substance of Fire (1996)
DIANA RIGG:	Genghis Cohn (1994)
JILL RILEY:	True Confections (1991)
WALTER RILLA:	Mr. Emmanuel (1944)
MIRIAM RISELLE:	The Singing Blacksmith (1938);
	Tevye (1939)
EMMANUELLE RIVA:	Kapo (1959)
JASON ROBARDS JR:	Julia (1977)
	Reunion (1988)
SAM ROBARDS:	Not Quite Paradise (1986)
	The Man Who Captured Eichmann (1996)
ERIC ROBERTS:	Descending Angel (1990)
RACHEL ROBERTS:	The Wall (1982)
TONY ROBERTS:	Annie Hall (1977)
EDWARD G. ROBINSON:	The Stranger (1946)
	The Ten Commandments (1956)
SAM ROCKWELL:	Safe Men (1998)
WILL ROGERS JR.:	The Eddie Cantor Story (1953)
ESTHER ROLLE:	Summer of my German Soldier (1978)
	Driving Miss Daisy (1989)
GUNILLA ROOR:	Freud Leaving Home (1991)
ERIC ROSEN:	The Wooden Gun (1979)
MICHAEL ROSENBERG:	His Wife's Lover (1931)
CANTOR MAX ROSENBLATT:	Yiddishe Mama (1939)
MARINA ROSETTI:	The Summer of Aviya (1988)
KATHARINE ROSS:	Voyage of the Damned (1976)
TIM ROTH:	Little Odessa (1994)
RICHARD ROUNDTREE:	Diamonds (1972)
JOHN RUBENSTEIN:	The Boys from Brazil (1978)
	Skokie (1981)
JAN RUBES:	Charlie Grant's War (1980)
	The Outside Chance of Maximilian Glick (1988)

SUSAN DOUGLAS RUBES:	The Outside Chance of Maximilian Glick (1988)
TALYA RUBIN:	Miracle at Moreaux (1986)
FANIA RUBINA:	The Living Orphan (1939)
SAUL RUBINEK:	Ticket to Heaven (1981)
	The Outside Chance of Maximilian Glick (1988);
	Falling Over Backwards (1990)
	The Quarrel (1992)
PETER RUDOLF:	The Revolt of Job (1983)
MERCEDES RUEHL:	Lost in Yonkers (1993)
MARK RUFALLO:	Safe Men (1998)
BARBARA RUSH:	The Young Lions (1958)
GEOFFREY RUSH:	Shine (1996)
ROSALIND RUSSELL:	A Majority of One (1961)
ROBERT RYAN:	Crossfire (1947)
JONATHAN SAGALLE:	Drifting (1982)
	Schindler's List (1993)
EVA MARIE SAINT:	Exodus (1960)
	Voyage of Terror (1990)
JESPER SALEN:	The Slingshot (1993)
SYDA SALMONAVA:	The Golem (1920)
JAIME SANCHEZ:	The Pawnbroker (1965)
DOMINIQUE SANDA:	The Garden of the Finzi-Continis (1971)
	Joseph (1995)
OTTO SANDER:	Rosa Luxemburg (1986)
GEORGE SANDERS:	Samson and Delilah (1949)
	Ivanhoe (1952)
	Solomon and Sheba (1959)
MIA SARA:	A Stranger Among Us (1992)
CHRIS SARANDON:	Forced March (1990)
MICHAEL SARRAZIN:	Joshua Then and Now (1985)
HERBERT SASSE:	My Mother's Courage (1996)
LUDWIG SATZ:	His Wife's Lover (1931)
JOHN SAXON:	Raid on Entebbe (1977)
ALAN SCARFE:	Joshua Then and Now (1985)
	Iron Eagle 2 (1988)
SAM SCHACHT:	A Secret Space (1988)
REBECCA SCHAEFFER:	The End of Innocence (1990)
	Voyage of Terror (1990)
MARIA SCHAFFEL:	I Love You...Don't Touch Me (1998)
ROGER SCHAUER:	The Inheritors (1985)
ROY SCHEIDER:	Marathon Man (1976)

MARIA SCHELL:	Voyage of the Damned (1976)
	Inside the Third Reich (1982)
MAXIMILIAN SCHELL:	The Young Lions (1958)
	Judgment at Nuremberg (1961)
	The Odessa File (1974)
	Julia (1977)
	The Chosen (1982)
	The Assisi Underground (1984)
	The Rose Garden (1989)
	Miss Rose White (1992)
	Abraham (1994)
	Little Odessa (1994)
JOSEPH SCHILDKRAUT:	The Wandering Jew (1920)
	The Diary of Anne Frank (1959)
RUDOLF SCHILDKRAUT:	The Wandering Jew (1920)
DANIEL SCHLACHET:	Swoon (1991)
ROMY SCHNEIDER:	The Hero (1969)
YISROEL SCHUMACHER:	Undzere Kinder (1948)
MAURICE SCHWARTZ:	Uncle Moses (1932)
	Tevye (1939)
HANNA SCHYGULLA:	Warszawa (1993)
PAUL SCOFIELD:	The Attic (1988)
GEORGE C. SCOTT:	Descending Angel (1990)
HARRY SECOMBE:	Oliver (1968)
KYRA SEDGWICK:	War and Love (1984)
	Miss Rose White (1992)
GEORGE SEGAL:	Ship of Fools (1965)
SHAHAR SEGAL:	Late Summer Blues (1987)
IRENA SELEZNIOVA:	The Wordmaker (1991)
CONNIE SELLECCA:	Brotherhood of the Rose (1989)
PETER SELLERS:	I Love You Alice B. Toklas (1968)
DAVID SEMADAR:	Prisoner in the Middle (1974)
EKATERINA SEMENOVA:	To See Paris and Die (1993)
RADE SERBEDZIJA:	The Truce (1997)
MUNI SEREBROFF:	Eli Eli (1940)
JANE SEYMOUR:	The Only Way (1970)
	War and Remembrance (1988)
DINA SFAT:	The Jew (1995)
OMAR SHARIF:	Funny Girl (1968)
	Funny Lady (1974)

RAY SHARKEY:	Willie & Phil (1980)
WILLIAM SHATNER:	Judgment at Nuremberg (1961)
HELEN SHAVER:	Zebrahead (1992)
ROBERT SHAW:	Diamonds (1972)
	Black Sunday (1977)
YASIN SHAWAD:	Hamsin (1983)
DICK SHAWN:	The Producers (1968)
WALLACE SHAWN:	Radio Days (1987)
JOHN SHEA:	The Impossible Spy (1987)
	Unsettled Land (1988)
IRIT SHELEG:	Fictitious Marriage (1988)
BEN SHENKMAN:	Pi (1998)
CYBILL SHEPHERD:	The Heartbreak Kid (1972)
JACK SHEPPERD:	Escape From Sobibor (1987)
ANTONY SHER:	Genghis Cohn (1994)
BAS SHEVA:	Catskill Honeymoon (1949)
MICHAEL SHILO:	Hill 24 Doesn't Answer (1955)
SHMUEL SHILO:	Noa at Seventeen (1982)
	Goodbye New York (1984)
YOSEPH (JOSEPH) SHILOAH:	I Love You Rosa (1972)
	Eagles Attack at Dawn (1974)
	Rosebud (1974);
	Passover Fever (1995)
DALIA SHIMKO:	Noa at Seventeen (1982)
ZE'EV SHIMSHONI:	Soldier of the Night (1984)
YISROEL SHUMACHER:	The Jolly Paupers (1937)
SYLVIA SIDNEY:	Raid on Entebbe (1977)
	Used People (1992)
OLIVER SIEBERT:	The White Rose (1983)
CASEY SIEMASZKO:	Biloxi Blues (1988)
SIMONE SIGNORET:	Ship of Fools (1965)
	Madame Rosa (1977)
RON SILVER:	Enemies: A Love Story (1989)
	Mr. Saturday Night (1992)
JONATHAN SILVERMAN:	Brighton Beach Memoirs (1986)
	Broadway Bound (1992)
JEAN SIMMONS:	Mr. Emmanuel (1944)
MICHEL SIMON:	The Two of Us (1968)
PAUL SIMON:	Annie Hall (1977)
ROBERT F. SIMON:	The Benny Goodman Story (1955)
FRANK SINATRA:	Cast A Giant Shadow (1966)

STELLEN SKARSGARD:	Good Evening Mr. Wallenberg (1992)
	The Slingshot (1993)
HANA SLIVKOVA:	The Shop on Main Street (1965)
MARYA SMALL:	American Pop (1981)
ALEXIS SMITH:	Rhapsody in Blue (1945)
KURTWOOD SMITH:	The Nightmare Years (1989)
PAUL SMITH:	21 Hours at Munich (1976)
WILL SMITH:	Independence Day (1996)
DANA SMUTNA:	Sweet Light in a Dark Room (1960)
WESLEY SNIPES:	Streets of Gold (1986)
KRISTINA SODERBAUM:	Jud Suess (1940)
IKA SOHAR:	I Don't Give a Damn (1988)
JUDITH SOLE:	The Wooden Gun (1979)
PAUL SOLES:	Falling Over Backwards (1990)
JACK SOMACK:	Portnoy's Complaint (1972)
JOSEF SOMMER:	Forced March (1990)
LOUISE SOREL:	When Every Day is the Fourth of July (1978)
LINDA SORENSON:	Joshua Then and Now (1985)
THOMAS JUNGLING SORENSON:	Mendel (1997)
MIRA SORVINO:	Amongst Friends (1993)
RENEE SOUTENDIJK:	The Murderers Among Us (1989)
	Forced March (1990)
KEVIN SPACEY:	The Murder of Mary Phagan (1987)
	The Doomsday Gun (1994)
JOE SPANO:	The Dunera Boys (1985)
SEBASTIAN SPENCE:	Family of Cops (1995)
	Family of Cops II: Breach of Faith (1997)
DOUGLAS SPENCER:	The Diary of Anne Frank (1959)
DAVID SPIELBERG:	War and Love (1984)
GUNTER SPOERRIE:	The Wannsee Conference (1984)
ROBERT STACK:	To Be or Not To Be (1942)
TERRENCE STAMP:	Mindbender (1995)
HARRY DEAN STANTON:	Private Benjamin (1980)
MAUREEN STAPLETON:	Sweet Lorraine (1987)
	Miss Rose White (1992)
RAY STARKEY:	Zebrahead (1992)
IMELDA STAUNTON:	Antonia and Jane (1991)
MARY STEENBURGEN:	The Attic (1988)
RENATE STEIGER:	The Boat is Full (1980)
ROD STEIGER:	The Pawnbroker (1965)
	The Chosen (1982)
	The Glory Boys (1984)

	Sword of Gideon (1986)
MARGARET SOPHIE STEIN:	Enemies: A Love Story (1989)
ALBERT STEINRUCK:	The Golem (1920)
PHILIP STERLING:	The Wall (1982)
DANIEL STERN:	Hannah and Her Sisters (1986)
DEAN STOCKWELL:	Gentleman's Agreement (1947)
	Compulsion (1959)
GUY STOCKWELL:	Tobruk (1967)
ERIC STOLTZ:	A Woman at War (1994)
LENA STOLZE:	The White Rose (1983)
	The Nasty Girl (1989)
CHRISTOPHER STONE:	Prisoner in the Middle (1974)
SHARON STONE:	War and Remembrance (1988)
OPHELIA STRAHL:	The Wooden Gun (1979)
SUSAN STRASBERG:	Kapo (1959)
MORRIS STRASSBERG:	Where is My Child? (1937)
DAVID STRATHAIRN:	Lost in Yonkers (1993)
	Mother Night (1996)
PETER STRAUSS:	Masada (1981)
	Brotherhood of the Rose (1989)
MERYL STREEP:	Julia (1977)
	Holocaust (1978)
	Sophie's Choice (1982)
BARBRA STREISAND:	Funny Girl (1968)
	The Way We Were (1973)
	Funny Lady (1974)
	Yentl (1983)
BARBARA SUKOWA:	Rosa Luxemburg (1986)
NICOLAS SUROVY:	The Man Who Captured Eichmann (1996)
DONALD SUTHERLAND:	The Assignment (1997)
JANET SUZMAN:	The House on Garibaldi Street (1979)
	Leon the Pig Farmer (1992)
PATRICK SWAYZE:	Dirty Dancing (1987)
D.B. SWEENEY:	A Day in October (1992)
LORETTA SWIT:	The Execution (1985)
	Miracle at Moreaux (1986)
SYLVIA SYMS:	Conspiracy of Hearts (1960)
SAID TAGHAOUI:	Hate (1995)
JEFFREY TAMBOR:	The Man Who Captured Eichamann (1996)
MARY TAMM:	The Odessa File (1974)
TURIA TAN:	Prisoner in the Middle (1974)

JESSICA TANDY:	Driving Miss Daisy (1989)
	Used People (1992)
SHLOMO TARSHISH:	Hamsin (1983)
BRADFORD TATUM:	Not In This Town (1997)
WALTER TAUB:	David (1979)
CHAIM TAUBER:	Motel the Operator (1939)
DORON TAVORI:	Hide and Seek (1980)
VIC TAYBACK:	Lepke (1974)
BENEDICT TAYLOR:	Every Time We Say Goodbye (1986)
ELIZABETH TAYLOR:	Ivanhoe (1952)
	Victory at Entebbe (1976)
NOAH TAYLOR:	Shine (1996)
ROBERT TAYLOR:	Ivanhoe (1952)
LEIGH TAYLOR-YOUNG:	I Love You Alice B. Toklas (1968)
INNA TCHOURIKOVA:	Adam's Rib (1991)
HEDI TEMESSY:	The Revolt of Job (1983)
JON TENNEY:	Twilight of the Golds (1996)
ODED TEOMI:	They Were Ten (1961)
LAURENT TERZIEFF:	Kapo (1959)
ERIC THAL:	A Stranger Among Us (1992)
	Samson and Delilah (1996)
DANNY THOMAS:	The Jazz Singer (1952)
R.H. THOMPSON:	Charlie Grant's War (1980)
	Ticket to Heaven (1981)
	The Quarrel (1992)
RON THOMPSON:	American Pop (1981)
INGRID THULIN;	The Damned (1969)
	Moses (1975)
KEVIN TIGHE:	School Ties (1992)
MARC TISSOT:	The Proprietor (1996)
OLIVER TOBIAS:	Romance of a Horsethief (1971)
AVI TOLEDANO:	The Heritage (1993)
ANDREI TOLOUBEIEV:	Adam's Rib (1991)
MARISA TOMEI:	Slums of Beverly Hills (1998)
JOHANNA TOMEK:	The Inheritors (1985)
LILY TOMLIN:	Getting Away with Murder (1996)
DAVID TOPAZ:	Goodbye New York (1984)
TOPOL:	Sallah (1965)
	Fiddler on the Roof (1971)
	The House on Garibaldi Street (1979);
	The Winds of War (1983)

	War and Remembrance (1988)
DAN TOREN:	Finals (1983)
RIP TORN:	The Execution (1985)
SPENCER TRACEY:	Judgment at Nuremberg (1961)
AMI TRAUB:	Drifting (1982)
CLAIRE TREVOR:	Marjorie Morningstar (1958)
JEAN-LOUIS TRINTIGNANT:	Les Violons Du Bal (1974)
ELISABETH TRISSENAAR:	Angry Harvest (1985)
EUGENE TROOBNICK:	The Imported Bridegroom (1990)
GISELA TROWE:	The Blum Affair (1948)
TOM TRYON:	The Story of Ruth (1960)
YOAV TSAFIR:	Late Summer Blues (1987)
MICHAEL TUCCI:	The Man Who Captured Eichmann (1996)
MICHAEL TUCKER:	Radio Days (1987)
ULRICH TUKER:	The White Rose (1983)
	My Mother's Courage (1996)
ROBIN TUNNEY:	Rescuers: Stories of Courage: Two Families (1998)
DAN TUREN:	Atalia (1984)
DAN TURGEMAN:	Crossfire (1989)
ZYGMUND TURKOW:	Der Purimshpiler (1937)
	The Vow (1937)
JOHN TURTURRO:	Unstrung Heroes (1995)
	The Truce (1997)
ARNON TZADOK:	One of Us (1989)
ASHER TZAFATI:	Newland (1994)
TUVIA TZAFIR:	Festival at the Pool Room (1975)
LIV ULLMANN:	The Serpent's Egg (1978)
	Dangerous Moves (1984)
	Gaby: A True Story (1987);
	The Rose Garden (1989)
LEE VAN CLEEF:	The Young Lions (1958)
JAMES VAN DER BECK:	I Love You, I Love You Not (1997)
JO VAN FLEET:	I Love You Alice B. Toklas (1968)
PETER VAN NORDEN:	Scandal in a Small Town (1988)
DIANE VARSI:	Compulsion (1959)
TATYANA VASILIYEVA:	To See Paris and Die (1993)
RON VAWTER:	Swoon (1991)
CONRAD VEIDT:	Power (1934)
BEN VEREEN:	Funny Lady (1974)

JOHN VERNON:	Justine (1969)
	Heavy Metal (1981)
PABLO VERON:	The Tango Lesson (1997)
MARIO VIEGAS:	The Jew (1995)
JAN-MICHAEL VINCENT:	The Winds of War (1983)
NIKOLAS VOGEL:	The Inheritors (1985)
JON VOIGT:	The Odessa File (1974)
MAX VON SYDOW:	Voyage of the Damned (1976)
	Hannah and Her Sisters (1986)
	Father (1990)
FRANK VOSPER:	Power (1934)
YORGO VOYAGIS:	The Little Drummer Girl (1984)
STEVEN WADDINGTON:	Ivanhoe (1997)
MICHAEL WAGER:	Hill 24 Doesn't Answer (1955)
CHRISTOPHER WALKEN:	Next Stop Greenwich Village (1976)
	Annie Hall (1977);
	Biloxi Blues (1988)
	Day of Atonement (1992)
ALLY WALKER:	The Seventh Coin (1992)
NANCY WALKER:	The World of Sholom Aleichem (1959)
LEE WALLACE:	War and Love (1984)
ELI WALLACH:	Romance of a Horsethief (1971)
	Skokie (1981)
	The Wall (1982)
	The Impossible Spy (1987)
SHANI WALLIS:	Oliver (1968)
JESSICA WALTER:	The Execution (1985)
	Slums of Beverly Hills (1998)
SAM WANAMAKER:	Voyage of the Damned (1976)
	Holocaust (1978)
	Private Benjamin (1980)
SELA WARD:	Rescuers: Stories of Courage: Two Women (1997)
SIMON WARD:	Children of Rage (1975)
JACK WARDEN:	The Apprenticeship of Duddy Kravitz (1974)
	Raid on Entebbe (1977)
DAVID WARNER:	The Fixer (1968)
	Holocaust (1978)
	Masada (1981)
	Hanna's War (1988)
JULIE WARNER:	Mr. Saturday Night (1992)

LESLEY ANN WARREN:	Joseph (1995)
MENASHE WARSHAVSKI:	Laura Adler's Last Love Affair (1990)
SAM WATERSTON:	The Nightmare Years (1989)
	Crimes and Misdemeanors (1990)
	The Proprietor (1996);
	Miracle At Midnight (1998)
JACK WATSON:	Tobruk (1967)
NATHAN WATT:	Unstrung Heroes (1995)
AL WAXMAN:	Rescuers: Stories of Courage: Two Women (1997)
ANAT WAXMAN:	I Don't Give a Damn (1988)
	The Wordmaker (1991)
	Romantic Stories (1992)
DAVID WAYNE:	The Last Angry Man (1959)
JOHN WAYNE:	Cast A Giant Shadow (1966)
FRITZ WEAVER:	Black Sunday (1977)
	Rescuers: Stories of Courage: Two Women (1997)
SIGOURNEY WEAVER:	Madman (1979)
	Eyewitness (1981)
PAUL WEGENER:	The Golem (1920)
FLORENCE WEISS:	The Cantor's Son (1937)
	The Singing Blacksmith (1938)
	Overture To Glory (1940)
RAQUEL WELCH:	Scandal in a Small Town (1988)
TUESDAY WELD:	Once Upon a Time in America (1984)
JOHANAN WELLER:	Echoes of Conflict (1989)
ORSON WELLES:	The Stranger (1946)
	Compulsion (1959)
	Voyage of the Damned (1976)
CAROLE WELLS:	Funny Lady (1974)
FRITZ WEPPER:	Cabaret (1972)
OSKAR WERNER:	Ship of Fools (1965)
	Voyage of the Damned (1976)
OTTO WERNICKE:	Long Is The Road (1948)
CHANDRA WEST:	True Confections (1991)
SAMUEL WEST:	Reunion (1988)
JUSTIN WHALIN:	Miracle At Midnight (1998)
SHEILA WHITE:	Oliver (1968)
MITCHELL WHITFIELD:	I Love You...Don't Touch Me (1998)
STUART WHITMAN:	The Story of Ruth (1960)
JAMES WHITMORE:	The Serpent's Egg (1978)
RICHARD WIDMARK:	Judgment at Nuremberg (1961)

ELIZABETH WIENER:	Marry Me Marry Me (1969)
DIANNE WIEST:	The Wall (1982)
	Hannah and Her Sisters (1986)
	Radio Days (1987)
	The Birdcage (1996)
MARY WILCOX:	Lepke (1974)
JACK WILD:	Oliver (1968)
GENE WILDER:	The Producers (1968)
	Blazing Saddles (1974)
	The Frisco Kid (1979)
TOM WILKINSON:	The Governess (1998)
BARBARA WILLIAMS:	Tell Me That You Love Me (1984)
	Family of Cops (1995);
	Family of Cops II: Breach of Faith (1997)
BILLY DEE WILLIAMS:	The Last Angry Man (1959)
EMLYN WILLIAMS:	Ivanhoe (1952)
ROBIN WILLIAMS:	The Birdcage (1996)
TREAT WILLIAMS:	Once Upon a Time in America (1984)
	Max and Helen (1990)
LAMBERT WILSON:	Warszawa (1993)
SCOTT WILSON:	The Passover Plot (1975)
TEDDY WILSON:	The Benny Goodman Story (1955)
MARIE WINDSOR:	The Eddie Cantor Story (1953)
SHELLEY WINTERS:	The Diary of Anne Frank (1959)
	Diamonds (1972);
	Next Stop Greenwich Village (1976)
	The Magician of Lublin (1979)
	Over the Brooklyn Bridge (1984)
JOSEPH WISEMAN:	Zalman or the Madness of God (1975)
KELLY WOLF:	A Day in October (1992)
SIMON WOLF:	Yiddishe Mama (1939)
ELIJAH WOOD:	Avalon (1990)
NATALIE WOOD:	Marjorie Morningstar (1958)
PEGGY WOOD:	The Story of Ruth (1960)
JAMES WOODS:	Raid on Entebbe (1977)
	Holocaust (1978)
	Eyewitness (1981);
	Once Upon a Time in America (1984)
	Joshua Then and Now (1985)
MAXINE WOODS:	The Plot Against Harry (1989)
MICHAEL WOODS:	War and Remembrance (1988)

EDWARD WOODWARD:	King David (1985)
IRENE WORTH:	Forbidden (1984)
	Lost in Yonkers (1993)
N'BUSHE WRIGHT:	Zebrahead (1992)
PATRICK WRIGHT:	Fate (1990)
JANE WYATT:	Gentleman's Agreement (1947)
ED WYNN:	Marjorie Morningstar (1958)
	The Diary of Anne Frank (1959)
YOSI YADIN:	The Hero (1969)
	Lies My Father Told Me (1975)
LIOR YAENI:	But Where is Daniel Wax? (1974)
JEAN YANNE:	Hanna K. (1983)
	A La Mode (1994)
NATALYA YEGOROVA:	Luna Park (1991)
MICHAEL YORK:	Justine (1969)
	Cabaret (1972)
	Sword of Gideon (1986)
SUSANNAH YORK:	Fate (1990)
BERT YOUNG:	Once Upon a Time in America (1984)
	Over the Brooklyn Bridge (1984)
LORETTA YOUNG:	The Stranger (1946)
ROBERT YOUNG:	Crossfire (1947)
SEAN YOUNG:	The Proprietor (1996)
LEO YUNG:	The Wooden Gun (1979)
AMON ZADOK:	Beyond the Walls (1985)
	Unsettled Land (1988)
	Torn Apart (1989)
STEVE ZAHN:	Safe Men (1998)
GAL ZAID:	The Wordmaker (1991)
PIOTR ZAITCHENKO:	Taxi Blues (1990)
VANESSA ZAOUI:	Alan & Naomi (1992)
ASHER ZARFATI:	The Secret of Yolanda (1982)
EDMUND ZAYENDA:	A Brivele Der Mamen (1939)
	Mamele (1938)
RENEE ZELLWEGER:	A Price Above Rubies (1998)
FERENC ZENTHE:	The Revolt of Job (1983)
ESTHER ZEVKO:	But Where is Daniel Wax? (1974)
ORLI ZILBERSHATZ:	Song of the Siren (1994)
STEPHANIE ZIMBALIST:	The Triangle Factory Fire Scandal (1979)

J. ZLOTNICK:	Border Street (1948)
NESSIM ZOHAR:	The Wordmaker (1991)
RITA ZOHAR:	Laura Adler's Last Love Affair (1990)
	The Man Who Captured Eichmann (1996)
URI ZOHAR:	Blazing Sand (1960)
IDIT ZUR:	Noa at Seventeen (1982)
DOR ZWEIGENBOM:	Late Summer Blues (1987)
YETTA ZWERLING:	Motel the Operator (1939)
NOAM ZYLBERMAN:	The Outside Chance of Maximilian Glick (1988)
ELSA ZYLBERSTEIN:	Mina Tenanbaum (1994)

FILMS

ACTORS
ALPHABETICAL
CHRONOLOGICAL
DIRECTORS
GENRES
LANGUAGES
DISTRIBUTORS

IVAN ABRAMSON:	East and West (1923)
ALAN ADELSON:	Lodz Ghetto (1998)
ROBERT ALDRICH:	The Frisco Kid (1979)
WOODY ALLEN:	Annie Hall (1977)
	Hannah and Her Sisters (1986)
	Radio Days (1987
	Crimes and Misdemeanors (1990)
MICHAEL ANDERSON:	Sword of Gideon (1986)
IRENE ANGELICO:	Dark Lullabies (1985)
ALEXANDRE ARCADY:	Day of Atonement (1992)
EMILE ARDOLINO:	Dirty Dancing (1987)
DARREN ARONOFSKY:	Pi (1998)
ALEXANDER ASKOLOV:	Commissar (1968)
HY AVERBACK:	I Love You, Alice B. Toklas (1968)
JOHN D. AVILDSEN:	Save the Tiger (1973)
JOM TOB AZULAY:	The Jew (1995)
RALPH BAKSHI:	American Pop (1981)
WALTER BANNERT:	The Inheritors (1985)
URI BARBASH:	Beyond the Walls (1985)
	Unsettled Land (1988)
	One of Us (1989)
MICHAL BAT-ADAM:	Boy Takes Girl (1983)
VERA BELMONT:	The Lover (1990)
JACOB BEN-AMI:	Green Fields (Grine Felder) (1937)
JACK BENDER:	A Call To Remember (1997)
ROBERTO BENIGNI:	Life Is Beautiful (1997)
NOMI BEN NATAN:	Born in Berlin (1991)
RICHARD BENJAMIN:	My Favorite Year (1982)
EDWARD BENNETT:	A Woman at War (1994)
BRUCE BERESFORD:	King David (1985)
	Driving Miss Daisy (1989)
PAMELA BERGER:	The Imported Bridegroom (1990)
INGMAR BERGMAN:	The Serpent's Egg (1978)
JOSEF BERNE:	Mirele Efros (1939)
	Catskill Honeymoon (1949)
CLAUDE BERRI:	The Two of Us (1968)
	Marry Me, Marry Me (1969)

FRANK BEYER:	Jacob the Liar (1974)
SASANNE BIER:	Freud Leaving Home (1991)
TONY BILL:	Rescuers: Stories of Courage: Two Families (1998)
JON BLAIR:	Anne Frank Remembered (1995)
BEN K. BLAKE:	Two Sisters (1938)
REX BLOOMSTEIN:	The Longest Hatred (1991)
DON BLUTH:	An American Tail (1986)
CARLE BOESE:	The Golem (1920)
PAUL BOGART:	Torch Song Trilogy (1988)
	Broadway Bound (1992)
PETER BOGDANOVICH:	Rescuers: Stories of Courage: Two Women (1997)
FERIO BOUGHEDIR:	Summer of La Goulette (1996)
HAIM BOUZAGLO:	Fictitious Marriage (1988)
MATTHEW BRODERICK:	Infinity (1996)
MEL BROOKS:	The Producers (1968)
	Blazing Saddles (1974)
	History of the World, Part I (1981)
ZBYNEK BRYNYCH:	Transport from Paradise (1965)
KEN CAMERON:	Miracle at Midnight (1998)
MICHAEL CAMPUS:	The Passover Plot (1975)
DYAN CANNON:	The End of Innocence (1990)
CHARLIE CHAPLIN:	The Great Dictator (1940)
BRENDA CHAPMAN:	Prince of Egypt (1998)
MARVIN J. CHOMSKY:	Victory at Entebbe (1976)
	Holocaust (1978)
	Inside the Third Reich (1982)
	Brotherhood of the Rose (1989)
DAN COHEN:	Madman (1979)
ELI COHEN:	The Summer of Aviya (1988)
	The Wordmaker (1991)
	The Quarrel (1992)
	Under the Domim Tree (1995)
PETER COHEN:	The Architecture of Doom (1989)
PETER COLLINSON:	The House on Garibaldi Street (1979)
MARTHA COOLIDGE:	Lost in Yonkers (1993)
CONSTANTIN COSTA-GAVRAS:	Hanna K. (1983)
	The Music Box (1989)

ALAN CROSLAND:	The Jazz Singer (1927)
BILLY CRYSTAL:	Mr. Saturday Night (1992)
GEORGE CUKOR:	Justine (1969)
DAN CURTIS:	When Every Day Was the Fourth of July (1978)
	Long Days of Summer (1980)
	The Winds of War (1983)
	War and Remembrance (1988)
MICHAEL CURTIZ:	The Jazz Singer (1952)
BOAZ DAVIDSON:	Festival at the Poolroom (1975)
	Tzanafi Family (1976)
VALENTINE DAVIES:	The Benny Goodman Story (1955)
JULIE DAVIS:	I Love You...Don't Touch Me (1998)
ASSI DAYAN:	King for a Day (1982)
	Finals (1983)
RICHARD DEMBO:	Dangerous Moves (1984)
CECIL B. DEMILLE:	Samson and Delilah (1949)
	The Ten Commandments (1956)
VITTORIO DE SICA:	The Garden of the Finzi-Continis (1971)
GIANFRANCO DE SOSIO:	Moses (1975)
THOROLD DICKINSON:	Hill 24 Doesn't Answer (1955)
BARUCH DIENAR:	They Were Ten (1961)
	Take Two (1985)
EDWARD DMYTRYK:	Crossfire (1947)
	The Young Lions (1958)
MICHAEL DRACH:	Les Violons du Bal (1974)
ANTHONY DRAZAN:	Zebrahead (1992)
REMY DUCHEMIN:	A la Mode (1994)
MARTINE DUGOWSON:	Mina Tenanbaum (1994)
CHRISTIAN DUGUAY:	The Assignment (1997)
BILL DUKE:	Cemetery Club (1993)
JULIEN DUVIVIER:	Le Golem: The Legend of Prague (1935)
JOLANTA DYLEWSKA:	Chronicle of the Uprising in the Warsaw Ghetto According to Mark Edelman (1994)
JACQUES EHRLICH:	Flames in the Ashes (1986)
JUDIT ELEK:	To Speak the Unspeakable: The Message of Elie Wiesel (1996)
ROLAND EMMERICH:	Independence Day (1996)
ERICH ENGEL:	The Blum Affair (1948)

JOHN ERMAN:	The Attic: The Hiding of Anne Frank (1988)
ROBERT FAENZA:	Jonah Who Lived in the Whale (1993)
BEDA DOCAMPO FEIJOO:	Under the World (1987)
MICHAEL FERGUSON:	The Glory Boys (1984)
JACK FISHER:	Torn Apart (1989)
RICHARD FLEISCHER:	Compulsion (1959)
	The Jazz Singer (1980)
ARI FOLMAN:	Saint Clara (1996)
ALEXANDER FORD:	Border Street (Ulica Granicza) (1948)
BOB FOSSE:	Cabaret (1972)
EYTAN FOX:	Song of the Siren (1994)
JESS FRANCO:	Angel of Death (1986)
JOHN FRANKENHEIMER:	The Fixer (1968)
	Black Sunday (1977)
HERBERT B. FREDERSDOF:	Long Is the Road (1948)
SIDNEY J. FURIE:	Iron Eagle 2 (1988)
GIDEON GANANI:	Crossfire (1989)
	Flames of Revolt: The Irgun (1990)
HERB GARDNER:	I'm Not Rappaport (1997)
ALAN GIBSON:	A Woman Called Golda (1982)
BRIAN GIBSON:	The Murderers Among Us (The Simon Wiesenthal Story) (1989)
LEWIS GILBERT:	Not Quite Paradise (1986)
YITZHAK GINSBERG:	Romantic Stories (Tel Aviv Stories) (1992)
PETER GLENVILLE:	Me and the Colonel (1958)
WOLFGANG GLUCK:	'38: Vienna Before the Fall (1988)
JIM GODDARD:	The Impossible Spy (1987)
	Lupo (1970)
MENAHEM GOLAN:	Diamonds (1972)
	Escape to the Sun (1972)
	Eagles Attack at Dawn (1974)
	Lepke (1974)
	Kazablan (1974)
	Operation Thunderbolt (1977)
	The Magician of Lublin (1979)
	Over the Brooklyn Bridge (1984)
	Hanna's War (1988)
	Hit the Dutchman (1992)

JACK GOLD:	Escape from Sobibor (1987)
SANDRA GOLDBACHER:	The Governess (1998)
SIDNEY GOLDIN:	East and West (1923)
	His Wife's Lover (Zayn Vaybs Lubovnik) (1931)
	Uncle Moses (1932)
	The Cantor's Son (Dem Khazn's Zindl) (1937)
MICHAEL GOLDMAN:	Jumpin' Night in the Garden of Eden (1998)
ALLAN A. GOLDSTEIN:	The Outside Chance of Maximilian Glick (1988)
MAREK GOLDSTEIN:	Long Is the Road (1948)
JACOB GOLDWASSER:	Over the Ocean (1992)
STEVE GOMER:	Sweet Lorraine (1987)
KEITH GORDON:	Mother Night (1996)
AMIT GOREN:	Echoes of Conflict (1989)
LEONID GOROVETS:	Ladies' Tailor (1990)
SHAUL GOSKIND:	Undzere Kinder (1948)
HAIM GOURI:	The Last Sea (1980)
	Flames in the Ashes (1986)
WILLIAM A. GRAHAM:	21 Hours at Munich (1976)
	The Man Who Captured Eichmann (1996)
LEE GRANT:	Tell Me a Riddle (1980)
JAMES GRAY:	Little Odessa (1994)
KJELL GREDE:	Good Evening Mr. Wallenberg (1992)
ALFRED E. GREEN:	The Jolson Story (1946)
	The Eddie Cantor Story (1953)
DAVID GREENE:	Family of Cops II: Breach of Faith (1997)
JOSEPH GREEN:	Yidl Mitn Fidl (A Jew with His Fiddle) (1936)
	Der Purimshpiler (The Jester) (1937)
	A Brivele der Mamen (A Letter to Mother) (1938)
	Mamele (Little Mother) (1938)
GRIGORI GRICHER-CHERIKOVER:	Laughter Through Tears (1928)
TOM GRIES:	QB VII (1974)
NATAN GROSS:	Undzere Kinder (1948)
KRYSZTOF GRUBER:	Greta (1986)
AMOS GUTTMAN:	Drifting (1982)
IMRE GYONGYOSSY:	The Revolt of Job (1983)
MELISA HACKER:	My Knees Were Jumping: Remembering the Kindertransports (1996)

BILLY HALE:	The Murder of Mary Phagan (1987)
JOHN HAMBURG:	Safe Men (1998)
JOHN HANCOCK:	Steal the Sky (1988)
VEIT HARLAN:	Jud Suess (1940)
MARK J. HARRIS:	The Long Way Home (1997)
RICHARD HARRIS:	The Hero (1969)
RIVKA HARTMAN:	Bachelor Girl (1987)
AVRAM HEFFNER:	But Where Is Daniel Wax? (1974)
	Laura Adler's Last Love Affair (1990)
STEVE HICKNER:	Prince of Egypt (1998)
SCOTT HICKS:	Shine (1996)
GEORGE ROY HILL:	Thoroughly Modern Millie (1967)
	The Little Drummer Girl (1984)
PETER HILL:	Jacob (1994)
ARTHUR HILLER:	Tobruk (1967)
ROBERTA HODES:	A Secret Space (1988)
ANGNIESZKA HOLLAND:	Angry Harvest (1985)
	Europa, Europa (1991)
BILLY HOPKINS:	I Love You, I Love You Not (1997)
E. MASON HOPPER:	Hungry Hearts (1922)
HUGH HUDSON:	Chariots of Fire (1981)
TIM HUNTER:	Rescuers: Stories of Courage: Two Couples (1998)
	Rescuers: Stories of Courage: Two Families (1998)
SHMUEL IMBERMAN:	I Don't Give a Damn (1988)
MARKUS IMHOOF:	The Boat Is Full (1981)
SIMCHA JACOBOVICI:	Deadly Currents (1991)
	Hollywoodism: Jews, Movies and the American Dream (1997)
TAMARA JENKINS:	Slums of Beverly Hills (1998)
NORMAN JEWISON:	Fiddler on the Roof (1971)
ALAN JOHNSON:	To Be or Not to Be (1983)
KAREL KACHYNA:	The Last Butterfly (1990)
JAN KADAR:	The Shop on Main Street (1965)
	Lies My Father Told Me (1975)
JEREMY P. KAGAN:	The Chosen (1982)
	Descending Angel (1990)
TOM KALIN:	Swoon (1991)
LEORA KAMENETZKY:	Born in Berlin (1991)

ALBERT H. KAMINSKY:	Aaron's Magic Village (1997)
RUSS KAREL:	Almonds and Raisins (1984)
MATHIEU KASSOVITZ:	Cafe au Lait (1993)
	Hate (1995)
JERZY KAWALCROWICZ:	Austeria (1988)
ELIA KAZAN:	Gentleman's Agreement (1947)
DIANE KEATON:	Unstrung Heroes (1995)
IRVIN KERSHNER:	Raid on Entebbe (1977)
BEEBAN KIDRON:	Antonia and Jane (1991)
	Used People (1992)
JANUSZ KIJOWSKI:	Warszawa (1993)
HENRY KING:	David and Bathsheba (1951)
RICK KING:	Forced March (1990)
EPHRAIM KISHON:	Sallah (1965)
ELMAR KLOS:	The Shop on Main Street (1965)
AMOS KOLLEK:	Goodbye, New York (1984)
	Double Edge (1991)
HENRY KOSTER:	The Story of Ruth (1960)
TED KOTCHEFF:	The Apprenticeship of Duddy Kravitz (1974)
	Joshua Then and Now (1985)
	Family of Cops (1995)
ANDRAS KOVACS:	Cold Days (1966)
STANLEY KRAMER:	Judgment at Nuremberg (1961)
	Ship of Fools (1965)
VIATCHESLAV KRICHTOFOVITCH:	Taxi Blues (1991)
CLAUDE LANZMANN:	Shoah (1985)
MARTIN LAVUT:	Charlie Grant's War (1980)
ABRAHAM LEFF:	Where Is My Child? (1937)
ERNEST LEHMAN:	Portnoy's Complaint (1972)
CLAUDE LELOUCH:	Les Misérables (1995)
SERGIO LEONE:	Once Upon a Time in America (1984)
MERVYN LEROY:	A Majority of One (1961)
HENRY LEVIN:	Jolson Sings Again (1949)
MEYER LEVIN:	The Illegals (1947)
BARRY LEVINSON:	Avalon (1990)
NADAV LEVITAN:	Intimate Story (1981)
	The 17th Bride (1984)

SAM LEWIN:	The Dunera Boys (1985)
PETER LILIENTHAL:	David (1979)
WILLY LINDWER:	The Last Seven Months of Anne Frank (1988)
LYNNE LITTMAN:	Rescuers: Stories of Courage: Two Couples (1998)
NORMAN LLOYD:	Actor: The Paul Muni Story (1978)
JOSEPH LOSEY:	Mr. Klein (1991)
PAVEL LOUNGUINE:	Taxi Blues (1990)
	Luna Park (1991)
ERNST LUBITSCH:	To Be or Not to Be (1942)
SIDNEY LUMET:	The Pawnbroker (1965)
	A Stranger Among Us (1992)
HARRY LYNN:	Where Is My Child? (1937)
	Mothers of Today (Hayntike Mames) (1939)
JOHN MACKENZIE:	The Infiltrator (1994)
KENNETH MADSEN:	A Day in October (1992)
LOUIS MALLE:	Au Revoir les Enfants (1987)
DAVID MAMET:	Homicide (1991)
ROBERT MANDEL:	School Ties (1992)
LUIS MANDOKI:	Gaby: A True Story (1987)
DANIEL MANN:	The Last Angry Man (1959)
	Judith (Conflict) (1966)
	Playing for Time (1980)
ROBERT MARCARELLI:	I Don't Buy Kisses Anymore (1992)
ROBERT MARKOWITZ:	The Wall (1982)
ROSS MARKS:	Twilight of the Golds (1996)
GARRY MARSHALL:	Beaches (1988)
MARIAN MARZYNSKI:	Shtetl (1996)
ELAINE MAY:	The Heartbreak Kid (1972)
PAUL MAZURSKY:	Next Stop, Greenwich Village (1976)
	Willie & Phil (1980)
	Enemies: A Love Story (1989)
DEEPA MEHTA:	Sam & Me (1991)
AYELET MENAHEMI:	Romantic Stories (Tel Aviv Stories) (1992)
LOTHAR MENDES:	Power (1934)
ISMAIL MERCHANT:	The Proprietor (1996)
HARVEY MILLER:	Getting Away with Murder (1996)
MOSHE MIZRAHI:	I Love You, Rosa (1972)

	The House on Chelouche Street (1973)
	Madame Rosa (1977)
	War and Love (1984)
	Every Time We Say Goodbye (1986)
EGON MONK:	The Oppermanns (1982)
ILAN MOSHENSON:	The Wooden Gun (1979)
ELIJAH MOSHINSKY:	Genghis Cohn (1994)
A. MOSKALYK:	Dita Saxova (1967)
ILYA MOTYLEFF:	The Cantor's Son (Dem Khazn's Zindl) (1937)
RONALD NEAME:	The Odessa File (1974)
ALBERTO NEGRIN:	Voyage of Terror: The Achille Lauro Affair (1990)
ABBEY NEIDIK:	Dark Lullabies (1985)
JAN NEMEC:	Diamonds of the Night (1964)
MIKE NICHOLS:	Biloxi Blues (1988)
	The Birdcage (1996)
RON NINIO:	Auditions (1995)
ORNA BEN-DUR NIV:	Because of that War (1988)
	New Land (1994)
MAX NOSSECK:	Overture to Glory (Der Vilner Shtot Khazn) (1940)
RAPHAEL NUSSBAUM:	Blazing Sand (1960)
	Sinai Commandos (1968)
JOHN O'CONNOR:	Prisoner in the Middle (1974)
KATSUMI OHYAMA:	The Visas that Saved Lives (1992)
MARCEL OPHUIS:	The Sorrow and the Pity (1970)
	Hotel Terminus (1987)
STUART ORME:	Ivanhoe (1997)
ANTHONY PAGE:	Forbidden (1984)
	Scandal in a Small Town (1988)
	The Nightmare Years (1989)
ALAN J. PAKULA:	Sophie's Choice (1982)
STUART PAUL:	Fate (1990)
LARRY PEERCE:	Goodbye, Columbus (1969)
DAVID PERLOV:	Ben Gurion: An Appointment With Destiny (1968)
SYDNEY POLLACK:	The Way We Were (1973)
ABRAHAM POLONSKY:	Romance of a Horsethief (1971)
GILLO PONTECORVO:	Kapo (1959)
SALLY POTTER:	The Tango Lesson (1997)

GERALD POTTERTON:	Heavy Metal (1981)
JOHN POWER:	Father (1990)
ANER PREMINGER:	Blind Man's Bluff (1993)
	On My Way to Father's Land (1995)
OTTO PREMINGER:	Exodus (1960)
	Rosebud (1974)
ALEXANDER PROSHKIN:	To See Paris and Die (1993)
FONS RADEMAKER:	The Rose Garden (1989)
ALVIN RAKOFF:	Mr. Halpern & Mr. Johnson (1983)
ALEXANDER RAMATI:	The Assisi Underground (1984)
MORT RANSEN:	Falling Over Backwards (1990)
IRVING RAPPER:	Rhapsody in Blue (1945)
	Marjorie Morningstar (1958)
CAROL REED:	Oliver (1968)
ZEEV REVACH:	Loan Me Your Wife (1988)
DON RICHARDSON:	The World of Sholom Aleichem (1959)
ERAN RIKLIS:	Cup Final (1992)
MARTIN RITT:	The Front (1976)
ERIC ROCHANT:	Les Patriotes (1994)
NICOLAS ROEG:	Samson and Delilah (1996)
MICHAEL RUEMER:	The Plot Against Harry (1989)
STUART ROSENBERG:	Voyage of the Damned (1976)
SCOTT ROSENFELT:	Family Prayers (1993)
ALAN ROSENTHAL:	Israel: A Nation Is Born (1992)
FRANCESCO ROSI:	The Truce (1997)
ALEXANDER ROSLER:	Mendel (1997)
GAELEN ROSS:	Blood Money: Nazi Gold (1987)
HERBERT ROSS:	Funny Lady (1974)
EUGENE ROSOW:	Routes of Exile: Moroccan Jewish Odyssey (1982)
JOE ROTH:	Streets of Gold (1986)
AMNON RUBINSTEIN:	Nadia (1987)
	The Heritage (1993)
KEN RUSSELL:	Prisoner of Honor (1991)
	Mindbender (1995)
BORIS SAGAL:	Masada (1981)
GENE SAKS:	Brighton Beach Memoirs (1986)
AKE SANDGREN:	The Slingshot (1993)

JOSEPH SARGENT:	Never Forget (1991)
	Miss Rose White (1992)
	Abraham (1994)
PIERRE SAUVAGE:	Weapons of the Spirit (1990)
PHILIP SAVILLE:	Max and Helen (1990)
FRANKLIN J. SCHAFFNER:	The Boys from Brazil (1978)
JERRY SCHATZBERG:	Reunion (1988)
HEINZ SCHIRK:	The Wannsee Conference (1984)
JOHN SCHLESINGER:	Marathon Man (1976)
RENEN SCHORR:	Late Summer Blues (1987)
MAURICE SCHWARTZ:	Tevye (1939)
STEFAN SCHWIETERT:	A Tickle in the Heart (1996)
MARTIN SCORSESE:	King of Comedy (1983)
AUBRAY SCOTO:	Uncle Moses (1932)
ARTHUR ALLAN SEIDELMAN:	Children of Rage (1975)
	Friendship in Vienna (1988)
JOSEPH SEIDEN:	Eli Eli (1940)
	God, Man and Devil (1949)
PAUL SHAPIRO:	Miracle at Moreaux (1986)
IAN SHARP:	Secret Weapon (1990)
MELVILLE SHAVELSON:	Cast a Giant Shadow (1966)
RIKI SHELACH:	The Last Winter (1984)
YOEL SILBERG:	Kuni Lemel in Tel Aviv (1977)
	Hershaleh (1977)
	The Secret of Yolanda (1982)
	Kuni Lemel in Cairo (1983)
JOAN M. SILVER:	Hester Street (1974)
	Crossing Delancey (1988)
	In The Presence of Mine Enemies (1997)
GAIL SINGER:	True Confections (1991)
GARY SINYOR:	Leon the Pig Farmer (1992)
ORI SIVAN:	Saint Clara (1996)
EDWARD SLOMAN:	His People (1925)
JACK SMIGHT:	Remembrance of Love (Holocaust Survivors: Remembrance of Love) (1982)
PETER SOLAN:	The Boxer and Death (1963)
TODD SOLONDZ:	Welcome to the Dollhouse (1996)

DROR SOREF:	The Seventh Coin (1992)
STEVEN SPIELBERG:	Schindler's List (1993)
JOHANNA SPECTOR:	Two Thousand Years of Freedom and Honor: The Cochin Jews of India (1992)
	About the Jews of Yemen: A Vanishing Culture (1986)
JUAN BAUTISTA STAGNARO:	Under the World (1987)
GEORGE STEVENS:	The Diary of Anne Frank (1959)
OLIVER STORZ:	Three Days in April (1995)
BARBRA STREISAND:	Yentl (1983)
YALE STROM:	The Last Klezmer (1995)
	Carpati (1996)
MEL STUART:	The Triangle Factory Fire Scandal (1979)
DANIEL SULLIVAN:	The Substance of Fire (1996)
HENRYK SZARO:	The Vow (1937)
SAMY SZINGERBAUM:	Brussels Transit (1980)
AKIVA TEVET:	Atalia (1984)
DAVID THACKER:	Broken Glass (1996)
RALPH THOMAS:	Conspiracy of Hearts (1960)
RALPH L. THOMAS:	Ticket to Heaven (1981)
J. LEE THOMPSON:	The Ambassador (1984)
RICHARD THORPE:	Ivanhoe (1952)
GILBERTO TOFANO:	Siege (1970)
TZIPI TROPE:	Tell Me That You Love Me (1984)
FRANÇOIS TRUFFAUT:	The Last Metro (1980)
DORON TSABARI:	Underdogs: A Sports (War) Movie (1996)
MICHAEL TUCHNER:	Summer of My German Soldier (1978)
ZYGMUND TURKOW:	The Jolly Paupers (Freylekhe Kabtsonim) (1937)
RINO TZROR:	Underdogs: A Sports (War) Movie (1996)
LIV ULLMANN:	Sofie (1992)
EDGAR G. ULMER:	Green Fields (Grine Felder) (1937)
	The Singing Blacksmith (Yankl Der Schmid) (1938)
	The Light Ahead (1939)
	American Matchmaker (American Shadchen) (1940)
ADAH USHPIZ:	Not Like Sheep to the Slaughter: The Story of the Bialystock Ghetto (1990)
STERLING VAN WAGENEN:	Alan & Naomi (1992)
MICHAEL VERHOEVEN:	The White Rose (1983)

	The Nasty Girl (1989)
	My Mother's Courage (1996)
KING VIDOR:	Solomon and Sheba (1959)
LUCHINO VISCONTI:	The Damned (1969)
MARGARETHE VON TROTTA:	Rosa Luxemburg (1986)
LAURENCE VULLIAMY:	The State of Israel (1998)
DANIEL WACHSMAN:	Hamsin (Hot Desert Wind) (1983)
ANDRZEJ WAJDA:	A Generation (1954)
	Korczak (1990)
JOSH WALETZKY:	The Partisans of Vilna (1986)
RAOUL WALSH:	Esther and the King (1960)
MICHAL WASZYNSKI:	The Dybbuk (1937)
PAUL WEGENER:	The Golem (1920)
JIRI WEISS:	Sweet Light in a Dark Room (1960)
ROB WEISS:	Amongst Friends (1993)
ORSON WELLES:	The Stanger (1946)
SIMON WELLS:	Prince of Egypt (1998)
PAUL WENDKOS:	The Execution (1985)
MICHELLE WIART:	A Wall in Jerusalem (1970)
HERBERT WISE:	Skokie (1981)
IRA WOHL:	Best Boy (1979)
DAN WOLMAN:	My Michael (1975)
	Hide and Seek (1980)
	Soldier of the Night (1984)
	Up Your Anchor (1985)
DONALD WRYE:	Not In This Town (1997)
WILLIAM WYLER:	Funny Girl (1968)
BOAZ YAKIN:	A Price Above Rubies (1998)
PETER YATES:	Eyewitness (1981)
ISAAC YESHURUM:	Noa at Seventeen (1982)
	Green Fields (1989)
ROGER YOUNG:	Joseph (1995)
	Moses (1996)
ROBERT M. YOUNG:	Triumph of the Spirit (1989)
	Doomsday Gun (1994)
SHEMI ZARHIN:	Passover Fever (1995)

YOLANDE ZAUBERMAN:	Ivan and Abraham (1993)
HOWARD ZIEFF:	Private Benjamin (1980)
	The Seventh Cross (1944)
FRED ZINNEMANN:	Julia (1977)
URI ZOHAR:	Three Days and a Child (1967)

FILMS

Genres

Drama

Abraham (1994)
Adam's Rib (1991) (R)
Alan & Naomi (1992)
The Ambassador (1984)
Amongst Friends (1993)
Angel of Death (1986)
Angry Harvest (1985) (G)
The Assisi Underground (1984)
Atalia (1984) (H)
The Attic (1988)
Au Revoir Les Enfants (1987) (F)
Auditions (1995)
Austeria (1988) (P)

Beyond the Walls (1985)
Blind Man's Bluff (1993)
The Blum Affair (1948) (G)
The Boat Is Full (1981) (G)
Border Street (1948) (P)
The Boxer and Death (1963) (CZ)
Boy Takes Girl (1983) (H)
Boys from Brazil (1978)
A Brivele der Mamen (1939) (Y)
Broken Glass (1966)
But Where Is Daniel Wax? (1974) (H)

A Call to Remember (1997)
Chariots of Fire (1981)
Charlie Grant's War (1980)
Children of Rage (1975)
The Chosen (1981)
Cold Days (1966) (HU)
Commissar (1968) (R)
Compulsion (1959)

A = Arabic
CR = Croatian
CZ = Czech
DAN = Danish
F = French
G = German
Y = Yiddish
H = Hebrew
HU = Hungarian
I = Italian
JAP = Japanese
NOR =Norwegian
P = Polish
POR = Portuguese
R = Russian
RU = Rumanian
SP = Spanish
SWE = Swedish
Silent

Conspiracy of Hearts (1960)
Crossfire (1947)
Crossfire (1989) (H)
Cup Final (1992) (H)

The Damned (1969)
Dangerous Moves (1984)
David (1979)
David and Bathsheba (1951)
A Day in October (1992)
Day of Atonement (1992)
Dead End Street (1983) (H)
Descending Angel (1990)
Diamonds (1972)
Diamonds of the Night (1964) (CZ)
The Diary of Anne Frank (1959)
Dita Saxova (1967) (CZ)
The Doomsday Gun (1994)
Double Edge (1991)
Drifting (1982) (H)
The Dunera Boys (1985)
The Dybbuk (1937) (Y)

Echoes of Conflict (1989) (H)
End of Innocence (1990)
Enemies: A Love Story (1989)
Escape from Sobibor (1987)
Escape to the Sun (1972)
Esther and the King (1960)
Europa, Europa (1991) (G) (R)
Every Time We Say Goodbye (1986)
The Execution (1985)
Exodus (1960)
Eyewitness (1981)

Family of Cops (1995)
Family of Cops II: Breach of Faith (1997)

Family Prayers (1993)
Father (1990)
Fictitious Marriage (1988) (H)
Finals (1983) (H)
The Fixer (1968)
Forbidden (1984)
Forced March (1990)
Freud Leaving Home (1991) (SWE)
Friendship in Vienna (1988)

Gaby: A True Story (1987)
The Garden of the Finzi-Continis (1971) (I)
A Generation (1954) (P)
Genghis Cohn (1994)
Gentleman's Agreement (1947)
The Glory Boys (1984)
God, Man and Devil (1949) (Y)
The Golem (1920) (Silent)

Good Evening, Mr. Wallenberg (1992) (SWE) (G) (HU)
The Governess (1998)
Green Fields (1937) (Y)
Green Fields (1989) (H)
Greta (1986) (P)

Hamsin (1983) (H)
Hanna K. (1983)
Hate (1995) (F)
The Heritage (1993) (H)
The Hero (1969)
Hester Street (1974) (Y)
Hide and Seek (1980) (H)
His People (1925) (Silent)
Holocaust (1978)
Homicide (1991)
The House on Chelouche Street (1973) (H)
The House on Garibaldi Street (1979)
Hungry Hearts (1922) (Silent)

Hunted (1979) (G)

I Don't Give a Damn (1988) (H)
I Love You, I Love You Not (1997)
I Love You, Rosa (1972) (H)
The Impossible Spy (1987)
In the Presence of Mine Enemies (1997)
The Infiltrator (1994)
Infinity (1996)
The Inheritors (1985) (G)
Inside the Third Reich (1982)
Intimate Story (1981) (H)
Ivan and Abraham (1993) (Y)
Ivanhoe (1952)
Ivanhoe (1997)

Jacob (1994)
Jacob the Liar (1974) (G)
The Jew (1995) (POR)
Jonah Who Lived in the Whale (1993)
Joseph (1995)
Joshua Then and Now (1985)
Judgment at Nuremberg (1961)
Julia (1977)
Justine (1969)

Kapo (1959)
King David (1985)
Korczak (1990) (P)

Ladies' Tailor (1990) (R)
The Last Angry Man (1959)
The Last Butterfly (1990)
The Last Metro (1980) (F)
The Last Winter (1984)
Late Summer Blues (1987) (H)
Laura Adler's Last Love Affair (1990) (Y) (H)

Le Golem: The Legend of Prague (1935)
Lepke (1974)
Les Misérables (1995) (F)
Les Patriotes (1994) (F)
Les Violons du Bal (1974) (F)
Lies My Father Told Me (1975)
The Light Ahead (1939) (Y)
The Little Drummer Girl (1984)
Little Odessa (1994)
The Living Orphan (1939) (Y)
Long Days of Summer (1980)
Long Is the Road (1948) (Y) (G) (P)
Lost in Yonkers (1993)
The Lover (1990)
Luna Park (1991) (R)

Madame Rosa (1977) (F)
Madman (1979)
The Magician of Lublin (1979)
Mamele (1938) (Y)
The Man Who Captured Eichmann (1996)
Marathon Man (1976)
Masada (1981)
Max and Helen (1990)
Mendel (1997) (N)
Mina Tenanbaum (1994) (F)
Mindbender (1995)
Miracle at Midnight (1998)
Miracle at Moreaux (1986)
Mirele Efros (1939) (Y)
Miss Rose White (1992)
Mr. Emmanuel (1944)
Mr. Halpern & Mr. Johnson (1983)
Mr. Klein (1977) (F)
Moses (1975)
Moses (1996)
Motel the Operator (1939) (Y)

Mother Night (1996)
Mothers of Today (Hayntike Mames) (1939) (Y)
The Murder of Mary Phagan (1987)
Music Box (1989)
My Michael (1975) (H)
My Mother's Courage (1996) (G)

Nadia (1987) (H)
The Nasty Girl (1989) (G)
Never Forget (1991)
Newland (1994)
The Nightmare Years (1989)
Noa at Seventeen (1982) (H)
Not In This Town (1997)

The Odessa File (1974)
Once Upon a Time in America (1984)
One of Us (1989) (H)
The Only Way (1970)
The Oppermanns (1982) (G)

The Passover Plot (1975)
The Pawnbroker (1965)
Pi (1998)
Playing for Time (1980)
Power (1934)
Prayer for Katarina Hurovitzova (1969) (CZ)
A Price Above Rubies (1998)
Prisoner in the Middle (1974)
Prisoner of Honor (1991)
The Proprietor (1996)

QB VII (1974)
The Quarrel (1992)

Remembrance of Love (1982)
Rescuers: Stories of Courage: Two Couples (1998)

Rescuers: Stories of Courage: Two Families (1998)
Rescuers: Stories of Courage: Two Women (1997)
Reunion (1988)
The Revolt of Job (1983) (HU)
Romantic Stories (1992)
Rosa Luxemburg (1986) (G)
The Rose Garden (1989)

Saint Clara (1996) (H)
Save the Tiger (1973)
Scandal in a Small Town (1988)
Schindler's List (1993)
School Ties (1992)
Secret of Yolanda (1982)
A Secret Space (1988)
Secret Weapon (1990)
The Serpent's Egg (1978)
The 17th Bride (1984)
Shine (1996)
Ship of Fools (1965)
The Shop on Main Street (1965) (CZ)
Siege (1970) (H)
Skokie (1981)
Slingshot (1993) (SWE)
Sofie (1992) (DAN)
Soldier of the Night (1984)
Solomon and Sheba (1959)
Song of the Siren (1994) (H)
Sophie's Choice (1987)
Steal the Sky (1988)
Story of Ruth (1960)
A Stranger Among Us (1992)
Streets of Gold (1986)
Substance of Fire (1996)
The Summer of Aviya (1988) (H)
Summer of My German Soldier (1978)
Sweet Light in a Dark Room (1960) (CZ)

Sweet Lorraine (1987)
Swoon (1991)

The Tango Lesson (1997)
Tell Me a Riddle (1980)
Tell Me That You Love Me (1984)
They Were Ten (1961) (H)
'38: Vienna Before the Fall (1980) (G)
Three Days and a Child (1967) (H)
Three Days in April (1995) (G)
To See Paris and Die (1993) (R)
Transport from Paradise (1965) (CZ)
The Triangle Factory Fire Scandal (1979)
Triumph of the Spirit (1989)
The Truce (1997)
21 Hours At Munich (1976)
Twilight of the Golds (1996)
Two Sisters (1938) (Y)
Tzanafi Family (1976) (H)

Uncle Moses (1932) (Y)
Under the Domim Tree (1995) (H)
Under the World (1987) (SP)
Unsettled Land (1988)

Voyage of the Damned (1976)
The Vow (1937) (Y)

The Wall (1982)
The Wandering Jew (1920) (Silent)
The Wannsee Conference (1984) (G)
War and Love (1984)
War and Remembrance (1988)
Warszawa (1993) (P)
When Every Day Is the Fourth of July (1978)
Where Is My Child? (1937) (Y)
The White Rose (1983) (G)

Willie & Phil (1980)
The Winds of War (1983)
A Woman at War (1994)
A Woman Called Golda (1982)
The Wooden Gun (1979) (H)
The Wordmaker (1991) (H)

Yiddishe Mama (1939) (Y)
The Young Lions (1958)

Zalman; or, The Madness of God (1975)
Zebrahead (1992)

Comedy

A la Mode (1994) (F)
Aaron's Magic Village (1997)
American Matchmaker (1940) (Y)
An American Tail (1986)
Annie Hall (1977)
Antonia and Jane (1991)
The Apprenticeship of Duddy Kravitz (1974)
Avalon (1990)

Bachelor Girl (1987)
Beaches (1988)
Biloxi Blues (1988)
The Birdcage (1996)
Blazing Saddles (1974)
Brighton Beach Memoirs (1986)
Broadway Bound (1992)

Cafe au Lait (1993) (F)
Cemetery Club (1993)
Crimes and Misdemeanors (1990)
Crossing Delancey (1988)

Driving Miss Daisy (1989)

East and West (1923) (Silent)

Falling Over Backwards (1990)
Fate (1990)
Festival at the Poolroom (1975) (H)
The Frisco Kid (1979)
The Front (1972)

Getting Away with Murder (1996)
Goodbye, Columbus (1969)
Goodbye, New York (1984)
The Great Dictator (1940)

Hannah and Her Sisters (1986)
The Heartbreak Kid (1972)
His Wife's Lover (1931) (Y)
History of the World, Part I (1981)

I Don't Buy Kisses Anymore (1992)
I Love You, Alice B. Toklas (1968)
I Love You...Don't Touch Me (1998)
I'm Not Rappaport (1997)
The Imported Bridegroom (1990)

Jewish Luck (1925) (Silent)
The Jolly Paupers (1937) (Y)

King for a Day (1982) (H)
King of Comedy (1983)

Laughter Through Tears (1928) (Silent)
Leon the Pig Farmer (1992)
Life Is Beautiful (1997) (I)
Loan Me Your Wife (1988) (H)
Lupo (1970) (H)

A Majority of One (1961)

Marjorie Morningstar (1958)
Marry Me, Marry Me (1969) (F)
Me and the Colonel (1958)
Mr. Saturday Night (1992)
My Favorite Year (1982)

Neighbors (1938) (Y)
Next Stop, Greenwich Village (1976)
Not Quite Paradise (1986)

The Outside Chance of Maximilian Glick (1988)
Over the Brooklyn Bridge (1984)
Over the Ocean (1992) (H)

Passover Fever (1995) (H)
The Plot Against Harry (1989)
Portnoy's Complaint (1972)
Private Benjamin (1980)
The Producers (1968)
Der Purimshpiler (1937) (Y)

Radio Days (1987)
Romance of a Horsethief (1971)

Safe Men (1998)
Sallah (1965) (H)
Sam & Me (1991)
Slums of Beverly Hills (1998)
Song of the Siren (1994) (H)
Summer of La Goulette (1996) (A) (F) (I)

Table Settings (1984)
Take Two (1985)
Taxi Blues (1990) (R)
Tevye (1939) (Y)
Thoroughly Modern Millie (1967)
Ticket to Heaven (1981)

To Be or Not to Be (1942)
To Be or Not to Be (1983)
Torch Song Trilogy (1988)
True Confections (1991)
The Two of Us (1968) (F)

Undzere Kinder (1948) (Y)
Unstrung Heroes (1995)
Up Your Anchor (1985) (H)
Used People (1992)

The Way We Were (1973)
Welcome to the Dollhouse (1996)
The World of Sholom Aleichem (1959)

Musicals

Actor: The Paul Muni Story (1978)
American Pop (1981)

The Benny Goodman Story (1955)

Cabaret (1972)
The Cantor's Son (1937) (Y)
Catskill Honeymoon (1949) (Y)

Dirty Dancing (1987)

The Eddie Cantor Story (1953)
Eli Eli (1940) (Y)

Fiddler on the Roof (1971)
Funny Girl (1968)
Funny Lady (1974)
Heavy Metal (1981)
Hershaleh (1977) (H)
The Jazz Singer (1927)

The Jazz Singer (1952)
The Jazz Singer (1980)
Jolson Sings Again (1949)
The Jolson Story (1946)

Kazablan (1974) (H)
Kuni Lemel in Cairo (1983) (H)
Kuni Lemel in Tel Aviv (1977) (H)

Oliver (1968)
Overture to Glory (1940) (Y)

Prince of Egypt (1998)

Rhapsody in Blue (1945)

The Singing Blacksmith (1938) (Y)

Yentl (1983)
Yidl Mitn Fidl (1936) (Y)

Documentaries

About The Jews of Yemen: A Vanishing Culture (1986)
Almonds and Raisins (1984)
Anne Frank Remembered (1995)
The Architecture of Doom (1989) (SWE)

Because of that War (1988) (H)
Ben Gurion: An Appointment With Destiny (1968)
Best Boy (1979)
Blood Money: Nazi Gold (1987)
Born in Berlin (1991) (H) (G) (SWE)
Brussels Transit (1980) (Y)

Carpati (1996) (Y)
Chronicle of the Uprising in the Warsaw Ghetto According to Marek Edelman (1994) (P)

Dark Lullabies (1985)
Deadly Currents (1991)

The Eighty-First Blow (1974) (Y) (H)

Flames in the Ashes (1986) (Y) (H)
Flames of Revolt: The Irgun (1987) (F)

Hollywoodism: Jews, Movies and the American Dream (1997)
Hotel Terminus (1987) (F)

The Illegals (1947)
Israel: A Nation Is Born (1992)

Jud Suess (1940) (G)
A Jumpin' Night in the Garden of Eden (1988)

The Last Klezmer (1995)
The Last Sea (1980) (Y) (H)
The Last Seven Months of Anne Frank (1988)
The Long Way Home (1997)
The Longest Hatred (1991)

My Knees Were Jumping: Remembering the Kindertransports (1996)

Not Like Sheep to the Slaughter: The Story of the Bialystok Ghetto (1990)

On My Way to Father's Land (1995) (H)

The Partisans of Vilna (1986)

Routes of Exile: Moroccan Jewish Odyssey (1982)

Shoah (1985)
Shtetl (1996)
The Sorrow and the Pity (1970) (F)
The State of Israel (1998)

A Tickle in the Heart (1996)
To Speak the Unspeakable: The Message of Elie Wiesel (1996) (HU) (RU)
Trial of Adolph Eichmann (1997)
2000 Years of Freedom and Honor: The Cochin Jews of India (1992)

Underdogs: A Sports (War) Movie (1996) (H)

The Visas that Saved Lives (JAP)

A Wall in Jerusalem (1970)
Weapons of the Spirit (1990) (F)

Action

The Assignment (1997)

Black Sunday (1977)
Blazing Sand (1960)
Brotherhood of the Rose (1989)

Cast a Giant Shadow (1966)

Eagles Attack at Dawn (1974)

Hannah's War (1988)
Hill 24 Doesn't Answer (1955)
Hit the Dutchman (1992)

Independence Day (1996)
Iron Eagle 2 (1988)

Judith (Conflict) (1966)

Operation Thunderbolt (1977)

Raid on Entebbe (1977)
Rosebud (1974)

Samson and Delilah (1949)
Samson and Delilah (1996)
The Seventh Coin (1992)
Sinai Commandos (1968)
Sword of Gideon (1986)

The Ten Commandments (1956)
Tobruk (1967)
Torn Apart (1989)

Victory at Entebbe (1976)
Voyage of Terror: The Achille Lauro Affair (1990)

FILMS

ACTORS

ALPHABETICAL

CHRONOLOGICAL

DIRECTORS

GENRES

LANGUAGES

DISTRIBUTORS

Languages

Films not listed below are in English.

Yiddish

American Matchmaker (American Shadchen) (1940)
A Brivele der Mamen (A Letter to Mother) (1939)
Brussels Transit (1980)
The Cantor's Son (Dem Khazns Zindl) (1937)
Carpati (1996)
Catskill Honeymoon (1949)
The Dybbuk (1937)
The Eighty-First Blow (1974)
Eli Eli (1940)
Flames in the Ashes (1986)
God Man and Devil (1949)
Green Fields (Grine Felder) (1937)
Hester Street (1974)
His Wife's Lover (Zayn Vaybs Lubovnik) (1931)
Ivan and Abraham (1993)
The Jolly Paupers (Freylekhe Kabtsonim) (1937)
The Last Sea (1980)
Laura Adler's Last Love Affair (1990)
The Light Ahead (1939)
The Living Orphan (1939)
Long is the Road (1948)
Mamale (Little Mother) (1938)
Mirele Efros (1939)
Motel the Operator (1939)
Mothers of Today (Hayntike Mames) (1939)
Neighbors (1938)
Overture to Glory (Der Vilner Shtot Khazn) (1940)
Der Purimshpiler (The Jester) (1937)
The Singing Blacksmith (Yankl der Schmid) (1938)
Tevye (1939)
Two Sisters (1938)
Uncle Moses (1932)
Undzere Kinder (1948)
The Vow (1937)
Where Is My Child? (1937)
Yiddishe Mama (1939)
Yidl Mitn Fidl (A Jew with His Fiddle) (1936)

Hebrew

Atalia (1984)

Auditions (1995)
Because of that War (1988)
Blind Man's Bluff (1993)
Born in Berlin (1991)
Boy Takes Girl (1983)
But Where Is Daniel Wax? (1974)
Crossfire (1989)
Cup Final (1992)
Dead End Street (1983)
Drifting (1982)
Echoes of Conflict (1989)
The Eighty-First Blow (1974)
Festival at the Poolroom (1975)
Fictitious Marriage (1988)
Finals (1983)
Flames in the Ashes (1986)
Flames of Revolt: The Irgun (1990)
Green Fields (1989)
Hamsim (1983)
The Heritage (1993)
Hershaleh (1977)
Hide and Seek (1980)
The House on Chelouche Street (1973)
I Don't Give a Damn (1988)
I Love You Rosa (1972)
Intimate Story (1981)
Kazablan (1974)
King for a Day (1982)
Kuni Lemel in Cairo (1983)
Kuni Lemel in Tel Aviv (1977)
The Last Sea (1980)
Late Summer Blues (1987)
Laura Adler's Last Love Affair (1990)
Loan Me Your Wife (1988)
Lupo (1970)
My Michael (1975)
Nadia (1987)
Newland (1994)
Noa at Seventeen (1982)
Not Like Sheep to the Slaughter: The Story of the Bialystok Ghetto (1990)
On My Way To Father's Land (1995)
One of Us (1989)
Over the Ocean (1992)
Passover Fever (1995)
Saint Clara (1996)
Sallah (1965)

Siege (1970)
Song of the Siren (1994)
The Summer of Aviya (1988)
They Were Ten (1961)
Three Days and a Child (1967)
Tzanafi Family (1976)
Under the Domim Tree (1995)
Underdogs: A Sports (War) Movie (1996)
Up Your Anchor (1985)
The Wooden Gun (1979)
The Wordmaker (1991)

Arabic

Summer of La Goulette (1996)

Croatian

The Ninth Circle (1960)

Czech

The Boxer and Death (1963)
Diamonds of the Night (1963)
Dita Saxova (1967)
A Prayer for Katarina Hurovitzova (1969)
The Shop on Main Street (1965)
Sweet Light in a Dark Room (1960)
Transport from Paradise (1965)

Danish

Sofie (1992)

French

A la Mode (1994)
Au Revoir les Enfants (1987)
Cafe au Lait (1993)
Hate (1995)
Hotel Terminus (1987)
The Last Metro (1980)
Le Golem: The Legend of Prague (1935)
Les Misérables (1995)
Les Patriotes (1994)
Les Violons du Bal (1974)
Madame Rosa (1977)
Marry Me, Marry Me (1969)
Mina Tenanbaum (1994)
Mr. Klein (1977)
The Sorrow and the Pity (1970)

Summer of La Goulette (1996)
The Two of Us (1968)
Weapons of the Spirit (1990)

German
Angry Harvest (1985)
The Blum Affair (1948)
The Boat Is Full (1981)
Born in Berlin (1991)
David (1979)
Europa, Europa (1991)
Good Evening, Mr. Wallenberg (1992)
Hunted (1979)
The Inheritors (1985)
Jacob the Liar (1974)
Jud Suess (1940)
Long is the Road (1948)
My Mother's Courage (1996)
The Nasty Girl (1989)
The Oppermanns (1982)
Rosa Luxemburg (1986)
38: Vienna Before the Fall (1988)
Three Days in April (1995)
The Wannsee Conference (1984)
The White Rose (1983)

Hungarian
Cold Days (1966)
Good Evening, Mr. Wallenberg (1992)
Revolt of Job (1983)
To Speak the Unspeakable: The Message of Elie Wiesel (1996)

Italian
The Damned (1969)
The Garden of the Finzi-Continis (1971)
Life Is Beautiful (1997)
Summer of La Goulette (1996)

Japanese
The Visas that Saved Lives (1992)

Norwegian
Mendel (1997)

Polish
Austeria (1988)

Border Street (Ulica Granicza) (1948)
Chronicle of the Uprising in the Warsaw Ghetto According To Marek Edelman (1994)
A Generation (1954)
Greta (1986)
Korczak (1990)
Long Is the Road (1948)
Warszawa (1993)

Portuguese
The Jew (1995)

Rumanian
To Speak the Unspeakable: The Message of Elie Wiesel (1996)

Russian
Adam's Rib (1991)
Carpati (1996)
Commissar (1968)
Europa, Europa (1991)
Ladies' Tailor (1990)
Luna Park (1991)
Taxi Blues (1990)
To See Paris and Die (1993)

Silent
East and West (1923)
The Golem (1924)
His People (1925)
Hungry Hearts (1922)
Jewish Luck (1925)
Laughter Through Tears (1928)
The Wandering Jew (1920)

Spanish
Under the World (1987)

Swedish
The Architecture of Doom (1989)
Born in Berlin (1991)
Freud Leaving Home (1991)
Good Evening, Mr. Wallenberg (1992)
Slingshot (1993)

FILMS

ACTORS
ALPHABETICAL
CHRONOLOGICAL
DIRECTORS
GENRES
LANGUAGES
DISTRIBUTORS

Distributors

The following is a list of video distributors mentioned in this book and their addresses and telephone numbers. Listings for such studios as MCA Universal, Fox, Warner, MGM, Paramount, Orion, HBO, Columbia Tristar, Disney, Hollywood, Touchstone, New Line, Miramax, Turner, Polygram, Media, Cannon, etc., are not included as they are, or were, in some cases, major studios, and their products are carried in video stores throughout North America. Contact your local video store or distributor if you wish to obtain copies of these videos.

A & E HOME VIDEO
c/o New Video Group
250 Park Avenue South
New York, NY 10010
212-582-9000
800-229-9994

ABC VIDEO
Distributed by WEA Corporation
9451 LBJ Freeway, Suite 107
Dallas, TX 75243
214-234-6200

ACADEMY ENTERTAINMENT
1 Pine Haven Shore Road
P.O. Box 788
Shelburne, VT 05482
802-905-2060

ACE VIDEO
19749 Dearborn Street
Chatsworth, CA 91311
818-718-1116

ALDEN FILMS
P.O. Box 449
Clarksburg, NJ 08510

908-462-3522

ALLIANCE INTERNATIONAL
121 Bloor Street East, Suite 1400
Toronto, ON
CANADA M4W 3M5
416-967-1141

APPLAUSE PRODUCTIONS INC.
85 Longview Road
Port Washington, NY 11050
516-883-7460

ASTRAL
c/o Coscient Astral Distributors
33 Yonge Street, Suite 1020
Toronto, ON
CANADA M5E 1S9
416-956-2000

ATLAS VIDEO INC.
4915 St. Elmo Avenue
Bethesda, MD 20814
301-907-0030

AUDIO FORUM
96 Broad Street
Guilford, CT 06437
203-453-9794

BFS VIDEO
350 Newkirk Road North

Richmond Hill, ON
CANADA L4C 3G7
416-884-2323

DMG
6363 Sunset Boulevard, 6th Floor
Hollywood, CA 90028-7318
213-468-4067

CBC ENTERPRISES
Box 500, Station A
Toronto, ON
CANADA M5W 1E6
416-925-3311

CHV COMMUNICATIONS INC.
3948 Chesswood Drive
Downsview, ON
CANADA M3J 2W6
416-633-9079

CABIN FEVER ENTERTAINMENT
100 West Putnam Avenue
Greenwich, CT 06830
310-393-9000

CFP HOME VIDEO (LIONS GATE HOME VIDEO)
2 Bloor Street West, Suite 1901
Toronto, ON
CANADA M4W 3E2
416-944-2212

CINEPLEX-ODEON HOME VIDEO
1303 Yonge Street
Toronto, ON
CANADA M4T 2Y9
416-323-6600

CONNOISSEUR VIDEO COLLECTION
1543 7th Street, Suite 202
Santa Monica, CA 90401-2636
203-863-5200

CORONET/MTI FILM & VIDEO
100 Wilmot Road
Deerfield, IL 60015
847-940-1260

DISCOUNT VIDEO TAPES INC.
P.O. Box 7122
Burbank, CA 91510
818-843-3366

ERGO MEDIA INC.
668 Front Street
P.O. Box 2037
Teaneck, NJ 07666
201-692-0404
800-695-3746

EUROPEAN VIDEO DISTRIBUTOR
2321 West Olive Avenue, Suite A
Burbank, CA 91506
818-848-5902

FACETS MULTIMEDIA INC.
1517 West Fullerton Avenue
Chicago, IL 60614
312-281-9075
800-331-6197

FIRST RUN (ICARUS FILMS)
153 Waverly Place, 6th Floor
New York, NY 10014
212-727-1711

FOX LORBER ASSOCIATION INC.
419 Park Avenue South
New York, NY 10016
212-686-6777

FRIES HOME VIDEO
6922 Hollywood Boulevard, 12th Floor
Hollywood, CA 90028
213-466-2266

GLENN VIDEO VISTAS LTD
6924 Canby Avenue, Suite 103
Reseda, CA 91335
818-881-8110

GOODTIMES/KIDS CLASSICS
DISTRIBUTION CORPORATION
401 Fifth Avenue
New York, NY 10016
212-889-0044

HEMDALE HOME VIDEO
7966 Beverly Blvd.
Los Angeles, CA 90048
213-966-3758

HOME VISION CINEMA
5547 North Ravenswood Avenue
Chicago, IL 60640-1199
312-878-2600

HORIZON ENTERTAINMENT
45030 Trevor Avenue
Lancaster, CA 93534
805-940-1040

IGNATIUS PRESS
15 Oakland Avenue
Harrison, NY 10528-9974
914-835-4216

INGRAM INTERNATIONAL FILMS
1123 Heil Quaker Boulevard
La Vergne, TN 37086
615-793-5000
800-759-5000

INTERNATIONAL HISTORIC FILMS (IHF)
P.O. Box 29035
Chicago, IL 60629
312-927-2900

IVE (INTERNATIONAL VIDEO ENTERTAINMENT)
15400 Sherman Way, Suite 500
Van Nuys, CA 91406
818-908-0303

JEF FILMS INC.
Film House
143 Hickory Hill Circle
Osterville, MA 02655-1322
508-428-7198

JEWISH BOOK CENTER
45 East 33rd Street
New York, NY 10016
212-889-6800, ext. 285
800-WC-CALL-US, ext. 285

KINO ON VIDEO
333 West 39th Street, Suite 503
New York, NY 10018
212-629-0871 / 212-629-6880

KOL AMI INC.
18 West 27th Street, 10th Floor
New York, NY 10001
212-779-7944

LEARNING CORPORATION OF AMERICA
c/o Coronet/MTI
108 Wilmot Road
Deerfield, IL 60015
847-940-1260

LIVE HOME VIDEO
15400 Sherman Way
P.O. Box 10124
Van Nuys, CA 91410-0124
818-988-5060

LUMIVISION CORPORATION
1490 Lafayette Street, Suite 407
Denver, CO 80218
303-860-0400

MALOFILM (BEHAVIOUR) HOME VIDEO
2221 Yonge Street, Suite 400
Toronto, ON
CANADA M4S 2B4
416-480-0453

MONARCH HOME VIDEO
1123 Heil Quaker Boulevard
La Vergne, TN 37086-7006
615-793-5000

MONGREL MEDIA
901 Manning Avenue
Toronto, ON
CANADA M6G 2X4
416-516-9775

MOORE VIDEO
P.O. Box 5703
Richmond, VA 23220
804-745-9785

MUSEUM OF TOLERANCE
9786 West Pico Boulevard
Los Angeles, CA 90035-4701
800-553-4474 / 310-553-8402

NATIONAL CENTER FOR JEWISH FILMS
Brandeis University
Lown Building 102
Waltham, MA 02254-9110
617-899-7044

NATIONAL FILM BOARD OF CANADA
1251 Avenue of the Americas, 16th Floor
New York, NY 10020-1173
212-586-5131 / 212-596-1770

NEW YORKER VIDEO
16 West 61st Street, 11th Floor
New York, NY 10023
212-247-6110
800-447-0196

NOSTALGIA FAMILY VIDEO
P.O. Box 506
Baker City, OR 97814
503-523-9034

PROFESSIONAL MEDIA SERVICES CORP.
19122 South Vermont Avenue
Gardena, CA 90248
310-532-9024

PUBLIC MEDIA VIDEO
5547 North Ravenswood Avenue
Chicago, IL 60640-1199
312-878-2600

QUINTEX ENTERTAINMENT
345 North Maple Drive, Suite 358
Beverly Hills, CA 90210
310-281-2600

SGE HOME VIDEO
Division of Shapiro Glickenhaus Entertainment
12001 Ventura Place, 4th Floor
Studio City, CA 91604
818-766-8500

SINISTER CINEMA
P.O. Box 4369
Medford, OR 97501-0168
503-773-6860

SMA DISTRIBUTION
5600 Ambler Drive
Mississauga, ON
Canada L4W 2K9
905-624-4840

SONY PICTURES CLASSICS
550 Madison Avenue, 8th Floor
New York, NY 10022
212-833-8833

STARMAKER ENTERTAINMENT
151 Industrial Way East
Eatontown, NJ 07724
908-389-1020

SULLIVAN ENTERTAINMENT
110 Davenport Road
Toronto, ON
CANADA M5R 3R3
416-921-7177

SULTAN ENTERTAINMENT
335 North Maple Drive
Suite 351
Beverly Hills, CA 90210-3899
310-285-6000

TAPEWORM VIDEO DISTRIBUTORS
12420 Montague Street
Suite B
Arleta, CA 91331
818-896-8899

TRANS WORLD ENTERTAINMENT
3330 Cahuenga Boulevard West, Suite 500
Los Angeles, CA 90068
213-969-2800

VIDAMERICA
231 East 55th Street
New York, NY 10022
212-685-1300

VCL HOME ENTERTAINMENT INC.
13418 Wyandotte Street
North Hollywood, CA 91605
818-764-1777

VIDEO CITY PRODUCTIONS
4266 Broadway
Oakland, CA 94611
510-428-0202

VIDEO COMMUNICATIONS INC.
6535 East Skelley Drive
Tulsa, OK 74145
918-622-6460

VIDEO GAMA
12228 Venice Boulevard, No. 504
Los Angeles, CA 90066

VIDEO TREASURES
2001 Glenn Parkway
Batavia, OH 45103
513-732-2790

VIDEO YESTERYEAR
Box C
Sandy Hook, CT 06482
203-426-2574

VIDMARK ENTERTAINMENT
2644 30th Street
Santa Monica, CA 90405-3009
310-314-2000

WNET/THIRTEEN NON BROADCAST
356 West 58th Street
New York, NY 10019
212-560-3045

WORLDVISION HOME VIDEO
1700 Broadway
New York, NY 10019-5905
212-261-2700